What's New That's Old

By the Same Author

Treasure At Home

New Horizons in Collecting

The Coming Collecting Boom

What's New That's Old

Offbeat Collectibles

by John Mebane

South Brunswick and New York: A. S. Barnes and Company

London: Thomas Yoseloff Ltd

© 1969 by A. S. Barnes and Co., Inc.
Library of Congress Catalogue Card Number: 71-85663

A. S. Barnes and Co., Inc.
Cranbury, New Jersey 08512

Thomas Yoseloff Ltd
108 New Bond St.
London W1Y OQX, England

SBN: 498 06834 X
Printed in the United States of America

For Eva Mae, who will know who she is.

Contents

⟦1⟧

A Word About Sundry Matters

☞ Though it's often said that a book's dullest part is its prefatory matter, this contention—to lapse into the vulgar parlance—ain't necessarily so. Those who skip Prefaces often miss tidbits of information that could be mulled to advantage on a midsummer morning or a gray winter afternoon.

In the Preface you are now reading, for example, you'll find mention of a number of American companies whose early catalogues (some of which are still available if you'll hunt for them) are no less than treasurehouses of information for those interested in scores of objects either now beginning to be collected or destined for rescue from the rubbish heap in the near future. It would have been difficult to write this book, and even more difficult to adequately illustrate it, had I not had access to these remarkable catalogues originally published at various times between 1880 and the First World War.

Some of these early companies are still in operation, a few of them under changed names; others have gone out of business, and a number have been absorbed into and have become a part of larger enterprises. I should now like to express my gratitude (and, I am sure, the gratitude also of others who seek contemporary collectibles) to the business establishments listed below (among others), which issued such delightful and fascinating merchandise catalogues in the years gone by. Many of them continue to publish fine catalogues of the wares they manufacture or distribute. The street addresses of those I could locate are listed here, along with their headquarters cities. I have received cordial letters from a number of them, confirming these addresses. If you are interested, you will occasionally find early catalogues issued by these firms and others offered for sale in the advertising columns of various collector periodicals:

11

Adelphi Silver Plate Co., New York City

A. C. Becken Co., Chicago

Belknap Hardware & Manufacturing Company, 111 East Main Street, Louisville, Kentucky

Benj. Allen Co., Chicago

A. E. Benary, New York City

M. S. Benedict Mfg. Co., East Syracuse, New York

Hamilton S. Gordon, New York City

John H. Graham Co., Inc., 105 Duane Street, New York City

Harry Greenwold, Wallenstein-Mayer Co., 31 East Fourth Street, Cincinnati, Ohio

E. I. Horsman Co., New York City

Lyon & Healy, Wabash Avenue at Jackson Boulevard, Chicago

B. F. Norris, Alister & Co., Chicago

Oskamp, Nolting & Co., 26 West Seventh Street, Cincinnati, Ohio

Sargent and Company, 100 Sargent Drive, New Haven, Connecticut

Simpson, Hall, Miller & Co., originally of Wallingford, Connecticut (now merged into International Silver Company, Meriden, Connecticut)

A. G. Spalding & Bros., Inc. (with executive offices on Meadow Street, Chicopee, Massachusetts)

John F. Stratton, New York City

Thayer & Chandler, 215 West Ohio Street, Chicago

Tower Manufacturing & Novelty Company, New York City

Otto Young & Co., Chicago

Nor do I want to neglect paying tribute to that most interesting of magazines for young people, *The Youth's Companion,* whose issues through its thriving years were filled with illustrations and descriptions of so many objects for which collectors now yearn.

In addition, numerous other businesses, individuals, and institutions were helpful to me in preparing this book through their contributions of information, illustrations, and permissions. I should like to acknowledge my gratitude to the following:

American Optometric Association, 7000 Chippewa Street, St. Louis, Missouri (for illustrations and information); *Better Homes & Gardens,* Des Moines, Iowa (for permission to include some background about match safes similar to that included in an article of mine appearing in that magazine under the title *Treasure Hunt*); June Blythe, 1418 East 54th Place, Chicago (for help in locating addresses); Brown & Bigelow, 1286 University Avenue, Saint Paul, Minnesota (for illustrations); The Coca-Cola Company, Atlanta,

Georgia (for an illustration); Colgate-Palmolive Company, 300 Park Avenue, New York City (for permission to reproduce an illustration); George Eastman House, 900 East Avenue, Rochester, New York (for making accessible and permission to reproduce an illustration); Miss Betty Gau, 11209 South Sawyer Avenue, Chicago for illustrations and background material).

Also, *Harper's Bazaar,* 572 Madison Avenue, New York City (for permission to reproduce an illustration); Lamont Henry, M.D., 1293 Peachtree Street, N.E., Atlanta, Georgia (for reviewing editorial material); Lyon & Healy, Inc., Wabash Avenue at Jackson Boulevard, Chicago (for permission to reproduce some early photographs); Maico Hearing Instruments, 7375 Bush Lake Road, Minneapolis, Minnesota (for illustrations and permission to quote from *Hearing Progress,* published by this firm for the hard of hearing); Pickard, Incorporated, Antioch, Illinois, and Henry A. Pickard, Jr., President (for illustrations and editorial assistance); RCA Sales Corporation, 600 North Sherman Drive, Indianapolis, Indiana (for illustrations); Don and Charlotte Smith, 4624 T Street, Sacramento, California (for illustrations and background material); A. G. Spalding & Bros., Chicopee, Massachusetts (for illustrations and background material); John Sullivan, 3748 North Damen Avenue, Chicago (for illustrations); Dave Weiler, Route 2, Box 52, Auburn, Illinois (for an illustration and background material); Westmoreland Glass Company, Grapeville, Pennsylvania, and J. H. Brainard, President (for the loan of its early catalogues); and Wm. Wrigley Jr. Company, 410 North Michigan Avenue, Chicago (for permission to quote from one of its publications).

I also am indebted to Atlanta Newspapers, Inc., Atlanta, Georgia, which publishes my column on collecting in its Sunday editions and in which appeared some of the original research which I have expanded into fuller studies in one or two chapters of this book.

Finally, I should like to express my appreciation publicly to Hannah K. Mebane, for a special dispensation that permitted me to litter our living room and kitchen with catalogues, clippings, and assorted miscellany during the months that this book was in process of gestation. The litter has disappeared, but the memory lingers on.

[2]

Love Makes the World Go 'Round

In this generation we have witnessed the phenomena of hippies, beatnicks, nogoodnicks, and a wondrous variety of other assorted cults whose followers have worshiped at such curious shrines as those of hallucination, illusion, wishfulness, and ennui. There are those of us who think we have attained a reasonable majority and who disavow with exclamation that we are part or parcel of the offbeat generation. Nevertheless, we are caught up with it; our present and our future whirl intriguingly in the cross-currents created by a strange but dynamic young society that may not know where it is going but is nonetheless in a hurry to get there.

Since, despite our disclaimers, we are trapped in the corridor traversed so vigorously by this offbeat generation, perhaps—though we may not trip the light fantastic so buoyantly as they—we may find a sort of timorous joy in negotiating its confines. Though we may view with trepidation a sudden plunge into the River Styx, most of us surely experience a certain titillation in contemplating the wetting of our toes in the tantalizing waters. Let us consider, therefore, an excursion into offbeat collecting.

Even those prone to march steadfastly to the right will find that the pursuit of this largely uncharted course has certain compensations to offset the agony, imagined or real, of an expedition into the nonconformist world. As an item, you may follow the scent of a veritable host of novel collectibles without becoming addicted to LSD, growing a beard or hair that affronts the eyebrows, or playing a guitar. Not that I have anything against playing a guitar, as I shall presently make clear.

In this book we shall consider the offbeat collector to be, simply, one who finds fascination in discovering and/or pursuing things that normally haven't been considered in the category of antiques.

14

We shall discuss the man who has as much fun tracking down pro-
hibition-era hip flasks as a well-heeled counterpart has in seeking
an eighteenth-century Chippendale chair. And we shall talk about
the woman who takes as much delight in finding an early parasol
whose handle is adorned with the carved head of a bonneted lady
as a wealthy dowager takes in locating a choice early Sevres vase.

What a host of seductive opportunities lie ahead for the wary!
The offbeat collector may look for intriguingly decorated poker
chips, early twentieth-century tintypes, porcelain holders for condensed milk, paper doll cutouts, or Wells Fargo Bank draft checks.
He or she may seek college or professional football programs, celluloid advertising lapel pins, pictorial dice, Blickensderfer typewriters, home medical apparatus, or implements associated with the
once-flourishing art of pyrography.

You may be surprised by the offbeat collectibles that almost
lurk in wait for you. Have you ever possessed a Bandonion? Now
for goodness sake, Gwendolyn, don't tell me you don't know what
a Bandonion is! If you must confess ignorance, stop right where
you are and read the chapter about musical instruments. Then
think what a lift it would give you to rush over to Marilyn's house
and exclaim: "I found the sweetest Bandonion today—and you'll
never guess how little I paid for it!"

Or how about a nineteenth-century letterhead electro? You'll
have to admit, George, that almost no one has an outstanding collection of these. Yet, you can probably pick them up for a pittance.
If you possessed, say, just an even hundred of them—all different,
naturally—you could bring your Boy Scout troop to your home and
derive truly immense satisfaction from the astonishment on those
chubby little faces. If I've caught you off base, George, turn to the
next chapter and find out what these electros are and why you will
enjoy collecting them.

You'll be surprised by the factors in favor of offbeat collecting.
Moreover, being wealthy doesn't bar you from membership in the
offbeat collecting fraternity; you'll simply have to become accus-
tomed to spending less for your purchases. And you'll no longer be
snubbed by your impecunious acquaintances. Should you decide
to collect nutpicks, you may find that your less affluent neighbor
in the next block collects sponge cups and may, therefore, be will-
ing to rub noses with you.

Young married couples and even unmarried teenagers should
find offbeat collecting both a joy and a promise. I'm among the
oldsters who has high hopes for the young and the hip. Many a
male who has barely attained voting age has learned more about
more things in his young life than I have in mine. Many a female

who has just penned her first *avant garde* rhyme and quavers deliciously at the prospect of reading it in public already has more questions on her lips about life's purpose than many of her ancestors had voiced at their life's end. For the young generation the artifacts of their parents are ancient and sometimes marvelously quaint. The space craft and the computer may be commonplace to them, but the buttonhook and Rose O'Neill's Kewpies are creations of a lost civilization. For this young generation offbeat collecting will provide an eye-opening excursion into the wondrous days of yore. Moreover, a collection of late nineteenth- and early twentieth-century "antiques" begun now may afford an investment that could pay off handsomely when they reach retirement age, if indeed they ever do.

I don't mean that those who turn to the offbeats we will be discussing herein necessarily need stop their purchases of Cezannes, or Wistarburg topaz-and-white double glass flasks, or even William and Mary seventeenth-century marqueterie cabinets. Plow your money into these choice antiques if you wish, because, unless we eradicate ourselves, they'll probably be worth more next year than they are today. But give a thought while paying your tax bill or watching reruns on television to the hot-poker-painted tabourette, the fancy bead bag of the pre-flapper era, or the quaint round flask adorned with the words "Here's a smile to those I love." As John Cameron Swayze and I always say, you'll be glad you did. And this is a good way to widen your horizons if you're a bit on the thin side knowledgewise about those days when your grandmother was a child.

Some of us think that if we know all there is to know about George Ravenscroft and his lead glass, or the production of the china manufactories at Chantilly, Mennecy, Meissen, Worcester, and Bristol, or the output of the Goldsmith's Company during the regimes of the early Stuarts and the Protectorate, or the furniture of our own Pilgrims, we know enough to last us a lifetime. If we are familiar with all these things, we certainly know enough to qualify us to make speeches before the ladies' clubs. But is it entirely satisfying to know a great deal about the handicrafts and the tastes of our ancient forebears and very little indeed about those of our parents and our grandparents? Now there is nothing wrong with weltering in the murky mists of the Renaissance, but why not let our inquisitive little minds also ponder some of the marvels of the Gay Nineties and pry at least a little into the amazing exploits of those who pioneered the twentieth century?

Which brings us to this point:

Let's get hip, baby, and learn a little about those perfectly delightful and intriguing gadgets, accouterments, accessories, and necessities that gave Grandmother a warm glow and a lovely smile and induced Grandfather to snap his fingers just like they do in the cigarette commercials.

This stuff is still all around us, and if we don't research it and salvage it while it's still available, a hundred years from now we won't know any more about it than we do about the beads that Captain William Norton made for traffic with the Indians around Jamestown, Virginia, in 1621, which is very little indeed. That is a depressing thought, and one that need not be tolerated.

I don't suggest, even faintly, that you rush out and start collecting things that don't appeal to you. But I do suggest that you may not know how many things produced less than a century ago may appeal to you until you begin looking for some of them and scrutinizing them (perhaps with the aid of a magnifying glass if your beady little eyes are weak) and then trying to learn at least a trifle about their history.

Some years ago a lady fascinated by primitives displayed for me a short and peculiarly curved piece of wood, asking me rather breathlessly, "What is it?" I replied that I·hadn't the foggiest notion —and you may obtain an idea of my embarrassment when I tell you that it turned out to be a niddy noddy. Now anyone who purports to know anything about antiques ought to know a niddy noddy when one stares him in the face. So I escaped in silence, my conscience and my pride wounded to the quick, and set myself about the serious study of niddy noddies. Now, I can identify your niddy noddy even if it is wearing a jacket and smoking a pipe. I may not be the world's greatest living authority on niddy noddies, but I come close. Had the good lady confronted me with a vial of glass from a tomb at Beni Hasan, near Thebes, and I hadn't been able to identify it, my pride wouldn't have take such a beating. But a niddy noddy. . . !

I cite this discomfiting incident merely to illustrate how depressing a paucity of knowledge about the intimate household items of our rather recent forebears can be—and what a joy it is to be able to identify and talk about Bandonions, Zobos, Equipoise waists, Kensington art painting, mantel lambrequins, and Miss Parloa's cook books!

I certainly don't want you to infer that all of the collectibles we will talk about in this book are priceless gems or that if you hold them for a century, you can then sell them for a vast sum. Some of them are gems, and the value of a good many of them will undoubtedly increase. But what I want to do is to get you interested in some of them, and then if you do go out and start stalking them, I hope you will do so because you find it fun to learn about such things as advertising teaspoons, Aristinas, and patented scorchers.

Should any of the names I've mentioned be unfamiliar to you, don't let it throw you. They are explained in the chapters that follow.

In addition to the offbeat collectibles, I've thrown in for good measure some intelligence about certain objects that already are being collected and that somehow fascinate me and, I suspect, may also fascinate you. These include handpainted china, match safes, certain writing adjuncts, and a few others. Perhaps you'll find some information about these here that you haven't encountered elsewhere.

Confidentially, I think you'll find many of these offbeat collectibles as exciting as a Turkish water pipe filled with pot, and probably more exhilarating than smoking a banana. They'll probably turn you on as effectively as methedrine but without shooting holes in your brain.

Well, now that we have introduced you to this hobby horse, let's get in the groove and ride it.

Giddap, Dobbin! We may love this ride—and love makes the world go 'round.

[3]

Free Enterprise:
A World of Collectibles

Despite its shortcomings, this nation's business system, operated on the principle of free enterprise, constitutes perhaps the most eloquent of all expressions of American ingenuity. Examples of extraordinary adroitness in selling goods and services have multiplied through the years more abundantly than rabbits; today a whole world of collectible objects is available for those interested in preserving Americana at its imaginative best.

Certain articles related intimately to free enterprise business are already being collected. These include, for example, advertising cards, business ledgers and account books, and other items linked to advertising. Still, the surface has been barely scratched, and those reluctant to follow the well-beaten paths of collecting will find a beguiling sphere awaiting them in the dazzling, though sometimes confounding, realm of American business.

Have you seen the re-creation of an American business establishment of the nineteenth century? There is a fellow in the small Georgia town of Clarkston, who specializes in creating displays of businesses of past years. He is Harald J. Torgesen, and over a period of a good many years he has assembled hundreds of articles of furniture and furnishings, examples of goods sold, and implements and devices used in preparing articles for sale in mercantile and other business houses of the last century and early in this one. Mr. Torgesen has re-created for business conventions, special meetings, and other gatherings the interiors (and even the exteriors) of establishments which flourished a century or less ago.

These displays have completely fascinated those who have viewed them. For many they have generated nostalgia—perhaps even a

19

vague longing for a return to more leisurely days of doing business. While photographs and drawings of some of our business houses of years ago can help us visualize what they were like and give us some indication of how business was handled, they lack the four-dimensional reality which Mr. Torgesen's re-creations give.

Piled high in his large residence and in additional buildings that he controls, one will literally find thousands of objects associated with the American merchandising past. These include such things as chairs, tables, benches, counters, display racks, packaged merchandise, bottles filled with scores of concoctions ranging from medicines to soft drinks, account books, letterheads, calendars, trays, prints, barber chairs, drug and spice grinding machines—these and many other reminders of free enterprise as it was conducted in years gone by.

Mr. Torgesen first sketches the display as he visualizes it should appear, then puts it together to conform largely to the sketch. Hardly a day passes in which he does not acquire additional business objects from the past. He buys a single article or an entire store.

For many years our ingenuity has run rampant in the field of advertising. The art of persuasion has flourished in no other country as it has in ours. Ingenious minds have devised advertising gimmicks by the millions, and these tangible adjuncts of advertising in themselves offer choice opportunities for the imaginative collector.

I have written of advertising cards, broadsides, posters, and handbills in my *New Horizons in Collecting*, but there are dozens of other advertising appurtenances about which little or nothing has been written and on which little research thus far has been done.

Take advertising calendars. These were manufactured by the millions years ago, and of course, continue to be produced today. Some of today's calendars may become collectors' items of the future, but thousands of calendars turned out 50, 60 or 75 years ago are available for collecting right now.

We all know that calendars are not recent inventions. The Babylonians, and even primitive civilizations,, utilized calendars of a sort. Those of concern to us here, however, date from the last half of last century up until the First World War. Advertising calendars were used by soap manufacturers, stationers, meat packers, life insurance companies, buggy makers, railroads, seedsmen, and numerous other establishments to promote their wares or services or to keep their name before a fickle public. Some were decorated with appealing lithographs or were produced by chromolithography, which made possible the use of colors. Some depict fashions of the years in which they were issued. Others are graced with outdoor scenes, whimsical children, flowers, or likenesses of historic personages or animals.

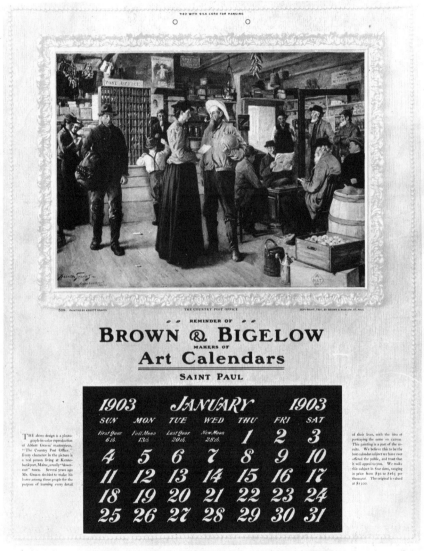

Brown & Bigelow, pioneer producer of advertising calendars by distinguished artists, produced this one for 1903 with the painting, "The Country Post Office," by the artist Abbott Graves. (Courtesy of Brown & Bigelow, Saint Paul, Minnesota)

Beautiful women have long been a favorite illustration for advertising calendars, and this one, issued in 1905, is no exception. (Courtesy of Brown & Bigelow, Saint Paul, Minnesota)

Calendars have been made in many sizes and shapes. Of prime interest are mechanical calendars, which could be manipulated, and fold-out calendars, some of which were costly to produce. Famous artists painted or drew some of the illustrations. Among them was Kate Greenaway, whose work is now again in vogue and increasing in demand. Another was Frederick Remington. Look for names of other well-known artists at the bottoms of the illustrations on early advertising calendars you may chance across.

You can frame some of the better calendar illustrations and use them as decorative accessories in your home just as you may have done with the colored fashion prints that originally appeared in *Godey's Lady's Magazine, Peterson's Magazine,* and other periodicals of the last century. Some of the more desirable calendars were made by the English firm of Raphael Tuck, which also produced many of the early greeting cards for which collectors are now scrambling. Brown & Bigelow, Saint Paul, Minnesota, was a pioneer in this field too.

Some companies gave their calendars away. Others exchanged them for box tops or wrappers from their products. The N. K. Fairbank Company, of Chicago, offered its 1904 Fairy Calendar in exchange for 10 box fronts from its soap. These particular calendars were decorated in the so-called Art Nouveau style, about which a rash of articles has lately appeared. The year before, Swift & Company had offered its 1903 calendar for either 10 cents in cash or stamps or 10 wrappers from its Wool soap.

These attractive early advertising calendars should be worth from 50 cents to $5, although unusually good ones may bring a little more.

Another gimmick was the advertising tray, many of which bear the names of soft drink or beer manufacturers. These were frequently lithographed in colors. The beverage companies concentrated on illustrations of pretty girls as adornment for the top surfaces of their trays. Some illustrations of girls in bathing suits were considered a trifle risqué for their times, but we wouldn't bat an eye at them in this topless era. Early advertising trays of this type can be bought for four or five dollars each in good condition, excepting the more elaborately decorated ones that are valued higher. Simple tin advertising trays were sold in 1915 at $1.95 a dozen.

Some of the more ambitious firms had their trays lithographed in 10 or 12 colors. In addition to publicizing beverages, some trays promoted cigars and other commodities.

Some time ago, Don Smith, of Sacramento, California, and his wife, Charlotte, became interested in collecting bottles once issued

Advertising calendar for 1896 by Brown & Bigelow, by whose courtesy it is reproduced here. The painting "Horses at Drinking Trough" is by Dagnan-Bouveret.

1905 insurance advertising calendar with choice Charles M. Russell painting. Originally issued by Brown & Bigelow, by whose permission it is reproduced.

by the old Buffalo Brewery Company and the Ruhstaller Brewery, of Sacramento. After assembling a large number of these old bottles, they decided to try to match them with the advertising trays, glasses and similar items once issued by the same companies.

Their success spurred them on to seeking bottles, trays, glasses and other advertising items issued by other beverage firms and by producers of bitters, tonics, and soft drinks in years past.

Today, the Smith home at 4624 T Street displays abundant evidence of the success of their endeavors. The Sacramento mementoes have been arranged attractively around an early Buffalo Brewery ice box that Don cut down to convenient cabinet size and refinished. Beautifully lithographed trays adorn walls in their home, and the bottles (including some fine figurals) are arranged on special shelves and elsewhere to enable them to share their collecting hobby with friends and visitors.

These items constitute part of the outstanding collection of advertising trays, bottles and kindred items belonging to Don and Charlotte Smith, Sacramento, California. The trays were issued by the Buffalo Brewing Company and Ruhstaller's Brewery. Beer bottles, glasses and other items are shown on an old Buffalo Brewing Company ice box cut down to cabinet size.

The lithographed beverage trays, Don points out, were customarily issued in matching sets that contained one large serving tray and six individual trays (about 4 inches in diameter) currently called "tip" trays. Today, it is difficult to find complete sets in the same place, but the Smiths have managed finally to locate a number of "starter" sets, finding one piece in one location and other matching trays elsewhere.

Both Don and Charlotte are members of several antique bottle collecting clubs, and bottles remain their primary "love," but no longer their exclusive one. They devote a good bit of their leisure time to seeking the trays and glasses as well as some kindred advertising items. They even have a cribbage board once issued as a

A part of the fine collection of bottles, beverage advertising trays and allied items collected by Don and Charlotte Smith, of Sacramento, California. A free-blown demijohn is seen in the foreground on table at left. Bottles on the shelves behind the leaded glass lamp shade on the left include bitters, soda, beer, whiskey and other early ones. Many are choice items such as the Fish Bitters, shown fourth from left on the bottom row. Trays on the wall include some fine lithographed ones issued by breweries and soda water firms. The three bottles on the cabinet on the right are Cathedral Pickles.

gift advertising piece by the Buffalo Brewing Company's San Francisco Agency!

Other associated advertising items in their collection include match safes, flasks, demijohns, a clock, and bitters, beer, whiskey, tonic, and soda bottles. They also have some of the much-sought-after Cathedral pickle bottles. Among their choice bottles are Drake's Plantation Bitters, Napoleon figural, Jester figural, a double-eagle Stoddard flask, a Hunter-Fisherman calabash, a DeWitt Clinton flask, a free-blown chestnut flask, the Fish bitters, John Ryan soda, a Pineapple whiskey decanter, and Big Bill Best Bitters, to list only a small part of them.

Both Don and Charlotte Smith are "collectors" in the proper sense of the word: they are not content merely to assemble bottles, trays and allied advertising items but engage in research about the companies once producing them. This has added both to their knowledge and their enjoyment. They frequently correspond with other collectors of similar items—and this correspondence not only often adds to their knowledge but sometimes to the enlargement of their collection.

A diversity of inexpensive gift items was made for advertising purposes. These ranged from rulers to paperweights. The latter offer opportunities for an excellent collection for those who cannot afford carefree indulgence in the far costlier weights made by the millefiori and other complicated glass techniques.

Many advertising paperweights were made in oblong or round glass shapes with an illustration in the bottom, usually magnified by the thickness of the glass above it. These illustrations quite often are of commodities, including early buggies, bicycles, and gasoline-propelled vehicles. Other weights contained pictorial representations of factories and stores, and also of individuals.

Among glass plants specializing in advertising paperweights was Westmoreland Specialty Company (known as Westmoreland Glass Company since 1923), of Grapeville, Pennsylvania. A 1900 catalogue loaned to me by the company shows a group of such weights in oblong, oval, round, octagonal and scalloped shapes. The catalogue had three comments about the weights:

"Beautiful and Artistic. The finest advertising devices in the world. Indestructible, unfading, and unchanging. They last forever. We can insert in these paper weights any desired advertisement, with or without cuts, or of any special design, either plain or engraved, or in reproduction of any sketch, engraving, lithograph or photograph, which we can reduce to the proper size."

Weights of this type may still be picked up for a very few dollars. One weight promoting Remington typewriters was advertised for sale not long ago at $3.75. This same price was asked for one advertising a tailor's services. A weight advertising Doughtery's & Son rye whiskey is valued at $5.50. Another, commemorating the 50th anniversary of a meat-packing company, was offered for $3.25, and one promoting bicycles was priced at $4.50. Recently I have picked up several at prices of $1.50 to $3, but ornate ones are higher.

Advertising rulers are fairly plentiful. A metal ruler decorated on one side with a group of early ink bottles and on the other with a replica of a steel pen is tendered at $7.50, but you should be able to find many wooden rulers at lower prices.

Strap-type advertising watch fobs were once popular. They were produced and distributed in behalf of various types of businesses, including machinery manufacturers. Most of them are still inexpensive. However, since the pocket watch seems to have lost much ground to the wrist watch in modern times, advertising fobs have been replaced by other types of advertising gimmicks, and the early ones may soon become quite scarce.

Dave Weiler, of Route 2, Box 52, Auburn, Illinois, began collecting the leather strap-type advertising watch fobs a few years ago and currently has a fabulous collection. By the end of 1967, he had amassed about 600, all different, and the total collection has been mounting since. All the fobs in his collection bear advertising. He continues buying but doesn't sell any of his collection.

Match safes of various types were once designed to advertise numerous commodities and services. One of these in the shape of a shoe was once utilized to advertise a shoe repair concern, and what could have been more appropriate? The shoe was hinged to the case, which could be opened for the insertion and extraction of matches. There were many novelty types of this sort, which should be worth from $5 to $10 or more. Match safes in general are discussed in detail in a subsequent chapter in this book.

Very few persons, apparently, are collecting advertising mirrors, but a large number are still around. They were once used to ballyhoo almost everything, from chewing gum to patent medicines. Most of them were small hand mirrors with celluloid backs. The Sterling Remedy Company once offered them at two cents each! Those with brass or other metal backs were costlier when they were made and are of more value now, but some of these have been found recently priced at only $2 each. One such advertised the New Home Sewing Machine and was dated 1890. Patriotic motifs are found on the backs of some advertising mirrors. One produced during World War I featured a display of the flags of the Allies. A rather naughty mirror issued by a patent medicine company pictured a cherub seated on a potty with a legend beneath it that has no place in a family book of this kind!

Celluloid advertising buttons were turned out by the ton early in this century. One featured a clay pigeon in its center to publicize the Western Cartridge Company. Others containing illustrations or mottoes, ballyhooed bicycles, automobile tires, ammunition, the services of seamstresses, dynamite, whiskey, and numerous other commodities and services. The average run of these should be worth $1 to $3 each. Tokens were used for similar advertising purposes.

Also quite desirable are advertising spoons. These, made in both teaspoon and demitasse sizes, promoted food products, fairs, merchandise shows, and other events and products. The souvenir spoon collector may find many of them of interest. They should be worth two or three dollars each, excepting truly unusual ones.

Novelty knives were used to promote both products and individual stores. One of these with a picture of Buster Brown and his dog on one side of the celluloid handle and advertising Brown's shoes also doubled as a bottle opener. It was made in the shape of a woman's leg. One owner recently asked $5 for this type. Simple knives used in early promotions are worth a dollar and up.

Advertising booklets constitute a field into which neither the antiques addict nor the book collector has looked sufficiently yet. Various companies had these booklets printed, some of them in color. Their contents covered a diversity of subjects. For example, there were booklets that contained modern versions of traditional fairy tales, slanted to promote products and services. A delightful one of this type with colored illustrations, *The Shop that Jack Built,* was used as a promotional piece for Milennium Flour and Bread. The William Wrigley Jr. Company, of Chicago, in 1915 issued a color booklet entitled *Wrigley's Mother Goose,* which introduced the "Sprightly Spearmen"—those spear-shaped elves that have been so widely used through the years to identify the company's gum. This booklet adapted well-known nursery rhymes to ballyhoo jingles, such as:

> *Old King Spear was a merry old Dear!*
> *And a very old Dear was he!*
> *He called for his gum*
> *Till they brought him some,*
> *Then he shouted "Hurrah for Wrig-LEY!"*

Although not the sort of poetry likely to go down to posterity, the booklet was very popular and several subsequent editions were printed.

C. I. Hood and Company, of Lowell, Massachusetts, a major advertiser early in this century, used booklets to promote its sarsaparilla. One of these, *A Day with a Circus: and Other Stories, Sketches, etc., including Something about a Peculiar Medicine,* relates several circus stories which were undoubtedly interesting to children and also includes promotional comments about several Hood products.

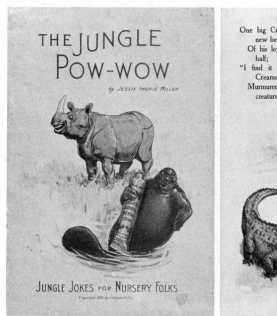

The front cover and a typical illustrated page from The Jungle Pow-Wow, *an advertising booklet published by Colgate & Company in 1911.*

At about the same time, Colgate & Company published a series of booklets for young people, all of them charmingly illustrated in color. Titles included *The Jungle School, The Jungle Pow-Wow,* and *Dental Lectures.*

Within the past year or two, I have picked up a number of these delightfully illustrated little booklets for a pittance and am sorely tempted to try to assemble a library of them. This project could ultimately constitute a valuable library of a promotional method for American business. Such a collection might even vie in interest with one of early American school books.

Railroads and trolley companies published a number of sight-seeing and travel booklets and brochures. Sometimes these were illustrated with maps of the period, and these will interest map collectors. Others contained drawings or photographs of historic spots, shrines, public buildings, and homes, many of which have now made way for "progress" so that the early illustrations constitute a valuable record and will help preserve history. One of these, a 75-page booklet entitled *Seeing Denver,* was issued by the American Trolley Sight Seeing Coach Company, in 1903, and contained pictures of major attractions in that Colorado area. A copy was recently offered in mint condition for $3. The *Travellers Guide Book from Boston to Portland by the Eastern Railroad and the Portland, Saco & Portsmouth Railroad,* a hardbound book of 204 pages published in 1857, is advertised at $6. Similar booklets are now valued at $1 to around $10. A library of travel and sightseeing books and booklets published by transportation firms could provide both a valuable and enlightening collection.

Many businesses, including railroads, once issued lithographs as promotional and good will gifts. Some of these are of historic interest. Chromolithographs once given away by businesses may often be framed and used in home or office decoration. The New York Central & Hudson River Railroad issued a series of interesting lithographs in 1893, published as the *Four Track Series* and available then on request and a two-cent stamp. Some time ago the Chesapeake Western Railway gave away photographic reproductions of "old No. 199," a Camelback locomotive that had been confiscated in West Virginia by General "Stonewall" Jackson and was later recaptured by Federal troops. This locomotive was hauled by horses over the highway extending from Martinsburg, West Virginia, through Harrisonburg, Virginia, to Staunton and became the first locomotive to pass through Harrisonburg. When the Valley Railroad (which subsequently became a part of the Chesapeake Western Railway) was built in 1869, this locomotive, which had been returned to its owners, was operated along the same route by rail that it had traveled earlier by highway.

In addition, of course, there have been scores of lithographs, paintings, and other pictorial representations delineating aspects of numerous American businesses, some of them done by famous artists and many well worth preserving.

Thousands of thermometers were once distributed free to advertise firms or specific products. These were put to good use in homes and offices. Over many years lead pencils in varied designs have been given away as publicity gimmicks as they still are today. A tremendous collection could be made of advertising pencils alone at a cost that would be almost negligible. The same goes for match covers.

Novel advertising gifts ranged from stick pins to shoe horns. The H. J. Heinz Company gave away miniature replicas of cucum-

Business cards of the late 1800's, showing stock cards at left and similar ones imprinted on the right.

Lithographed advertising or trade cards such as these helped publicize many a product or company in earlier years.

bers that were mounted as stick pins or as other jewelry-type dress accessories. There are many thousands of imprinted pens awaiting collectors. Another once-important ballyhoo item was the paper or celluloid fan. Some companies distributed these by the hundreds to churches and other organizations, and all were put to good use before the advent of air conditioning.

Other advertising gifts worth collecting now include aprons, charms, billfolds, caps and bonnets, banks, school bags and book straps, pennants, toothpick holders, letter openers, paper umbrellas, game counters (usually made of celluloid), puzzles and tricks, simple games, various items of crockery, can openers and bottle openers, corkscrews, ash trays, blotting pads, key chains, inexpensive tools, coin purses, diaries, cigar cutters, soap dishes, clocks, post cards, cigarette silks, dominoes, sheet music, and kites. These items, however, provide merely an introduction to the types once handed out by merchants and manufacturers practicing the art of persuasion. You will encounter dozens of others.

Business billheads and letterheads, especially those with lithographed illustrations, may one day become prime collectors' items. Many of these are now available almost for the asking. Thousands will be found stored away in musty files of old business establishments and manufacturing plants. In a similar category are the engravings or plates used in printing and called "electros." Many will still be found in old stores and printing shops. Some of these electrotypes depict merchandise ranging from jewelry and glasswares to boxes and grocery items. Stock electros were sold for advertising purposes and for use in printing letterheads. Not long ago I bought 2,000 lithographed letterheads and billheads containing letters and bills in manuscript for just a few dollars, sold them almost immediately for twice what I had paid, and now wish I had them back again at twice what I sold them for. Hindsight doesn't help much in such a situation.

Early bank draft checks and bills of exchange are worth seeking. Quite recently a Wells Fargo bank draft check dated 1864 and with a bank stamp attached was offered for sale at $8.50. The same price was asked for a Wells Fargo bill of exchange drawn on San Francisco and cashed in New York. It was dated in 1868.

Don't neglect such items as railroad and steamship bonds and certificates, business incorporation papers, early insurance policies, and annual transportation company passes. In fact, insurance company policy forms with their printed blanks filled in, in manuscript, will bring tidy sums if they are early enough. One such form insuring a sea voyage and dated 1775 was offered by a dealer some months ago for $22.50. Another dated 1776 and insuring a schooner was offered for $15. What was insured is a factor in the value.

Copies of railroad company stock certificates dated toward the end of the Civil War have been offered recently at prices of only a dollar or two but may be selling for more by the time you read this.

Another major business collectible is the early package—tin, glass, pottery, and others. Those interested in collecting the early

Lithographed billheads dating in the first quarter of this century, showing the warehouses or processing plants of wholesale companies.

tin can packages will find an illustrated chapter devoted to them in my *New Horizons in Collecting.* In 1952, the *Spinning Wheel* published a series of interesting articles about commercial antique packages, pointing out, among other things, that fine early druggists' jars were produced by the famous Whitall-Tatum firm of Millville, New Jersey, where the well-known Millville Rose paperweight also was devised.

On these boards are almost 600 advertising watch fobs with leather straps, representing a part of the collection assembled by Dale Weiler, Route 2, Box 52, Auburn, Illinois. There are no duplicates in this astonishing collection.

Thousands of different types and shapes of packages of various materials were produced last century to hold everything from cosmetics and patent medicines to tea and stationery. Even the early decorated paperboard and heavy paper containers are worth watching for. So are such diverse containers as those for powder, coffee, dentifrices, hair-grooming substances, and soaps. Drug bottles of numerous types are collectible as are the early containers for alcoholic beverages and soda pop.

Both shelf and display jars of numerous kinds can be included in a collection of business mementoes as can various apothecary shop objects such as mortars and pestles, and display bottles. Decorted barber bottles have been sought for years. Begging to be collected are soda fountain items, including dispensers, sundae glasses, ice cream spoons, and so on.

The business collector who comes across early models of business inventions would probably have been "living right," as we used to say in our family—and still do. Some years ago, the Fine Arts Department of International Business Machines Corporation employed Dr. Roberto Guatelli, a distinguished authority on Leonardo da Vinci, to construct models of some of the famous inventions by the extremely versatile Italian artist and inventor, who lived 500 years ago. Centuries ahead of his time, Leonardo da Vinci conceived and drew sketches for such things as the helicopter, the air conditioner, and an excavating machine.

The average collector certainly won't encounter such priceless treasures as these early drawings, but he has a chance of coming across nineteenth-century working or patent models of a number of inventions that are in use today. And he should be able to locate without too much trouble nineteenth-century published reports from the Patent Office, which list and describe thousands of inventions. I have purchased several volumes of these within recent years for a few dollars each.

In addition, early types of machines used by businesses are fairly easy to come by. Some well-outmoded models are still in use. These include such things as duplicating machines, used by many establishments to print letters and circulars used in mail advertising; check protectors; canceling and perforating devices utilized to mark bills paid or debts canceled; dating and time stamps and machines and also numbering devices; wax seals, and seal presses utilized for various purposes by banks, railroads, notaries public, jewelers, and others.

Although early tavern, hostelry and a few other assorted types of signs and signboards have been collected for some time, there are a multitude of nineteenth- and early twentieth-century signs which should be detoured from the rubbish heap. Among the more fascinating of these are signs in the shape of watches, clocks, and spectacles which have hung over or in front of hundreds of opticians', jewelers', and watch repairers' shops. These were usually made of wood, iron, or tin. Probably thousands of these have found their way to the discard since the beginning of this century. If you're a private collector, you won't have room for very many, but you might be surprised to find out how interesting a few can be hung on the walls of a playroom, den, or professional or business office. The history of advertising signs is a fascinating one, and those who would want to know about it will find a wealth of information in *The History of Signboards,* written by Jacob Larwood and John Camden Totten and first published in London in 1866. A large number of early signboards are illustrated in this volume, which went through several editions and is not either excessively scarce or very high in price. A full chapter also is devoted to them in my *New Horizons in Collecting.*

Small business cards constitute a delightful area in which to collect. Printing establishments once produced stock cards of this kind by the thousands, and these were imprinted with the names of the businesses using them. Most such cards were about the same size as today's individual business cards and were illustrated in color with a white space left for imprinting. The majority were printed by the chromolithographic process. In the latter part of last century, blank assorted cards such as these could be purchased for as little as $1.40 per thousand. Printers offered them at 30 for 10 cents with names printed on them.

Hundreds of subjects were used as illustrations. Flowers constituted one favorite design, but some cards illustrated animals, children at play, sports, foreign vistas, and comic views. Many such cards can be picked up today for two or three cents each.

Those who would like to see a fine collection of early business memorabilia will find it in the Oldest Store Museum that opened a few years ago in St. Augustine, Florida. An increasing number of museums are now beginning to preserve and display business collectibles.

A visit to a few old business establishments will suggest numerous other items that you can add to those listed in this brief introduction to a broad field.

Here is an additional sampling of some recently asked prices for collectible business antiques; but remember that these, as is the case with all prices mentioned in this book, are merely guides and that quite often you will find the same or similar items offered for higher or lower prices:

Advertising mirrors: early cough drops, $2; barrel-shaped with celluloid back, clothiers, $2; early labor union promotional, $2.50; tools, 2 inches high, $2; 1913 Odd Fellows, 4 inches in diameter, $3.

Signs: tin, 21x33 inches, featuring a "Moxie" girl (soft drink), $30; wooden, 39x15 inches, gold lettering advertising boots and shoes, $25; wooden sanded, black, 45x12¼ inches, millinery, $10; jeweler, watch-shaped sign of cast iron and sheet metal, 22 inches in diameter, $200.

Watch fobs: whiskey, $3; Diesel Wimmer Company, featuring

This crock fountain dispenser was made for *The Coca-Cola Company* by a West Virginia firm in the early 1890's. These dispensers were given to operators of drug store soda fountains as an incentive premium for top gallonage sales but were distributed for a short time only and are now quite scarce. The decorated bowl on top held about a gallon of Coca-Cola syrup, and the faucet below drained off about an ounce of the syrup for each glass to be mixed with ice and carbonated water. They have been reproduced in plastic by *The Coca-Cola Company*. (Photo by courtesy of *The Coca-Cola Company*)

Watch, spectacle and jewelry signs are among the most intriguing of all types to collect. Those shown here date early in this century. The watch at top center was designated as being "Louis XIV" style. The spectacle sign at top right was made of glass, and those below it in the shape of pairs of spectacles were of metal. Sign at bottom of page was of beveled-edge plate glass with the illustration itself on paper.

Left to right at top: *wax seal handle with a typical wax seal below it; McGill's fastener press; and the Chicago check protector.* Second row: *the Grubler check protector; S. & P. check protector; and automatic bank punch.* Third row: *brass wheel ribbon ticket dater; a Follet time stamp; the Centennial ticket stamp; and a handled seal press (above) and Lever check protector (below).* Bottom row: *lead seal press; a lead seal used in sealing cars, cigar cases, large packages and so on, and a milled wax seal with deep routed letters to prevent counterfeiting. All these business items date in the first decade of this century.*

Business collectibles mostly from early twentieth century. Left to right, top row: *a Reid copy holder for the typist; a Bates numbering machine, and two fancy braided straw office waste baskets.* Second row: *oblong glass paper weight of type used for advertising purposes; the Tower bilateral letter scales; the Luce automatic copy holder, and two druggists' jugs.* Third row: *a series of illustrations from the Fairbank advertising Fairy Calendar of 1899. At bottom are a group of electro- plates made in stock patterns and used in printed advertising.*

Business adjuncts of the early 1900's. Left to right, top row: a coin cup, Staat's money changer, and a double change box. Second row: Universal cash register and a sample of a facsimile autograph stamp. Third row: pocket dater, pocket stamp, rubber hand stamp, and a self-inking stamper. Fourth row: tin billhead case, early Hektograph duplicator, and early Eureka duplicator. Fifth row: a Duplicator duplicator, and three daters.

eagle on shield, $4; motorcycles, brass, $3.50; sporting items, advertising outdoors magazine, $2; cement mixers, $2.50; earth-moving equipment, $2.50; automobile, $4; motorcycle, $3.50.

Knives: single blade, metal handle, brickyard, $3.50; knife manufacturing company, $2.50; pearl handle, cutlery company, $4.50.

Booklets: motor car manufacturer, 1906, $6; motor car manufacturer, 1909, $4.50; thread company, 50¢; clothing company, early, $1; patent medicine compounder, $2; coffee company, 50¢.

Miscellaneous: sewing machine company 4-part advertising calendar, $3.50; thimble advertising plating company, $2; pudding mold advertising flour, $14.25; glass paperweight advertising paper bags, $2.75; iron paperweight advertising insurance company, $7.50; glass goblet advertising patient medicine, $4.50; tin match safe advertising machinery firm, $3; tin tray advertising coffee, $8.50; pottery jug advertising cough medicine, $2.75; glass tumbler advertising petroleum, $3.

[4]

Everything Short of
Life Everlasting

Rube Goldberg's closest competitor in the field of zany inventions has been the quack doctor. Through the years charlatans in the field of medicine have assembled, through the use of such things as spare radio parts and assorted odds and ends of metal and wires, machines which, they have claimed, would both diagnose and cure almost any disease imaginable, and some unimaginable.

Impressed by flashing lights and whirring and buzzing noises emanating from the machines, gullible patients have enriched the pocketbooks of the quacks. More dismaying, the majority of those whose health has not been impaired through subjection to fake devices and medications have shown no physical improvement despite exorbitant expenditures.

Literally millions of dollars have been spent by men and women grasping for hope upon "medical" treatments and home remedies whose questionable merits have been heralded in every communications media. Quacks, sharpies, con men, and others have foisted upon the public machines, medicinals, recipes, and contrivances "guaranteed" to cure everything from fits to cancer—to achieve virtually every conceivable miracle short of providing life everlasting.

Even before the turn of the century, sharpsters capitalized upon the dawning of the age of science by utilizing some of the new scientific discoveries in the construction of weird machines for which they made utterly fantastic claims. The science of medicine had made great progress, so how were the uninformed to know that these devices just might not do what the "doctor" claimed?

Even though the heyday of worthless health machines was ear-

lier in this century, more sophisticated phonies have suckered the
public in recent years by selling worthless and sometimes harmful
gadgets and remedies.

*Patent medicine manufacturers were once large users of advertising
cards such as these attractive ones. All types of advertising cards are collected today.*

Both government and private agencies, including in particular the Food and Drug Administration and the Bureau of Drug Abuse Control, today are helping safeguard the public from drugs, concoctions, and devices that are either harmful or have no merit; but these safeguards didn't exist for our grandparents and great-grandparents, many of whom shelled out hard-earned dollars for such things as "cures" for baldness, consumption, epilepsy, and concoctions and machines whose vendors promised would enlarge their bust, remove their blemishes, or make them look 20 years younger. It hasn't been too many years since one medical imposter sold electric blankets as a cure for cancer and a get-rich-quick company offered a worthless "magic spike" as a cure for any and all diseases.

One of the tragedies resulting from these machinations, of course, has been that some patients have died because they placed faith in worthless cures and failed to seek treatment by licensed medical doctors. Another tragedy has been that elderly persons and those least able to afford it have most frequently been the victims of the money-milkers. In more recent years characters from the underworld, seeking to capitalize on the lifesaving antibiotics and other recently developed "wonder drugs," have been concocting and peddling misbranded drugs on the black market. A startling exposé of these practices was made by Margaret Kreig in 1967 in a book entitled *Black Market Medicine* (Prentice-Hall, Inc., Englewood Cliffs, New Jersey).

Inadequate laws and inadequate staffs of the investigative and policing agencies have hampered the arrest, prosecution, and conviction of those engaging in this nefarious business of preying upon the gullible. Medical quackery by mail was termed one of the top frauds dealt with by United States postal inspectors in an article, "The Menace of Mail-Order Medicine," by Ralph Lee Smith, condensed in the October, 1967, issue of *The Reader's Digest* from *Today's Health*. The author quoted the Arthritis Foundation, for example, as estimating arthritis quackery to be a $300-million-a-year fraud, most of it transacted by mail. Medical quacks continue to prey in particular, according to the article, upon females who seek to enlarge their bosoms and upon males concerned over problems of impotence or inadequate sexual adjustment.

Even so, progress has been made in recent years in reducing medical quackery with such groups as the American Medical Association, the Post Office Department, and the Better Business Bureau helping spearhead the war upon the quacks. The Drug and Food Administration has been a pioneer in this war.

In earlier years, some producers of diathermy machines, which produce heat in the body tissues by the use of high currents, were

Home "Turkish bath" cabinets such as those shown on the top row and at left on second row were advertised as cures for colds and other ailments in the 1880's and 1890's. In the center of the second row is an advertisement for a device which, it was claimed, supplied oxygen to the blood and cured diseases and pains, and at the right is an early bottle for Marshall's Catarrh Snuff, dated 1896, and now collectible. Third row from left: two types of electric belts of the 1890's advertised as cures for various ailments; a magnetic foot battery, and a dust protector. Fourth row: a toilet mask or "face glove"; a lady's back-supporting garment; anti-blizzard paper vests and chest protectors; and (above at right) a perforated frictional belt, and (below), a buckskin "lung protector." Bottom: a medical battery and a dynamo electric machine for home use.

enriched by the sale of these devices characterized as designed specifically for home use. But medical authorities have repeatedly stated that the use of such a machine for self-treatment can be dangerous and that diathermy treatment should be administered only by licensed medical doctors after careful diagnosis.

The newspapers and magazine of the late 1800's and early 1900's were filled with advertisements for inefficacious and often harmful substances and implements. This field affords a veritable circus for collectors who would like to preserve some of the examples of quackery, of hoaxes, and of gullibility of past years.

A collection of advertisements themselves—including newspaper and magazine publications, posters and broadsides, and advertising booklets—could provide a fascinating display. Even more interesting would be a collection of gadgets and devices used as home remedies, including a miscellany of electrical apparatus offered earlier in this century. Still another intriguing collection could be made of bottles, boxes, and jars containing home remedies of some decades ago. Of merit would be a file of recipes for concoctions used in the home in an effort, frequently vain, to effect cures of diseases and other ailments.

Since the flesh is heir to a host of afflictions, the field for quacks was wide open half a century or more ago, and hundreds of examples of the art of medicinal hoodwinking are still available if you'll just search for them.

Some "doctors" were so bold at the outset of this century as to advertise publicly that they would cure persons given up by other doctors as incurable. One of these advertised in 1900 as follows:

"If your physician has failed to cure you, write this eminent man, giving full name, age, sex, and your leading symptom, and receive a complete diagnosis of your case free of all cost."

The word "free" was abundantly used by the quacks of past years (and it is still being used by quacks of today), and it cost our forebears many a dollar.

Another advertised "free medicine to all" to cure "heart trouble," advising readers to:

"Place your finger on your pulse and see if your heart beats regularly and steadily. If there is a single skipping or irregularity of the beats, your heart is weak or diseased, and there is no telling how soon it will stop beating altogether. Heart troubles, dangerous as they are, can be instantly recognized by all. No doctor can tell better than you if your heart is out of order."

The advertiser then proceeded to advise all who had been treating themselves for stomach, lung, kidney or nervous diseases and had failed to find a cure that "the chances are 9 in 10 that your

Home electrical apparatus, such as shown here, was used by some persons in the early 1900's in a effort to ease their physical miseries. The outfits on the top row and on the left of the second row wholesaled originally at prices of $4 to $14.40. The two other household medical batteries were cheaper. Below is a collectible bottle, produced in 1893 to hold a beauty cream and chap specific.

These collectible bottles, produced in 1900, once held a food emulsion, a tonic, an expectorant, and medicinal jelly.

trouble is in your heart," and he offered to send them this "doctor's" box of "celebrated Heart Tablets absolutely free of charge."

Apparently about nine of every ten women today (and almost that percentage of men) want to lose weight, and probably most of them should. We are a nation of soft livers and big eaters. Had you been living 70 years ago, you could have purchased by mail various "home remedies" which promised you a swift loss of unwanted pounds. Some dealers offered recipes that you could whip up at home at a cost of a few cents. Legitimate medical authorities will tell you that most of these recipes were worthless.

One company solicited obstinate cases of blood poisoning, promising to cure permanently those so afflicted. Its advertisements, as were those of so many other companies of its day, were filled with words and phrases calculated to affright. The firm in question advertised:

Free Cure for Baldness

Prevents Hair Falling Out, Removes Dan
Hair to Natural Color, Stops Itchi
Growth to Eyebrows, Eyelash
---A Trial Pack

ASTHMA
AND
HAY-FEVER
CURED BY THE
Kola Plant

A New and Positive
Cure for ASTHMA and
HAY-FEVER has been
found in the Kola
Plant, a rare botanic
product of West Afri-
can origin. So great
are the powers of this

THE KOLA PLANT.

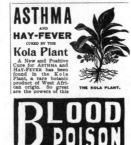

BLOOD POISON

RESCUED ON WAY TO GRAVE;
PROFESSOR STOPS FUNERAL;
RESTORES WOMAN TO LIFE.

DOES HE POSSESS DIVINE POWER?

Woman Threatened With Burial Is Revived by
This Man's Mysterious Mastery Over Disease.

MOST PHENOMENAL MIRACLE OF THE AGE.

Without the Use of Drugs, Medicines or the Sur-
geon's Knife He Defeats Death and Restores
Life and Health to Suffering Mankind.

Completely Upsets Modern Medical Practice.

Gives His Services to Rich and Poor Alike Without Charge—Refuses
Large Check From Grateful Husband—Cures Men and
Women Thousands of Miles Away as ꜱafely
as Those Who Call in Person.

BROTHER Let Me Be Your Friend

Read My
FREE
Offer and
Cure Yourself
Privately

STRONG VIGOROUS VITALITY.

What is Catarrh?

If You Have Any of the Following
Symptoms, Send Your Name
and Address To-day.

Is your breath foul? Is your voice husky? Is
your nose stopped? Do you snore at night? Do
you sneeze a great deal? Do you have frequent

pains in the forehead? Do you have pains across
the eyes? Are you losing your sense of smell?
Is there a dropping in the throat? Are you
losing your sense of taste? Are you gradually
getting deaf? Do you hear buzzing sounds? Do
you have ringing in the ears? Do you suffer
with nausea of the stomach? Is there a constant bad taste in the mouth? Do you have a
hacking cough? Do you cough at night? Do
you take cold easily? If so, you have catarrh.
Catarrh is not only dangerous in this way,
but it causes ulcerations, death and decay of
bones, loss of thinking and reasoning power,
kills ambition and energy, often causes loss of
appetite, indigestion, dyspepsia, raw throat
and reaches to general debility, idiocy and
insanity. It needs attention at once.

SICK LIVERS CURED FREE

Constipation, Headache, Dyspepsia,
Biliousness, Sour Stomach, Loss
of Sleep or Appetite, Sea-
sickness Cured by

DR. WARNER'S
HEALTH UNDERWEAR,
**Made of pure Camel's Hair and
fine Australian Wool.**
It is the best Underwear made.
It is the most durable.
It is free from all dye.
It will not irritate the skin.
It has special electric properties.
It is a protection against Colds,
Catarrh, Rheumatism and
Malaria.
Manufactured in all styles for Men, Women
and Children. For Sale by all Leading Mer-
chants. Catalogue, with prices, sent on appli-
cation.

*These were typical of the advertising claims made for both "remedies"
and individuals in the opening years of this century.*

"If you have taken mercury, iodide potash, and still have aches and pains, mucas patches in mouth, sore throat, pimples, copper colored spots, ulcers on any part of the body, hair or eyebrows falling out, write x x x"

Still another offered "free" treatment for those suffering with "consumption, weak lungs, catarrh, grippe and its deadly after effects, bronchitis, stubborn coughs and colds, wasting away, and pulmonary troubles." It published testimonials from "consumptives who had been given up to die."

All sorts of home cures were offered to women afflicted with drunkard husbands. Popular in this field was a "remedy" designed to be stirred into the husband's coffee and food without his knowledge. Most advertisers described the horrors of drunkenness in lurid detail and agonizing phrase.

There were preparations galore (and there still are) whose sellers promised would enlarge the female breasts, banish facial blemishes, or beautify the face in general. One manufacturer offered a "toilet mask" or "face glove" as "a natural beautifier for bleaching and preserving the skin and removing complexion imperfections."

"Free cures" for baldness were usually accompanied by gushing testimonials. "Before and after" illustrations also were published. It is interesting that these were customarily drawings, not photographs.

"Balmy oils" were proffered to cure cancer of the nose, eye, lip, ear, neck, breast, stomach, or womb.

There were "cures" said to never fail offered for "fits." Once advertised was an asthma "cure" which it was claimed had "cured thousands of cases that were considered incurable." Trial packages were offered—"free," naturally.

Advertised through the years have been thousands of brands of bitters, tonics and the like, the original bottles or boxes of which are highly collectible. That is particularly true of bottles lettered in the glass and containers with their original labels intact. Early bitters bottles have long been collected, but the general tonic bottles offer a good field. Those interested in bitters will find available a highly readable and most informative book on the subject by Richard Watson entitled *Bitters Bottles* (Thomas Nelson & Sons, Camden, New Jersey). Patent medicines and their containers were the subject of an informative article by Beverly J. Silva in the March, 1967, issue of *Western Collector* magazine. And of course, dozens of books have been written during the past two or three years on the collecting of bottles in general. You'll find some of these listed in the Selected Bibliography at the end of this volume.

Sudden Death

If you have heart disease you are in grave danger. Heart troubles, dangerous as they are, can be instantly recognized by all. No doctor can tell better than you if your heart is out of order. If you have any of the following symptoms, don't waste any time. Get my Heart Tablets at once.

Fluttering, palpitation, or skipping beats (always due to weak or diseased heart); shortness of breath from going upstairs, walking, etc.; tenderness, numbness or pain in left side, arm or under shoulder blade; fainting spells, dizziness, hungry or weak spells; spots before the eyes; sudden starting in sleep, dreaming, nightmare;

Heart Disease

choking sensation in throat; oppressed feeling in chest; cold hands and feet; painful to lie on left side; dropsy; swelling of the feet or ankles (one of the surest signs); neuralgia around the heart; sudden deaths rarely result from other causes.

They will restore you to health and strength as they have hundreds of other men and women.

FREE. To prove how absolutely I believe in them, to prove that they will do exactly what I say, I will send a box free to any name and address sent me. One trial will do more to convince you than any amount of talk. It will cost you nothing, and may save your life. Send for a trial box and enclose stamp for postage.

25,000 Packages Free.

Rheumatism Cured by a Simple Remedy That You May Try Without Spending a Cent---Cured Many Cases of 30 and 40 Years Standing.

62 Years of Age. Entirely Cured of Rheumatism
After Having Suffered 42 Years.

CANCER CURED
WITH SOOTHING, BALMY OILS.

Free to the Ruptured

EYESIGHT RESTORED

Failing Eyesight, Cataracts or Blindness Cured without the use of the knife.

MORPHINE OPIUM and Other DRUG HABITS Cured. Trial Free.

Drunkards Cured Secretly

Cancer Cured

Without Knife or Pain—No Pay Until Cured

IN WOMAN'S BREAST ANY LUMP IS CANCER

FREE BOOK—CURE YOURSELF AT HOME

I WILL GIVE $1000 IF I FAIL TO CURE ANY CANCER I TREAT BEFORE IT POISONS DEEP GLANDS

Without Knife or Pain, at Half Price for 30 days. Not a dollar need be paid until cured. Absolute Guarantee. 34 years' experience.

NEW CURE FOR EPILEPTIC FITS

CURE FOR THE DEAF
PECK'S PATENT IMPROVED CUSHIONED EAR DRUMS

Tobacco Cure.

How a Mother Banished Cigarettes and Tobacco With a Harmless Remedy. Costs Nothing to Try.

"If you can't sell 'em otherwise, scare 'em to death." This seems to have been the practice of some concoctors of drugs in the late 1800's and early 1900's. When it came to making claims, the sky was the limit, as witness these advertisements from early periodicals.

Also popular in the 1890's and the early 1900's were a variety of bath cabinets which were designed to yield something of a home-grown Turkish bath. Now this is the sort of thing that could well have been encouraged in those earlier days when taking a bath of any kind was something of a ceremony, set aside for special occasions such as Saturday nights.

These cabinets were made of various materials. The "Square Quaker Folding Thermal Bath Cabinet" opened up to create a sort of rubber-walled room. The bather rested on a chair inside the cabinet with his or her head outside. Entry could be gained through a hinged door. Heat was produced by the use of a small stove (lamps had been used earlier) placed beneath the chair. The stove could be regulated to provide a temperature of from 100 to 150 degrees within the cabinet. The bather sponged his or her body with warm water, alternately rubbing with heavy towels. Medication was available for use in the water. Top curtains could be opened so that the bather could cool off gradually while continuing to sponge and wield the towel.

Baths of this type could be quite wholesome but they didn't cure all the ailments some makers advertised they would. For example, one company claimed use of its cabinet bath would "cure a hard cold with one bath, and prevent Lagrippe, Fevers, Pneumonia, Lung Fever, Asthma, and is really a household necessity." It also offered a "head and complexion steaming attachment," whose use, it boasted, "makes clear skin, beautiful complexion, cures and prevents pimples, blotches, blackheads, skin eruptions, and diseases."

A similar contrivance, the Toledo Bath Cabinet, was advertised in January, 1900, at a price of only $4.50, as compared with its regular price of $10.

Smog-plagued residents of many—or perhaps most—areas of this country might have found an advertisement for one device of the early 1900's of great interest. This was Gibbs' Patent Dust Protector. In appearance it resembled a World War I gasmask. It was worn over the mouth and nose (attached by a band around the head) and, said its manufacturer, protected the nose and mouth "from inhalations of poisonous dust, which is killing thousands yearly." The protector sold for only a dollar, and a revival of it today might be appropriate for those of us who are assailed from dawn to dusk by noxious fumes and vapors that have made city living hazardous and do no good in the hinterlands either.

Home treatment apparatus of various types utilizing an electric current was touted as this century opened, and apparently a good many electrical devices were sold, some of them through well-established chain firms. A number of these contrivances were designed to alleviate "nervous" diseases. One type was an "electric belt," worn around the waist. This utilized an electrical current ("80-gauge current"), which, its sellers advertised, reached "every nerve, vein and muscle of the body" and was designed "for the permanent cure of all nervous, weak and debilitated conditions from any cause." It featured "four medium and one very large electroids, lever regulator for adjusting the current to any degree from 10 to 80 gauge" and came complete with a suspensory attachment. It was claimed that one of these battery-operated belts "afforded immediate relief . . . not reached by any amount of medicine." One brand was offered in 1900 at a price of $18.

In 1886, a magnetic shield and a foot battery were advertised, and some remarkable powers were claimed for them. The advertisement began as follows:

"Nothing is the absence of something. Neurasthenia, nerve exhaustion, is caused by a lack of magnetism in the blood. When the iron in the blood ceases to be a magnet, then polarity is gone and capillary circulation is imperfect, and the entire organism suffers. Polarity and magnetism energize the blood corpuscles and redouble the circulation of the venous system. To impart a powerful current of mineral magnetism to the body we must apply it direct, and in no other way can this be done so effectively as through the MAGNETIC SHIELD."

The manufacturers went on to claim that this shield is "a sure protection against diseases from without, and a powerful stimulating force within the body. The whole tone and character of the blood is changed in a few hours after wearing the shield. Lame Back, Weakness of Kidneys and Lumbar Muscles are positively cured in a few days by wearing these Shields."

Most shields appeared in belt or vest forms. The foot shield was designed to ward off diseases caused by wet, cold feet. It was in the form of an insole. You could buy a pair of these for a dollar.

A non-electric frictional perforated belt was also offered. It was made of rubber and wool, perforated throughout its length and width. The only claims made for it were that it would "counteract tendencies to congestive conditions of the stomach, bowels and kidneys." This, too, sold for a dollar.

Actually all sorts of wearing apparel and accessories designed either to prevent something or cure something abounded 75 years ago. For men and and women both there were shoulder braces, designed to "expand the chest, prevent round shoulders and promote respiration." One type was a combined shoulder brace-suspenders sold by general stores and druggists.

One manufacturer made "health underwear" of camel's hair and

*At top are three views of a 19th century machine used by an insti-
tute for the treatment of chronic diseases. It was said to transmit motion,
through attachments adjustable by means of a ratchet, to various parts
of the body. In the view at extreme left, the device was in a position to
apply movement to the upper portion of the human trunk. The next
illustration shows the same machine folded. The third illustration
shows the device rubbing a patient's chest and abdomen. The institute's director claimed that "motion, transmitted by the manipulator,
exerts a curative effect in* all *chronic affections . . ."* The italics are his.
*Below are pictured a nineteenth-century "Vibrating Kneader" and an
apparatus for rubbing in a recumbent position.*

wool with "special electric properties." This was termed a protection against colds, catarrh, rheumatism, and malaria.

One instrument was offered which, its makers claimed, "aug-
ments the supply of vitality by polarizing the body and causing it
to absorb oxygen from the air through the pores of the skin, thus
augmenting the work of the lungs to an almost unlimited degree."
Of this device, a lady in West Virginia reportedly wrote in 1893:

"I have had the most gratifying results from its use in neuralgia,
indigestion and in the re-building of broken-down females. We use
it for all ailments and find it superior to medicine and doctors."

Well, anything that will re-build broken-down females must
have some merit.

Varied types of electric battery machines were sold in earlier
years to "prevent disease" and "prolong life." These took advantage
of the therapeutic value of electricity in easing tension. But some
extravagant claims were made for some of the machines. One big
department store which sold machines of this type said, without
qualification: "Electricity is a specific for all sexual disorders," adding: "Female diseases, whether acute or chronic, yield readily to
this treatment."

Among those whose use of this type of machine was solicited

were ladies who were reluctant to submit themselves to medical examination!

Then this claim was made:

"It acts as a tonic, building up and strengthening the weakened organs and parts. All forms of female troubles, weakness, bearing down pains, sterility, etc., can be greatly relieved and even cured in this way. Even the wasted muscles and flattened breasts can be developed. Lost manhood and kindred diseases yield quicker to this treatment than any other known."

It was further claimed that the battery also cured asthma, bronchitis, catarrh, dispepsia, constipation, diarrhea, headache, epilepsy, locomotor ataxia, insomnia, varicocele, and lost vitality!

As a rule, the dry cell batteries were enclosed in wooden cases, most of which were constructed of oak. The current generated could be regulated from low to high. Appurtenances included nickel-plated hand electrodes, wood-handled sponge electrodes, cords, and a book of instructions for treatment.

A description of one of these battery devices may give a better indication of its construction:

"This battery is made with 10 cells or 15 volts, and measures 5 x 8 x 2½ and weighs 2½ pounds. The frame of battery is made of carefully selected, highly polished, quarter-sawed oak. All metal parts are nickel-plated, presenting a handsome and complete battery. The wiring of the battery is invisible, being placed in a false bottom of the box. A small, compact and neat coil furnishes the faradic current. . . . This battery is self-registering: that is, each cell represents a volt and a half, and either one or all of the cells can be utilized at a time. . . . Less than a teaspoon of liquid will fill a cell, and when through with the battery the cell is lifted out and the liquid thrown away."

A bottle of fluid for charging the battery was usually provided with the set.

The type of battery just described was used, among other things, for removing hair from the face—the electrolysis process in short. Another battery came equipped with an electric hair brush, electric facial massage roller, electric foot plate, and electric bust developer. This one was termed "as indispensable as the manicure outfit."

Electrical supply companies marketed these battery devices under the general name of household medical apparatus. Early in this century the sets sold at prices of $2.79 to around $15.

Many informative examples of quackery and deceit in the field of medicine and the healing arts are cited in two excellent studies of this field by an historian at Atlanta's Emory University, Dr. James Harvey Young. Dr. Young's books, *The Toadstool Millionaires,* published in 1961, and *The Medical Messiahs: a Social History of Health Quackery in Twentieth Century America,* which made its appearance in 1967 (both published by Princeton University Press) , relate how and why so many persons turn to quacks for help in spite of the tremendous advances made by medical science. The author emphasizes how quacks prey on the worries and the fears of thousands of individuals. Dr. Young served a three-year term on the National Advisory Food and Drug Council to the Food and Drug Administration.

Dr. Young, whose interest in quackery extends back to his days as a student when he was researching old newspaper files, has an interesting collection of examples of it.

A sort of "house of horrors" relating to medical quackery was published a good many years ago under the title *Nostrums and Quackery*. This two-volume work, the second edition of which appeared in 1912 under the imprint of the American Medical Association Press, Chicago, consisted of articles on nostrums and quackery reprinted, with additions and modifications, from *The Journal of the American Medical Association*.

These volumes are filled with accounts of quackery inflicted upon the public in the early years of this century and reproduce scores of illustrations of early advertisements. Chapters are devoted to fake cancer, consumption, drunkenness, "female weakness," obesity, rupture, asthma, diabetes, headache, and other cures. Other chapters deal with mechanical fakes, "cure-alls," cough medicines, hair dyes, kidney pills, laxatives, cosmetics, medical institutes, men's specialists, mineral waters, tonics and bitters, and related subjects.

This is a fascinating work to read, even today. Other excellent books relating to the subject of this chapter will be found in the Selected Bibliography.

This chapter serves merely as an introduction to some of the interesting, complicated, and even fantastic devices, gadgets, and medicinals offered to our forebears. Few collectors indeed have researched the field as yet. By no means all of the devices and medications used for home treatment in these earlier years were worthless; but the worthless ones obviously gave those of value a run for their money.

Except for bottles, so few of the articles discussed in this chapter have been widely traded in by collectors thus far that there are no standard prices for them at this time. This advertisement did appear in a publication not long ago: "A nice electrical shocking machine, measures $9 \times 8\frac{1}{2} \times 6$ box; this is a quack medicine cure-all item and gives one heck of a shock. $14.50."

[5]

Our Grandparents' Toys

Much has been written about mechanical and cast-iron toys of earlier days. Collectors are now paying prices for these which our grandparents would have considered outrageous if not incredible. Writers also have dealt with ancient playthings and toys from eras of which little is left but dust. There are many types of toys, however, from more recent times which, though they are not yet antiques, are collectible reminders of how toymakers labored to keep our grandparents out of mischief. These will be the primary, though not exclusive, concern of this chapter.

The steam toys of the 1880's and 1890's were truly fabulous contrivances. Certainly among the happiest of all boys at Christmas time of those years were the lads for whom Santa in his mystifying benevolence left a steam engine. When these were operated according to instructions, and with reasonable care, they didn't blow up and set the house afire.

In 1885, that treasured magazine *The Youth's Companion* introduced to thousands of young readers of its pages a miniature upright steam engine, which became so popular that more than 100,000 of them were made and sold during the ensuing six years. In 1891, this same publication helped acquaint additional thousands of youngsters with the Weeden Improved Horizontal Steam Engine, which it offered as a premium in exchange for one new subscription plus 15 cents additional for handling. Those preferring to purchase it outright could do so for $1.25 cash, plus 35 cents for postage.

At the same time, there was marketed Weeden's Double Mill Engine. Made by the Weeden Mfg. Company, New Bedford Massachusetts, one of the country's leading producers of steam toys of all types, the Improved Horizontal Double Steam Engine was imposing. The engine had two complete boilers, two lamps, two safety

61

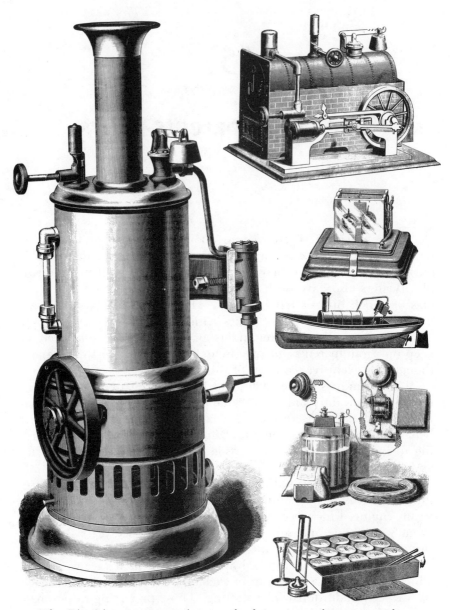

The Big Giant steam engine on the left ran on kerosene and was a big seller in 1900. Right, top to bottom: Weeden's Improved Horizontal steam engine, 1891; the Midget silverplating outfit of 1893; the steamboat "Porter," which had a brass boiler (1900); the Leclanche electric bell outfit, 1891; and the Cabinet of Chemical Wonders, 1891.

valves, a steam dome, and a whistle. Steam was conveyed by a pipe from both boilers through throttle valves to the steam chest. The engine was finished in bronze, scarlet, gilt, and black. The magazine offered the double engine in exchange for two new subscriptions and $1 additional, or it could be purchased outright for $3. It was sent by express, and charges were paid by the recipient.

The horizontal steam engines were made with a stationary instead of an oscillating cylinder. The steam chest was provided with a slide valve operated by means of an eccentric on the flywheel shaft. This added to the engine's power.

These various steam engines were capable of running toy machinery at a high rate of speed, a safety valve being present to prevent the danger of explosion.

Weeden's *upright* model steam engines were not as imposing in appearance but were effective and were sold by the thousands. These, along with the horizontal ones, were manufactured of light stamped metal.

Weeden and other makes of steam engines of the same period operated such devices as pile drivers, derricks, pumps, saws, and others.

Another steam engine making its appearance about the last of the nineteenth century was the "Big Giant." Instead of alcohol, which was used as fuel on most toy steam engines of that day, this one could be operated on ordinary kerosene and could be run continuously for ten hours at a cost of less than a penny. It also operated such models as forges, mills, machine shops, and other contrivances. The engine sold for about a dollar.

The American Steam Pile Driver, on the market about 1890, gave months of pleasure to thousands of boys. The pile driver was operated by steam generated by the attached steam engine. The operator pressed a lever after steam had been generated, and this set a drum to revolving at an increasingly rapid rate of speed. This, in turn, lifted a weight hung between two upright shafts and attached at the top to a rope. When the weight reached the top of the shaft, it released itself automatically from the hoisting rope and fell with impressive force. The lever was then released; the hoisting rope unwound itself from the drum and descended until its engaging hooks caught in the top eye of the weight, whereupon the whole process could be repeated. This machine sold for only $1.25.

The New Styles Company, which published a magazine of women's fashions in the opening years of this century, offered as a premium in exchange for 12 subscriptions a combined steam engine and steam force pump. The engine's boiler was of polished brass and steam was generated by the use of a lamp which burned either

Fascinating steam and electric toys of 1891 were favorites with boys. Top row, left to right: an upright steam engine and force pump, Weeden's No. 8 Mammoth engine, and the American Steam Pile-driver. Second row: Columbian electric generator, and a electric motor and battery outfit. Third row: the Rapid horizontal engine, the Edison electric lamp outfit, and the steamboat "Acushnet." At bottom is a steam locomotive and cars, model stage coach, station, figures, and other accessories.

alcohol or kerosene. The speed of the engine could be regulated by turning the wick up or down. Operating at ordinary speed, this machine could throw a stream of water about six feet. Suction hose, leading hose, and nozzles were provided with each pump. The machine illustrated admirably the manner of pumping water by steam pressure.

Various other makes of horizontal steam engines were advertised from 1900 to around 1905. Popular among these was the "Rapid," which measured 8 inches in height and had a boiler $3\frac{3}{4}$ inches long. It cost $2. A more powerful horizontal engine sold for $10. Its brass boiler was enveloped with a sheet iron jacket to prevent loss of heat.

In his informative work, *The Handbook of Old American Toys* (Mark Haber & Co., Wethersfield, Connecticut), Louis H. Hertz devotes a chapter to steam toys, in which he points out that, in addition to Weeden, other makes of early American steam toys included Ives, J. B. Flynt (Brooklyn), J. & E. Stevens Co., Jehu Garlick, James McNair, Buckman Mfg. Co., known subsequently as Union Mfg. Co., and Kraft & Huffington. Those who would like to know more about the history of the steam toys will find it advantageous to consult Mr. Hertz's book, the purpose of the chapter you are now reading being primarily to identify some of the interesting toys of a few generations ago and to indicate some which are definitely collectible.

Microscopes of various types composed an extremely popular category of gifts for boys and girls of the late nineteenth and early twentieth centuries.

Although microscopes had been known for years earlier, their first serious use as scientific instruments began in the latter part of the eighteenth century. Refinements of the instruments were made in the United States in the latter half of the nineteenth century, and the use of small, inexpensive microscopes to open up a fascinating new world of discovery for teen-agers was ushered in late last century. In 1887, microscope "packages" for the youngsters were available for as little as $1. One of these combination packages included a microscope with three lenses and an adjustable mirror, plus one mounted object, a glass slide, and a box for containing live insects or other objects to be studied under the magnifying lenses.

Another package consisted of a small imported brass microscope, a large horseshoe magnet, a round, handled magnifying glass (identified as a "burning glass"), and a "spyglass" (miniature telescope).

Small but serviceable microscopes in wooden cases sold for $1.25 to $2.25 in 1887. These were used to investigate the composition of leaves, the wings of flies, flowers, various small insects, minerals,

Youngsters of the 1890's enjoyed scientific toys, and optical outfits of various types experienced great popularity. Top, left to right: a compound microscope with case, the Young Naturalist's microscope, and a combination optical and magnetic package. Second row: another optical and magnetic package combination, a pocket microscope with stand, and a small microscope in a case. Third row: a microscope with a gallery of 100 slides of historic scenes; another Naturalist's microscope, a French microscope, and the Imperial Graphoscope, which gave an enlarged view of pictures. Bottom: a drawing of a French compound microscope in use, a Harvard microscope, and another French compound microscope with a specimen furnished for examination through the lens.

and numerous other objects. Thousands of these were imported from France and Germany. The stands were customarily made of lacquered brass, and the instruments usually came complete with a pair of small glass slides, one mounted object to study, and, often, a pair of forceps.

In 1900, *The Youth's Companion* offered as a premium (or for only a dollar cash) a "Symmetroscope," which it described as "a new invention which produces marvelous results," adding: "The power of observation and the beauty of color and form are only a few of the results which attend the use of this instrument. Artists and designers find it a never-failing source of new ideas of form and combinations of color and design, Manufacturers of carpets and wall-paper make use of it for striking and novel patterns for their latest styles." The magazine also offered a "Live Cage Microscope," which was a round glass container with brass fittings at top and bottom and a round lens at the top. It was designed for the examination of objects such as leaves, roots, flowers, grain, live insects and the like when a large field was required. The objects were placed in the bottom of the glass container and viewed through the magnifying lens which screwed on to the top.

Available for a dollar around 1890 was a package consisting of a "multiplying glass," small microscope, a pocket compass, horseshoe magnet, "spy glass," "burning glass," and some seeds for viewing. The same amount of money would buy a nickel-plated microscope and 100 pictures photographed on glass and mounted on cardboard strips. The microscope was fitted with a sliding tube for focusing and a reversible glass reflector. Good quality microscopes with rack-work attachments could be had for $5.

Popular during the same years were "spyglasses," or telescopes in various designs and with a magnifying power of about 12 times. These had lacquered brass tubes and achromatic lenses. Retail prices in 1902 ranged from $2.50 to $5, although simpler and less effectives ones were available at lower prices. These provided many hours of enjoyment for youngsters who focused them on everything from squirrels in distant trees to the goings-on in their neighbors' parlors.

Various other "scientific" types of toys appealed to boys and girls of the pre-space exploration era. There were all sorts of simple electric motors and batteries, for example. The motors, as were the steam engines, were utilized to run light toy machinery. A fine 1891 experimental toy was an Edison Electric Lamp Outfit. This consisted of an Edison one-candlepower lamp with carbons, zinc, wire and solution. This was used to illustrate the wonders of Edison's incandescent electric lamp. The materials and solution for making the lamp burn were placed in ordinary household jars or tumblers.

Various pieces of apparatus for minor but interesting experiments with electricity were produced by manufacturers. One outfit consisted of an "electrical machine" with a 14-inch plate glass disc, a brass conductor on a glass pillar for generating electricity, and a Leyden jar for storing the electricity. The jar was lined with tinfoil. There was also a brass discharge knob and chain with a glass handle, and an electroscope with two pith balls suspended by silk threads. The entire outfit sold for $3.

For a dollar and a half one could purchase in 1892 a toy silver-plating outfit with battery, electrodes and plating solution. This could be used to plate rings, charms, medals and other small objects.

For the girls there were toy sewing machines that actually sewed and made chain stitches. One of these was the New Century Toy Sewing Machine, which sold for $2 in 1900. It could be used to teach small girls the rudiments of dressmaking by letting them experiment with doll clothes.

Toy typewriters are not recent fabrications; they date back to the 1880's. The American Toy Typewriter sold for 85 cents in 1889. Letters of the alphabet and numerals were on a handled wheel, and the process of imprinting letters on paper was a slow one. However, it boasted an automatic paper feed, and the type disc was self-inking.

Feats of legerdemain were even more popular in the 1890's than they are today, and numerous outfits were manufactured for young magicians. One such outfit included two wands, a glass dish, a "Wizard's Furnace," three tin cones, large dice, an imitation rose, and other apparatus. With the use of this equipment the amateur magician could perform such feats as "eating" fire and blowing out smoke and sparks, causing a wand to remain suspended in the air without apparent support, causing a shower of candy to fall from an apparently empty plate, and making various objects mysteriously appear and disappear.

A larger outfit was available with which 25 tricks could be performed. These included stunts designated as the Enchanted Rose, Growing Rose-Bush, Phantom Ring, Charmed Handkerchief, Flying Dime and Orange, Sprightly Coin, Flying Gloves, and others.

When these outfits came on the market, there was a rush for them by youngsters who had been enchanted by the extraordinary feats performed earlier by such professionals as Houdini, Heller, and Anderson. Many owners of such apparatus staged their own backyard shows, making a small admission charge.

Of educational value was the "American Panorama," an early

A choice miscellany of late nineteenth-century toys, all of which were once given by The Youth's Companion as premiums. Top left is the Multitudinous Toy Set, featuring the famous Brownies created by Palmer Cox; a Brownie stamp (which came with a stamp pad); and the Pretty Village made of lithographed cardboard pieces which fit together. Second row from left: the American Panorama; Bradley's Panorama of American History; and Reed's Miniature Capitol and Historical Panorama. Third row: Boy's Fort of Amusement; a Rotographoscope (which gave a magnified view of photographic strips); and a set of three games— Toss, Tip-i-Tip, and Humpty Dumpty Marbles. Bottom: a set of indoor toys for boys; the Young Storekeeper's Outfit; and (above) a Punch and Judy show, and (below) the Lyceum Magic Lantern.

picture machine by whose use a series of chromolithographs depicting major events in American history could be viewed. The machine was operated with a crank handle. The scenes for viewing included the landing of Columbus, discovery of the Mississippi River, Braddock's defeat, the Boston Tea Party, Battle of New Orleans, baptism of Pocahontas, Defense of Fort Moultrie, Battle of Bunker Hill, and others. It cost 90 cents in the 1890's.

Another "forerunner" of the motion picture was the marvelous Zoetrope, which, when rotated, caused figures printed on simple strips of paper to appear animated. This cost a dollar complete with a set of 12 pictures strips in 1891.

Another instructional toy was the "Kindergarten and Mechanical Speller." In appearance, this resembled a miniature pinball machine or cash register. The top of this machine was equipped with a series of illustrations of identified animals and objects which were made to appear in view by turning a small wooden button on the side. The illustrations revolved inside the machine. On the bottom of the device was a set of keys that could be pressed to spell any words containing two to five letters. The words thus spelled appeared in view on a strip in the machine's center. If you find one of these early devices, it should be worth several dollars, but it cost only $1 retail in 1891.

To instill the principles of good salesmanship in young boys, "The Young Storekeeper's Outfit" was used about 80 years ago. Included in this was a box of toy money representing gold and silver coins totaling $100; sheets of labels designed to be cut up and attached with prices and names of commodities on boxes of sawdust or bran; an assortment of bag material and a form for making small paper bags; a price list of merchandise ranging from groceries to hardware; and a "Rapid Transit Cash Carrier." The last name was a container with two wheels at its top that traveled along a cord.

For younger boys and girls who wanted to keep store there was a toy cash carrier outfit, consisting of a car and a small cup in which notes or money could be enclosed; a coil of wire long enough to stretch across the room; two little springs with rubber bumpers designed to stop the traveling car gently at either end of the wire; an assortment of play money; and a group of pictures of commonplace commodities that could be "sold" as substitutes for the articles they depicted.

There also were numerous types of building toys that could be used to construct everything from miniature farms to churches. Some of these were made of wooden pieces (or blocks) and others of painted cardboard. One variation consisted of pieces to be cut out and mounted in slotted bases. Some of the slotted base strips

Toys for all ages. From left, top: a shadow pantomime set with movable figures, an illustration of Emerson's Boomerang Gun in action, and a home-made cornstalk doll. Second row: a silverplated card and linen marker outfit, Sunny Hill Farm, and Santa Claus and His Reindeer Team. Third row: a toy zither and banjo, spring pop cannon, and a three-toy set consisting of Ring Toss, a horse and wagon, and a Bagatelle board. Below at left is apparatus for scientific experiments, the Cabinet of Legedermain and Oriental Magic, and a set of West Point Cadets. Nearly all of these were featured by The Youth's Companion *in the late 1800's.*

could be manipulated to cause the objects mounted on them to move. For example, a small group of soldiers could be caused to go through various drill movements and marches.

One handsome set of building blocks was used to construct a village church. On the inside of the blocks composing this church scripture texts from the Bible were printed. Some sets of building blocks were made not of wood but of colored stone. A set of the latter type was offered for $1.75 in 1888 by F. Ad. Richter & Co., of New York City.

A truly fascinating train outfit, advertised in 1891, consisted of a steam locomotive, a car, and tender, all made of metal; a replica of a stage coach; a track; a flag house; and "people" and a station. The station was lithographed in color on paper, and the owner of this set cut out wooden boards and pasted the lithographed station on them. The "people" also were lithographed on paper and were cut apart and pasted on wood backings.

Some toy assembly sets were made of interchangeable blocks which could be fitted into one another by means of grooves. They could be used for building such things as train cars, stations, trucks, and even merry-go-rounds. As was the case with the station mentioned above, numerous other outfits for assembly by the recipient were printed or lithographed on cardboard or wood. Among these were farm buildings, animals, and fence for pastures.

Wooden painted toys included a good many of the items which also were made of cast iron or tin. Among these was a miniature horse-drawn car—a forerunner of the electric trolley. The car and horses were mounted on wheels, and the car seats were reversible.

Doll houses are beginning to return to popularity today, not so much among children, however, as among adult collectors, who can view them and visualize the exterior and interior appearance of the homes of the 1880's and 1890's. Many inexpensive but attractive doll houses were made of wood covered with lithographed paper. A large number of these originally sold for less than a dollar and will fetch many times that now.

Once available were numerous other types of wooden toys covered with lithographed paper; these ranged from pull vehicles to circuses. Many were mounted on wooden wheels so they could be pulled or pushed easily. The illustrations accompanying this chapter will show some of them, and they are all worth collecting. Particularly intriguing was a Punch and Judy show of 1891, complete with figures carved from wood and painted. This was an import from Germany. The set of five figures cost only $2, and was accompanied by a set of instructions for making the framework of a stage.

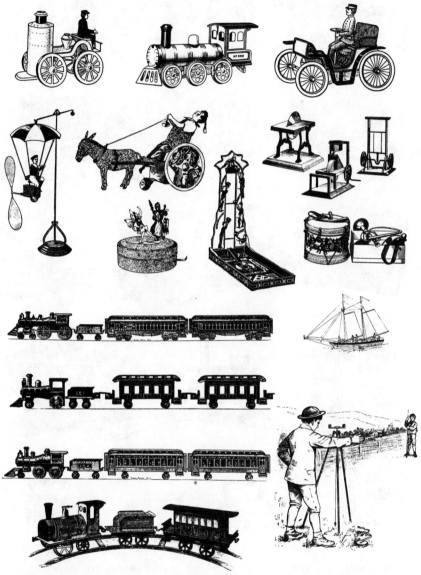

Action toys and others of the 1890's. Left to right, top: a horseless fire engine, bell locomotive, and automobile, all of which were operated with spring motors. Second row: mechanical air ship, balky donkey (top) and Magic Box (below), the Jolly Marble Game, three machines operated by steam engines (above) and snare drum and rein set (below). On the next four rows at left are shown various mechanical train sets. To the right of these is the sailboat "America" on wheels and a boys' surveying outfit.

Something for the girls. Top, left to right: young housekeeper's toy kitchen outfit (1893); 5 o'clock china tea set (1893), and tin kitchen (1891). Second row from left: another tin kitchen (1891); decorated china tea set (1891), and the "Saratoga" doll trunk (1893). Third row: three furnished doll apartments of 1891 and a fine doll's house of wood covered with paper of 1892. Fourth row: a knit doll and a motorized walking bear of 1901, and two fine toy ranges, about 1900. Bottom: a work kit for young girls (1893), and three toy sad irons of around 1900. These illustrations are from The Youth's Companion *and* Belknap Hardware & Manufacturing Co.

In addition to all types of dolls and doll accessories, many miniature toys were turned out in the late 1800's for girls. The collecting of miniaturia is heading toward a peak of interest right now so that these tiny pieces of last century may be expected to bring higher prices within the next few years. They included a diversity of tea sets made of china; castor sets of glass; wooden and cardboard furniture; and a great diversity of kitchen implements made of tin and iron. It will seem astonishing to today's collector of miniaturia that in 1891 a miniature set consisting of 15 pieces of china, a castor set with four bottles, and a tin kitchen equipped with a range could all be purchased for less than a dollar; A dollar bought a very handsome 21-piece tea set attractively decorated in colors and edged with gold leaf.

Of course, tinplate and iron train sets were popular with youngsters in the last century as they still are, and the collector in this field can read all about their development through the years in an informative book by Louis Hertz entitled *Riding the Tinplate Rails*.

There were dozens of other types of tin and iron toys, most of which bring quite high prices now when in good condition. One of these, incidentally, I have not seen in any of the antique shops lately. It was called the Aerial Revolving Railway. The action of a spring motor sent a small car with two tiny occupants from the top to the bottom of a steep incline and then back up again through a spiral course. It somewhat resembled the roller coaster.

The boys and girls of the last century apparently found more time to help out with various household chores than they do these days, and some gifts presented at Christmas were designed to enable them to extend their helpful activities, for which their doting parents undoubtedly were grateful. One of these was a silverplated card- and linen-marking set, accompanied by three sets of rubber type, ink, tweezers and an inking pad. With its use boys and girls could imprint calling and greeting cards and could place identification marks on the family clothing.

Cards and other items also could be imprinted with the use of small cylinder printing presses, available in 1908 and for several years thereafter for only a few dollars.

The so-called Magic Lantern saw widespread use over a period of years. It projected slides and was a forerunner of today's streamlined slide projectors. The Magic Lanterns were manufactured in numerous sizes and shapes and were available in models costing only a few dollars to professional outfits for use in schools and by professional lecturers. There are still a good many of these around, and interest in collecting them is likely to be aroused before long. Both Magic Lanterns and stereoscopes are discussed in some detail in my book *Treasure at Home*.

Sets consisting of a group of non-related toys were produced in quantities in the latter part of last century. One of these contained, for example, a bubble blower, a still savings bank, a plush dog activated by a bulb and air hose, a game of Tiddledy Winks, and a toy revolver. Numerous sets of this type were sold for a dollar or less.

Toy musical instruments were just as poplar 75 years ago as they are today. Produced were hundreds of thousands of snare drums, banjos, zithers, fifes, and other small reproductions of the larger popular instruments, including pianos. Some of the finest miniature pianos were made by the famous Schoenhut company, which also produced the well-known jointed figures and other delightful toys. These pianos came in various sizes, the finest ones originally selling for as much as $20 and the smallest and simplest ones selling for as little as a quarter! You'll find them retailing at antique shops now for perhaps around $7.50 to $75 or more. The Schoenhut firm was founded in Philadelphia by a German immigrant, Albert Schoenhut, less than a decade after the War between the States and became one of the largest and best-known toy-making companies in this nation.

Scores of games made to amuse young people of earlier generations are worth preserving, and I have devoted a chapter to these in my book *The Coming Collecting Boom*.

One outdoors' game not described in that book, however, has recently come to my attention. It must have provided many hours of fun for its participants. It was called "The Boomerang Gun." A boomerang of hard maple was shot from a wooden "gun" and proceeded to circle a pole while participants attempted to catch it with hand nets. The action of the boomerang was so fascinating and mysterious that in 1892 the inventor of this game offered $200 in gold as prizes for the first ten persons to give the correct answer to the question "What makes the boomerang come back?"

In contradictory statements, one encyclopedia of those days stated that the boomerang was thrown with the·flat side up, and another said it was thrown with the flat side down. But the boomerang used in the game just described had both sides flat!

In December, 1886, *The Youth's Companion* published an article on home-made toys. This described methods of making cornstalk dolls, cannons from spools, a moving rooster from cardboard and string, wagons from cigar boxes, and other toys from cardboard, newspaper, crepe paper, and buttons.

Other popular toys of the 1880's and 1890's included the Jolly Marble Game, Humpty Dumpty Marbles, the Never-Stop Seesaw, tops of various types, water and cap pistols, cork-shooting guns, and

Building and construction toys. Left to right, top row: The Village Church with windows in imitation of stained glass; another Village Church with scripture texts on the inside of the blocks; and Gilt Edge Building Blocks. Second row: Frost's Blocks (1903); the Famous Royal Guards (1892), and Anchor Stone Building Blocks (1888) (above), and Cannon's Detachable Toy Blocks, (1902) (below). Third row: the famous Erector building toy; Cement Block Manufactory, Fort Columbia (above), the well-known Meccano building set. All toys on the bottom row are 1917 versions except the 1894 Fort Columbia; those on the top row are all dated 1891.

On the top row from left are a toy package containing a jumping dog, toy revolver, bubble blower, savings bank, and a game of Tiddledy Winks; another package containing a doll's swinging hammock, folding round table, a doll house, doll settee, and game of Fox and Geese; and a game for small children called "Basalinda." Second row from left: an electric toy game called "Ano Kata"; a 1902 toy cash carrier-store outfit; the American Songster, a toy bird that could be made to imitate a canary; and a flexible backboard. Third row: a nursery rhyme mechanical toy whose figures could be made to move; a 1918 wooden express donkey and wagon; and (upper) a parlor floor croquet set. Bottom: a toy package consisting of a "mental education" board, a carbograph tracing frame, and a game of Donkey Party; an 1891 kindergarten mechanical speller; and the New Century toy sewing machine for girls (1900).

the Laughing Camera whose lenses gave individuals ludicrous-looking shapes.

Dozens of other games will be found illustrated and described in early toy manufacturers' catalogues, such as those of E. I. Horsman Company, and in catalogues of mail order houses and those of such popular retail establishments as F. W. Woolworth Company. All of these early toy catalogues are exceedingly scarce and, when found, will bring very high prices.

Because comparatively few of the toys described in this chapter have appeared on the antiques market, specific values have not been established for most of them, and you'll have to bargain with private owners.

[6]

Whoopee, Boys!
Elon's Got the Ball!

Athletic sports date back to the dawn of civilization. The ancient Greeks and the Egyptians, yearning for exciting entertainment, assembled in crowds to witness boxing and wrestling matches 5,000 years ago. The Coliseum sports of the early Christian era left something to be desired when it came to a display of what we now term sportsmanship, but they had their addicts by the thousands. Many early sports served to condition their participants for the arduous tasks of hunting for food and fighting for materialistic gain or defense of one's homeland.

Athletic contests of a more genteel nature evolved in the eighteenth century, began their maturity in the nineteenth, and reached their peak of perfection and interest in the twentieth. Baseball, this country's earliest national pastime, evolved into what is largely its present form in 1839 with Abner Doubleday, Alexander Cartright and others sharing in the credit for its rise as a spectator sport with a set of specific playing rules. Basketball had its beginnings in the early 1890's, and football, which was actually brought to this country from England, waddled around in a somewhat haphazard manner until after the Civil War when it then began to take form as the sport we know it today.

This chapter, however, will not be a treatise on sports. It will attempt to point up the fact that the collecting of sports mementoes, now limited to only a few individuals and institutions, deserves far wider attention. There are scores of items associated with sports through the years which should interest men and women, children and adults. There are numerous appealing keepsakes related to such sports as boxing, wrestling, bicycle and automobile racing, horse racing, track events, the various ball games, rowing, tennis, golf, skating, archery, ice hockey, and others, and the quest for these can be particularly satisfying.

Collecting can extend to memorabilia of such genteel sports as croquet and Saturn, the latter having been a late nineteenth-century lawn target game which required a little skill.

You may, in fact, be interested in some of these genteel sports which were features of many a social gathering or informal outdoors party of less than a century ago. A one-time favorite at resorts was called "lawn pool" or "Imperial Croquet," patented December 19, 1882, which was in effect a new form of croquet. However, instead of driving the ball through a wicket or arch as in the conventional game, the players attempted to strike a pedestal and dislodge a ball.

There were several target sports in addition to archery. Saturn, for example, provided a round target with pegs at which rings were tossed.

Parlor Tennis was played indoors with a flat bat and 24 colored balls, plus a mesh basket. Wise hostesses usually removed the bric-a-brac from the parlor before permitting indulgence in this sport.

For the young, there was a sport called Hooples, which consisted of rolling a large metal hoop with the aid of a stick. Although it originated in the nineteenth century, it had its devotees through my own childhood.

Though table tennis was played in the last century, it has continued in popularity through the years. Early table tennis equipment is now collectible.

Trophies, silver or silverplated, once awarded to outstanding athletes and sportsmen, compose one aspect of sports collecting. These trophies did not always remain in the possession of the winner or his heirs. Sometimes, under the duress of unpaid bills, they gravitated to hock shops. From hock shops they occasionally found their way into antique shops, coaxed along by dealers who found them unredeemed on pawn shop shelves.

The trophies are usually of some intrinsic merit, based upon the amount of silver they contain, but often of far more importance is the name engraved upon the trophy. If you are lucky, you may encounter the names of sports figures of past generations to whom the record books still pay tribute.

Of more interest than the traditionally fashioned two-handled loving cups are trophies featuring representations of the sport for which they were awarded. There were baseball trophies, for example, that were made in the shape of a group of bats supporting a baseball. Similarly, bowling awards sometimes represented a

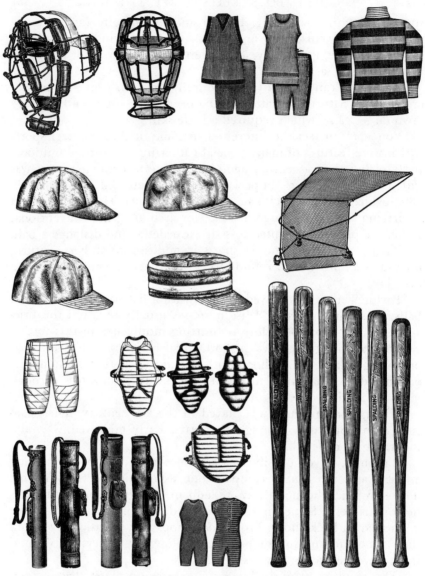

Sports paraphernalia of 1908 from the famous house of A. G. Spalding & Bros. Top row, left to right: an umpire's mask, "neck protecting" mask, two two-piece swim suits, and a striped jersey. Second row: Boston and Brooklyn style baseball caps, and a movable batting cage. Third row: Philadelphia and Chicago style baseball caps. Fourth row: padded basketball pants, and three inflated baseball body protectors. Fifth row: four caddy bags; a baseball umpire's body protector (and, at bottom, two one-piece swim suits), and Spalding's Players' Autograph bats. The bats are autographed, left to right, by Frank L. Chance, Ty Cobb, Roger Bresnahan, Geo. R. Stone, Miller J. Huggins, and Wm. H. Keeler.

Sporting fobs and chains and charms of pre-World War I vintage.

group of tenpins supporting a bowling ball. There were trophies featuring footballs of silver or silverplate with engraved lacing. Winners of automobile races were occasionally awarded cups with winged wheels at the base, and hunting trophies sometimes had genuine stag handles.

In addition to the two-handled loving cups, many were made with three handles. An outstanding collection of three-handled cups assembled by Kent B. Diehl was described by him in an article in the October, 1966, issue of *Western Collector*. Mr. Diehl's is reportedly the world's largest collection of such trophies, and among them are cups of porcelain, pottery, stoneware, and other materials. Some were produced by world-famous potteries, among these being one fashioned at Meissen with transfer prints made and

All of these trophies and loving cups date early in this century. They are silverplated, and some are lined with gold. At top right, in the center, and at left bottom are three of the traditional three-handled cups. These were manufactured by E. G. Webster & Son and Homan Manufacturing Company.

Trophies popular more than half a century ago are shown here. Note that some are designed to reflect the precise sport for which they were awarded, such as those for bowling, baseball, automobile racing, and football.

signed by the renowned Francois Bouche, whose painting attained fame in the eighteenth century. The early loving cups (or tankards) were used to hold strong drink and many a toast was drunk from them following festivities characterized by athletic prowess.

Some sports fans collect signed photographs of distinguished athletes—baseball and football players, boxers, and other figures in the world of athletics. Those athletes whose fame has lasted for a good many years occasionally find their own signed photos listed in the catalogues of dealers in autograph material. The autographed photos are valued according to the renown of the subject, and you'll encounter them priced at only a few dollars and up. Even signed photographs of outstanding sports stars of the present day usually bring two or three dollars.

In a vaguely allied category are sporting prints. Early ones done by noted artists often fetch quite high prices. These include many sporting lithographs turned out last century by Currier & Ives. Of prime value is the C&I colored lithograph entitled *The American National Game of Baseball: Grand Match for the Championship at the Elysian Fields, Hoboken, N.J.,* a very rare and perhaps the earliest representation of this game. It was published in 1866.

Currier & Ives produced numerous sporting lithographs in fields ranging from horse racing to boxing. Another scarce lithograph is *The Great Fight, between Tom Hyer & Yankee Sullivan,* published in 1849 by James Baillie, of New York City. The fight, in case you're interested, was won by Hyer. It took place on February 7, 1849, in Kent County, Maryland. Several other lithographers of the nineteenth century produced sporting prints, and by no means do all of them bring high prices today. Of interest, too, are books with sporting prints, particularly those with color plates rather than tinted plates, the latter being covered with a wash of color to soften the effect. A noted English illustrator of sporting books of the last century was Henry Alken. Among his own books was *National Sports of Great Britain,* published in 1821 and containing 50 colored plates. This volume has sold for around $250 to $300 at auction.

Naturally, fine examples of sports equipment and player accouterments should be of interest. Undoubtedly, there are thousands of examples around somewhere, although some of them now are being sought by museums. Things to look for include early baseballs, basketballs, footballs, tennis and soccer balls and others; athletic uniforms and caps of all types; tennis rackets and playing court markers; golf clubs and bags; baseball bats, bases, and home plates, and umpires' indicators; officials' badges and emblems; masks and face guards; and, of course, any adjuncts of games signed by players. These will suggest other items to you.

The interesting sport of Whooples, as it was played in 1889.

Cycling was a popular sport in the 1880's and 1890's, and many a bicycle race over long courses aroused the interest of large numbers of spectators. There are collectors of early bicycles, once called such names as "boneshakers" and "hobby horses." Other early cycling collectibles include collapsible cups, carrying bags, lights, and horns or other warning devices. There are even a few collectors of early bicycle brakes. For the history of some of the early bicycle events and cycling collectibles, the reader may be interested in an article of mine entitled *The Boneshakers Are Back,* which appeared in the magazine *Yankee* for April, 1965.

Early ice skates and skating lanterns are collectible as are other types of skates.

Souvenir programs of all types of sports events of past years not only may be collected but can often provide a wealth of information about players, teams, records, and rules. Fred Imhoff, of San Jose, California, began collecting football programs of college games in 1932 and assembled thousands of them. In the latter part of last century, many of these were published in cloth bindings by the more affluent colleges and universities. A collection of such programs can provide a veritable storehouse of fascinating statistics and other information of much interest to the sports enthusiast.

There is an excellent opportunity to collect early baseball guides, which have been issued for more than a century. Those turned out during the middle of last century are worth $20 or more each in good condition. An 1899 copy of *Spalding's Official Base Ball Guide* was recently offered at $10. Also available are numerous books about baseball (and other sports), including fiction and nonfiction. Henry Chadwick's *The Game of Baseball: How to Learn it, How to Play it, and How to Teach it,* published in 1868, is valued at $40 or more in first-class condition. The book of juvenile fiction *Won in the Ninth* by the renowned Christy Mathewson, published in 1910, is worth $5 or more. There are dozens of other early sports books whose values are ascending. Bear in mind that reprints, as a rule, are worth little: it is the original edition that fetches the top price.

Of course, autographs and letters written by famous sports figures are of value and this probably will be enhanced in the years ahead. Babe Ruth's signature on a menu for a dinner at which he was guest speaker sold some time ago for $5. An 1869 newspaper containing a baseball box score brought $4. Sports periodicals dated in the past century may be worth several dollars each—rare ones more. These include issues of the early *Police Gazette,* which also at one time published lurid accounts of events other than sports.

Merchandise catalogues featuring sports goods are highly desirable as are fishing tackle catalogues. For your information, here are a few prices asked in recent months for some catalogues in these categories:

Fine Fishing Tackle, a 92-page catalogue issued by James F. Marsters, Manufacturers, about 1869 and containing two color plates and numerous other illustrations, $22.50.

Hand-Made Fishing Tackle, Catalogue B, issued by the John J. Hildebrandt Company in 1910, and containing 24 pages, $15.

Catalogue No. 23, issued by Murray & Company, Chicago, in 1896 and containing 48 pages of tents, camping furniture, and so on, $12.50.

A sporting goods catalogue issued in 1903 by Roach, Hirth & Company with 118 pages of sporting goods, $15.

A catalogue of guns and other sports equipment published in 1904 by Von Lengerke & Antoine, Chicago, with 80 illustrated pages, $10.

However, many more recent catalogues may be purchased for smaller sums. Catalogues should be in good condition and should not have pages clipped.

A few other sports adjuncts to look for are stop watches, fencing foils, fishing lures, bowling balls, early wagering tickets, broadsides advertising early sports lotteries, and pre-1915 swimming suits.

Of interest also are pottery and porcelain plates, cups, mugs, and other items containing depictions of sports. Dr. Roland C. Geist, an authority on bicycles and author of *Bicycling as a Hobby,* began collecting fancy plates bearing pictures of cycling about 1934. As late as 1959, he was still able to buy some at around $2, but others cost up to about $50. Some of these plates were produced by American potteries and some were manufactured abroad.

Unusual sports items should be sought. These might include a pedespeed. According to a brief item in the *Spinning Wheel* for December, 1955, this unusual device was invented by one Thomas Luders in 1870 and consisted of a small monocycle for each foot. He made special ones for the ladies: they were fitted with shields to protect skirts. The devices were, said the magazine, "more bi-

Miscellaneous baseball paraphernalia dating from 1885 to 1907.

cycle than roller skate" and required considerable practice.

Although signed photographs of athletes and sports figures have been collected for a long time, these seem to be enjoying a spurt of popularity right now. Here are recent prices asked for some of these:

Ty Cobb, $25; Mickey Cochrane, $10; Hugh Duffy, $18.50; Lefty Grove, $9; Rogers Hornsby, $10; Harry Lajoie, $8; Connie Mack, $20; Honus Wagner, $15; Babe Ruth, $30; Al Simmons, $12; Edward A. Walsh, $10; Paul Waner, $10; Cy Young, $15. Note that all of these men were elected to the Baseball Hall of Fame.

Even signatures of famous players are of value, although normally a signature alone (often clipped from a letter or note) is of little interest as compared with an autograph letter signed. The value depends on the fame of the player and the scarcity of his autograph. The signature of Edward T. Collins was tendered by a dealer some months ago at $15 and that of Fred G. Clarke, also a member of the Baseball Hall of Fame, at $3.75. Many are valued somewhere between those two prices.

Collecting decoys can be a particularly satisfying hobby, because so many types have been made through the years. Some early ones are beautiful examples of the carver's art. Until the government outlawed their use some time ago, live tamed ducks were used to lure wild fowl into decoy ponds, where they were driven into a funnel net at one end and caught. With the outlawing of live ducks for the purpose, man-made decoys were substituted. Wild fowl calls also came into widespread use. These calls were crafted with precision, as they still are. They are quite simple in construction. A reed and a small wooden gutter are placed into a two-piece outer tube and are held in place by a small wedge. The basic sound emitted is largely determined by the manner in which the reed itself is tapered and fitted into the gutter or trough. The calls are usually made with either wooden or plastic tubes, although cane is sometimes used in Louisiana, where it is plentiful.

Paul Kalman, a public relations practitioner, sportsman, and free-lance writer of New Orleans, described in the November, 1962, issue of *Sports Afield* a call owned by Herb Parsons, a champion caller, as being made of Circassian walnut and checkered like the stock of a fine gun. He also mentioned that a call owned by a Texas oil man had an outer barrel of 14-karat gold!

Collectible are duck calls, snipe calls, turkey calls, dog calls, and various types of whistles.

The early decoy waterfowl were made of various materials, including wood, collapsible canvas, cork, papier-mâché, and a combination of wood and brass. A 1909 wholesale catalogue advertised collapsible canvas decoys with anchors at $12 a dozen, folding wood

Top row, left to right: Kankakee wood duck decoy mallard with a canvas back, and two papier-mâché mallards, a male and female. Second row: a solid cedar decoy, a decoy showing the attachment of a weight, and two collapsible canvas decoys. All these decoys date early in this century. Third row: Chesapeake folding decoys of 1907 and a turkey call of 1900. Fourth row: a duck call, snipe or duck call, and an echo call, all dating about the turn of the century. Fifth row: two duplex calls, and a metal whistle, all of about 1900. Below are pictured several collectible bicycle bells of around 1900, and a bicycle bugle and signal horn of about 1895.

duck decoys at $7 a dozen, and collapsible canvas decoy geese with new-style valves without wires at $24 a dozen. In 1907, papier-mâché mallard decoys with glass eyes wholesaled for $36 a dozen. Many decoys were strikingly realistic, painted in natural colors.

Some interesting decoys may now be picked up for a few dollars each, including some hand-carved ones. Refinished early mallard decoys have been offered in recent months at $14 a pair and metal geese decoys for $22.50 a pair. Others may cost you $25, $30, or more.

Here are recent prices asked for sports memorabilia:

Baseball broadside (*The Cincinnati Enquirer* baseball schedule for 1899), 14 by 22 inches, $5; Horace Partridge Company illustrated catalogue of baseball uniforms and supplies for 1897, $6.50; *Napoleon Lajoie's Official Base Ball Guide,* 1906, $12.50; *Spalding's Official Base Ball Guide,* 1912, $10; cyclist's brass collapsible cup, $6.75; *America's National Game: Historic Facts Concerning the Beginning, Evolution, Development and Popularity of Base Ball,* by Albert G. Spalding, 1911, first edition, $22.50; *Spalding's Official Foot Ball Guide, 1906,* edited by Walter Camp, $7.50; *Spalding's Official Soccer, Foot Ball Guide for 1908,* $2; celluloid baseball score keeper in shape of baseball, issued in 1920's by Massachusetts Breweries Company, $2; *Baseball Magazine* for April, 1920, with issue devoted to articles about Babe Ruth, $4.50.

Also, clamp-on ice skates, $2 a pair; Rose Bowl celluloid badges, 25 cents each; collection of 10 baseballs autographed by members of American and National League teams over past three decades, $350; pair of Wedgwood plates with golfing scenes (imported by Jones, McDuffee & Stratton), $10 each.

Not long ago, a bookshop offered for sale a collection of about 360 autograph letters, documents, and allied material dated in the period 1889-1891 and relating to football. The remarkable collection included letters signed by Alonzo Stagg and Walter Camp. The price asked for this group was $275. The same establishment offered two volumes of a rare English sporting periodical, *The Fancy,* published early in the nineteenth century and devoted largely to boxing at $275. The two volumes represented 55 numbers of the periodical with an added index and introduction and were bound in full red levant morocco by Zaehnsdorf.

An extremely rare publication, *The Complete Art of Boxing,* a 36-page pamphlet printed in Philadelphia in 1829 and said to have been the first work on boxing published in the United States, was offered by another dealer for $75. So don't pass up those early printed books about sports in this country; you may find a bonanza.

Among the commercial firms associated with sports and sports progress in the United States (as well as abroad), the name of

Spectator sports of the 1880's. Drawing at top left represents a La Crosse match in progress, while a game of Imperial Croquet or Lawn Pool is under way at right. The "racquet" at left is a La Crosse stick, and to the right is a Badminton set. Also shown are a polo shin guard and an abdomen protector; lawn tennis markers; a polo goal; tennis shoes of 1885; a tennis net of the same period attached to "Cavendish" posts; a patent dry court marker for tennis; a set of guy ropes and pins, a collapsible cyclist's cup and an illustration of its cover, and an 1889 lawn tennis ball.

Sports of an earlier day are represented here. At the top left is the Rugby football of 1902, which evolved into the 1917 football shown just below it. Beside the Rugby is another even earlier one and below it are two English association round footballs. Also seen near the top of this illustration are a megaphone, a football helmet and a uniform of 1902, and an 1885 football inflator. The young lady's basketball outfit in the center (extreme left) was regulation in 1917, and the tennis outfit next to it reflects the 1899 period. Seen to the right are a lawn tennis or polo shirt of 1885, a 1917 soccer ball, an Ayres tennis ball, a Wright & Ditson tennis ball, and a tennis racket of the late nineteenth century. The tennis drawing at bottom is dated 1889 as is the parlor tennis illustration. At right, the top cap was a regulation one for skating rink managers and the one below was a regulation skating cap. Both are dated 1885.

Baseball equipment of 1909. On the top row, left to right, are the St. Louis, Chicago, and Brooklyn style caps, while the Boston style is shown on the second row as are a uniform roll and a catcher's mask. The Thomas Jones mitt was named for the St. Louis first baseman who attained a fielding record of .986 in 1908. Below this glove are bat bags and to the right of the glove are a home plate, a base, a shoe showing the 1909 toe plate, and an umpire indicator. The pants shown at bottom left were worn in the early 1900's.

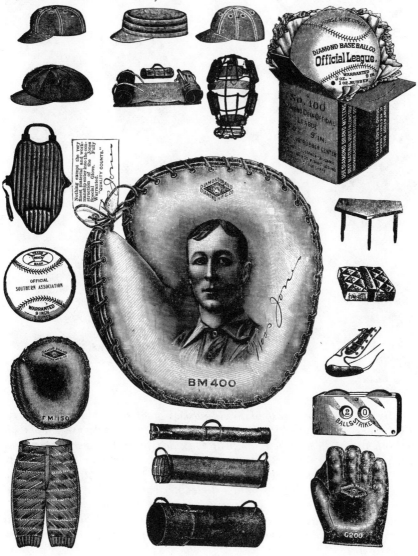

Bicycle racing and just plain riding was great sport late last century. The American Safety bicycle and American Star bicycle are shown on the top row with a bicycle lamp of the same period between them and a whistle on the right. Below from left are the Horsman bicycle lamp, a fine bicycle saddle seat, a Parvo bag designed to be strapped to the back of the saddle and to hold articles needed on a bicycle excursion, a handy tool bag (below the Parvo bag), a saddle bag below the seat saddle, and a cricket outfit of 1885, and cycling cap. Skating was as much fun as cycling. Three types of skates of the 1885 period are shown at bottom.

A. G. Spalding & Bros., Inc., with executive offices now in Chicopee, Massachusetts, is known to hundreds of thousands of people. This company was founded by Albert Goodwill Spalding, who attained fame as a pitcher for the Boston Red Stockings and the Chicago White Sox and later became manager and president of the White Sox. From 1871 to 1875, Spalding pitched 301 games and won 241 of them.

Spalding founded the company that bears his name in 1876. This firm boasts a number of notable "firsts." It created the first American-made golf club in 1894 and the first American-made golf ball four years later. The company introduced the first American-made tennis balls, the world's first basketball, and the first American-made football.

This company actually started in Chicago, shifting its offices to the East a few years later and subsequently acquiring the properties of the A. J. Reach Company in Philadelphia. It is interesting to note that this firm, which in a period of 30 years spent $30 million on sports promotion alone, started out with a shoestring capital of $800!

A number of the illustrations accompanying this chapter were taken from early A. G. Spalding & Bros. trade catalogues.

When President Eisenhower threw out the ten millionth major league baseball (made by Spalding) to start the 1957 baseball season in Washington, the ball was salvaged and placed in the Baseball Hall of Fame in Cooperstown, New York, and a replica of it is now housed in the Eisenhower Museum in Abilene, Kansas.

[7]

For the Ladies:
a Choice Miscellany

☞ Of course there are thousands of men and women who are attracted by the same types of collectible objects, but there are certain categories whose primary appeal is to the ladies. Take paper dolls, for example. Let's not fall into the error of thinking that the appeal of paper dolls today is limited to youngsters. On the contrary, it's their grown-up mammas who are beginning to scan them with a covetous eye.

This chapter, then, will concern itself with paper dolls and a completely unrelated group of additional miscellaneous items that should have a strong appeal to the female of the species, including decorated umbrella handles, vintage opera glasses, purses and hand-bags, fans, bonnet trimmings, and an interesting variety of special-purpose jars.

I have been assembling a file of intriguing background material about cut-out paper dolls for the past several years, though it has been difficult to come by. And I am beginning to find out how much fun I may have missed by not having played with them in my infancy, my sex notwithstanding. I think they would have been preferable to mudpies, and not nearly so messy. And had I played with them and saved a few of them, I wouldn't have had to look high and low for early examples to show you in this book.

Paper dolls actually date back a couple of centuries, but their heyday was the latter part of the nineteenth century. Their popularity by no means ended with the century's termination, because a number of popular women's magazines continued to publish them until well into the present century.

Early nineteenth-century producers of these dolls included the

Cut-out dolls of years ago. These were issued by (left to right top and bottom) Worcester Salt Company, Lion Coffee Company, Loose-Wiles Biscuit Company, and the Coats Thread Company.

Barbour Brothers Company and McLoughlin Brothers, the latter firm having been established by John McLoughlin at the beginning of the last century. Shortly after the middle of the nineteenth century, paper dolls began to appear in some abundance in the United States, particularly in magazines, from which they could be neatly cut out and dressed.

In England, the firm of Raphael Tuck, which made some of the most collectible Valentines and greeting cards, also produced paper dolls. A type similar to these was turned out in the United States by Amlico Publishing Company, headquartered in New York City in the latter part of the last century. Some years earlier, however, cut-out dolls had appeared in the famous *Godey's Lady's Book* and other periodicals and had made their appearance on trade cards and textile materials, serving primarily as good-will and promotional tools for business establishments. Some art publishers and dealers in this country had produced them in the early part of the last century. Most of the very early ones are scarce, but the dolls are still available from the late nineteenth and early twentieth centuries.

The late Carl W. Drepperd, a pioneer in researching Victorian collectibles, reported in the September, 1952, issue of *Spinning*

A sheet of paper doll cutouts published by the Decalco Lithographing Co., of Hoboken, New Jersey, half a century ago. Cutouts such as these are becoming increasingly scarce, though not rare.

Wheel that a magnificent collection of early paper dolls had been assembled by Herbert Hosmer, Jr., of South Lancaster, Massachusetts, and that these had been housed in a Memorial Museum in honor of John Green Chandler, one of the first United States publishers of paper dolls and kindred items. The article further reported that the vogue for paper dolls dates back to the reign of Louis XVI and Marie Antoinette and that these dolls were referred to then as "pantins." Other writers have repeated the statement. Mr. Hosmer, incidentally, authored several articles about paper dolls and doll cutouts in *Spinning Wheel* in 1952, and those interested in their early history will find these articles of interest.

Our concern here, however, is primarily with the later ones and particularly with the cutouts that were published in periodicals and are still available to collectors.

These dolls and cutouts are of special interest because in their dress they reflected the styles either of the times in which they first appeared or of an earlier day. Some of the best merit artistic interest and were drawn by well-known illustrators. Some were tiny figures, measuring only about an inch high, although in one of his articles Mr. Hosmer described one six feet tall.

Several types of manufacturers produced paper dolls to help induce the purchase of their products, among them thread firms, processors of breakfast foods, and coffee, and the like. There was once an "Aunt Jemima" doll issued by the makers of the pancake flour of that trade name. Some of these were made of cloth and might not be considered strictly as "paper" dolls, but the same company also made them of paper. One coveted series of such dolls was produced to help advertise McLaughlin's coffee in the 1890's with F. Kirsten as the artist. The company also issued cutout sheets of costumes for dolls.

When businesses issued dolls and doll costumes, these were usually accompanied by directions for cutting them out and putting them together. The primary processes involved were cutting and folding or bending along dotted lines. Whereas the cutouts appearing in magazines were almost altogether on thin paper, commercial ones were often printed on cardboard and could be made to stand up quite easily.

Some cutout sheets included not only dolls and clothing but assorted items of furniture and accessories. Though a number of these cutouts appeared in color, others were intended to be hand colored by budding young artists of tender years. Some of the dolls were so fashioned that they could stand or sit.

Many paper dolls were pictorial representations of famous persons, including members of royalty, statesmen, and adventurers. Others depicted characters in nursery rhymes, fables, and favorite stories for children. Some were issued whose dress represented costumes of various countries around the world. Many of these were both authentic and exquisite.

Some of the cutouts were issued in numbered series with different costumes available for each. Collectors may well wish to seek full sets of these series. The complete list of all dolls available in the sets was often printed on the reverse or inside covers of the dolls.

Among the commercial firms producing the dolls in series was a cocoa processing company, Volkmann Stollwerck and Company. Clara H. Fawcett, an authority on dolls, reported in an article in *Hobbies* for July, 1955, that this concern had issued a set of dolls depicting story book characters and consisting of 16 individual character cutouts, ranging from Little Boy Blue to Cinderella. A brief story about the particular character was printed on the inside cover of each.

The mass circulation women's magazines made paper dolls available to thousands, and you'll find still around cutouts from such periodicals as *Young Ladies Journal, Ladies' Home Journal, Pictorial Review,* and others. The Boston *Globe* and Boston *Herald* were among the newspapers that once published paper doll cutouts for their young readers.

Commercial firms issuing these dolls included, in addition to those already mentioned, Worcester Salt, Barney's Sandpaper, Decalco Lithographing Company, Lion Coffee Company, the widely known Clark Thread Company, Barbour Irish Flax Company, Duplex Corset Company, and the A. T. Company.

Among the most publicized series of cutouts were the Dolly Dingles, which appeared in the *Pictorial Review* during the "Roaring Twenties." Lettie Lane doll pages appeared in the *Ladies' Home Journal* during the first decade of this century. Several years later this publication carried the Betty Bonnett series, and also the Flossie Fisher Funnies.

Some of the old paper dolls are now being reproduced and are available for interested collectors.

Some of the hand-colored paper dolls you may find today were lithographed years ago in Germany. Tissue paper doll outfits were offered by department stores. These usually consisted of jointed dolls, crepe paper, ribbons, assorted tissue papers, and miscellaneous decorations and could be bought for as little as 25 cents a box. Patterns from which paper doll clothes could be cut were advertised by E. I. Horsman Company in 1906 in boxes wholesaling for $1.75 a gross. There were diagrams and printed instructions for each pattern. The same company also offered a combination called "The Smart Set Dolls and Crepe Paper Trousseau Combination," which wholesaled for $9 a gross. This set consisted of four dolls, an assortment of colored crepe papers and fancy trimmings, and patterns for making clothing and accessories.

The New York firm of Kaufman & Strauss Co. copyrighted its "Embroidery Dolls" in 1915. These had educational value in teaching children the use of the embroidery needle. An informative article about these embroidery dolls appeared in the October, 1966, issue of *The Antiques Journal* under the byline of Gladys Hollander.

You'll find the paper dolls and their accessories advertised today at a wide range of prices. The following, taken from recent dealer catalogues and advertisements, will serve to give some indication of the price variance for different types:

Dolly Dingle colored cutout appearing in the December, 1930, issue of the *Pictorial Review* (magazine complete), $1.75; *Ladies' Home Journals* with Lettie Lane cutouts, 1911 issues, $2 per copy; ten single clipped sheets of Dolly Dingle cutouts (1929), $10; supplement to the Boston *Globe* (1906) with cutouts of "See Saw Margery Daw," $2; single sheets from *Ladies' Home Journals* of 1912 to 1925 containing paper dolls, 75 cents a sheet; set of three different sheets with colored paper doll cutouts issued by Decalco Lithographing Company (around 1918), issued on stiff paper, each sheet containing 20 or more pieces, $7.50; Forbes paper doll outfit (about 1890), $2.50; box of Dolly Dingles, $3.50; set of Dutch paper dolls containing six figures and 14 outfits, $4.50; lot of nine Worcester Salt dolls with minor defects, $1; set of four McLoughlin Bros. paper doll sheets, $3; six early assorted advertising dolls, $3; complete set of Betty Bonnett series as published monthly in the *Ladies' Home Journal* in the 1913-1916 period, $35; 17-inch-tall A. T. Company doll with five dress outfits, $15; one sheet of Sunbonnet Baby paper dolls, $2.50; and set of Our Gang Comedy paper dolls, $16.50.

Prices often vary from dealer to dealer. For example, one dealer is asking $3.50 each for copies of *Ladies' Home Journals* (1909-1910) with the Lettie Lane dolls. In this field, as in so many others, it may save you a little money to shop around.

Leaving the subject of paper dolls after this rather brief treatment that may induce you to do some research on your own, let's consider early parasols and umbrellas, a field largely unexplored but one that offers possibilities for collecting fully as exciting as those of early canes, and primarily for the same reason—the shape and design of the head (and, occasionally, of the shaft).

In earlier years beautiful parasols were an adjunct of milady's dress when she went out of doors. Although umbrellas were designed chiefly to protect one from the rain, the parasol (which was lighter) served as a sunshade as well. A large percentage of the illustrations drawn to picture ladies' fashions in the late nineteenth century included a parasol, proof of which may be found by checking through such fashion magazines as the old *Harper's Bazaar, Godey's Lady's Book,* or *Peterson's Magazine.*

The handles of scores of early parasols and umbrellas as well were fashioned in intriguing forms and shapes, the variety of which may best be ascertained by thumbing through the pages of nineteenth- and early twentieth-century catalogues in which these sheltering articles were offered.

Among the fascinating volumes in the crazy-quilt assortment of books in my library is a two-part publication entitled *Abridgments of Specifications relating to Umbrellas, Parasols, and Walking Sticks,* published by the Commissioners of Patents' Sale Department of the British Government in 1871 and 1880. The books include patents for the manufacture of fabrics especially intended for umbrellas and parasols, inventions for the preparation of such materials to be used in these devices as cane, whalebone, horn, and others, and even patents for umbrella stands.

In the introduction to the first volume, it is stated that despite the fairly recent introduction of the umbrella into England, its use can actually be traced back to antiquity, and that the umbrella apparently originated in the East as a shade against the scorching rays of the sun. It is pointed out, for example, that the umbrella appears often in the Ninevite sculptures and that at one time it was an emblem of royalty. The early shape resembled closely that of the umbrellas of the late nineteenth century.

In Volume II of *Layard's Ninevah* it is stated, relative to the use of the umbrella by royalty:

"It was edged with tassels, and was usually ornamented at the top by a flower or some other ornament. On the later bas-reliefs, a long piece of embroidered linen or silk falling from one side like a curtain, appears to screen the king completely from the sun. The parasol was reserved exclusively for the monarch, and is never represented as borne over any other person."

The umbrella appears similarly in Egyptian sculptures, though its use in that country extended also to persons of noble birth or importance. Evidence also is found of the early use of the umbrella in India, China, Siam, and elsewhere in the East. In early Greece, parasols were used primarily by women, and Aristotle once wrote that it was considered a mark of effeminacy for a man to carry one. In the mid-nineteenth century the best umbrellas and parasols are reported to have been manufactured in France, where the folding umbrella was invented.

Early umbrella shades were made of paper or silk treated with oil or of glazed cotton cloth. The stretchers were of cane, and the ribs were made of whalebone, later of oak and finally of grooved steel. The material alpaca was introduced for use in umbrella coverings in the mid-nineteenth century.

Hooks and knobs generally featured the ends of the earlier umbrella sticks, but a great diversity of shapes began to appear in the latter part of last century.

In 1867, a patent was issued in England for a device that combined a fan, screen, and umbrella. It was constructed on the basic principle of a folding fan but was so designed that it opened to the entire circle of an umbrella.

Numerous other innovations and design variations have been introduced during the years. This concludes our concise lesson on umbrella history, and we proceed now to an examination of some types of collectible umbrellas and parasols produced during the past 100 years.

Gentlemen's umbrellas usually had larger and heavier handles than those intended for the ladies. A large variety of handles in crook, semi-crook, and "L" shapes featured gentlemen's umbrellas at the outset of this century. These were made of decorated horn, often with sterling silver mounts, of various woods (including one imitating ivory), and other materials.

Handles of the ladies' umbrellas and parasols of the same period featured the use of chased rolled gold plate, sterling silver, porcelain, coral, and boxwood. Mother-of-pearl was often used in the post below the head of the handle. Taffeta silk was ordinarily used for the covers of the best umbrellas and parasols, though the majority of collectors will concern themselves with the handles rather than the covers, since so many early umbrellas and parasols have long since had their covers damaged or lost. Thousands of the early twentieth-century umbrellas were made with detachable handles.

These fine protective devices were not particularly cheap in price. A 1909 catalogue offered them at prices up to $19.75 each, although others could be found at $5 to $12.50.

The best ones were made with rolled gold or silver handle caps or heads, the majority of which were etched or otherwise decorated in floral or geometrical designs. The metal or pearl posts on the shaft immediately below the heads were decorated or grooved. The wooden posts were frequently carved in designs. Tassels were invariably attached to the handles. Illustrations accompanying this chapter will give you an idea of various popular handle designs. Some handles, incidentally, had small plates attached on which the owner could have her name engraved. This was most helpful, since lapses of memory were as common among our forebears as among ourselves, and parasols were often left in the darndest places, including restaurants, business establishments, and the homes of one's friends.

About the time of World War I, some quite expensive small roll umbrellas with handsomely chased gold-filled shafts appeared on the market at prices of $20 to $25. These, too, had detachable and interchangeable handles. There also were some less expensive ones with rosewood or ebony handles. Some of these, however, had sterling silver inlays. The length of the handles varied from 7¼ to 14½ inches. A few of the umbrellas had handles with sterling silver loops at the end.

If one wanted to give an umbrella as a present, she could have it wrapped in a special umbrella box made of decorated paper at a charge of only about a dollar extra.

In 1900, umbrella handles appeared with replicas of human, animal, and bird heads. Otto Young & Co., Chicago, offered one with a bulldog head made of ivory, and another with an ivory head of a bonneted lady. These wholesaled at prices of $14 to $17.50 each, depending on whether the cover was of half twilled silk, half silk taffeta, silk taffeta, or all silk twill. The same company offered handles of "Congo" wood in the shape of a shepherd's crook. One with a pearl handle in the shape of a feather appeared in the 1905 catalogue of Benj. Allen & Co., of Chicago. The wholesale price was $8. Incidentally, quite early in this century you could buy the interchangeable handles separately without having to buy an entire umbrella.

Owners of fine umbrellas with handles featuring sterling or gold bands or entire handles of carved ivory or precious metals sometimes pawned them when they were short of ready cash. Top manufacturers of the finest handles included Luxenberg & Haskell, W. W. Harrison Company, and Allison & Lamson.

Even though it may be difficult to locate nineteenth-century parasols with their shades or covers intact, they certainly are worth searching for. A good many of the earlier covers measured only about a foot in diameter, but, after all, they were used as much for show as for protection from the sun's searing rays; and these dainty little affairs had much to commend them, including lightness of weight and beauty of color. Those with fancy fringes and ribbon trimmings were quite fashionable.

Ladies who joined the fashion parade, particularly on such occasions as Easter and other spring and summer holidays, sported parasols which matched or complemented the colors of their garments; a single parasol simply wouldn't do for those who wanted to be in swing with the styles of the day.

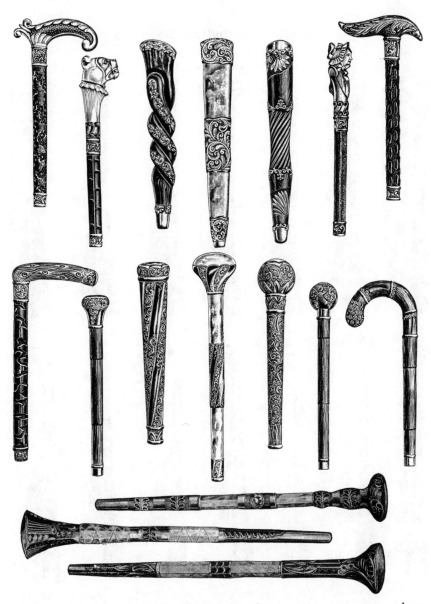

*The delightful umbrella handles on the two top rows were adver-
tised as the present century opened. Some of these handles were of ivory
with sterling bands and ornaments, others of wood. Note the bulldog
second from left on the top row and the bonneted lady second from
right. The three umbrella handles at bottom are of 1914 vintage.*

Ladies' Tight=Rolling Umbrellas.

Made of Fine Silk Taffeta, on Steel Rods.

PRICES EACH.

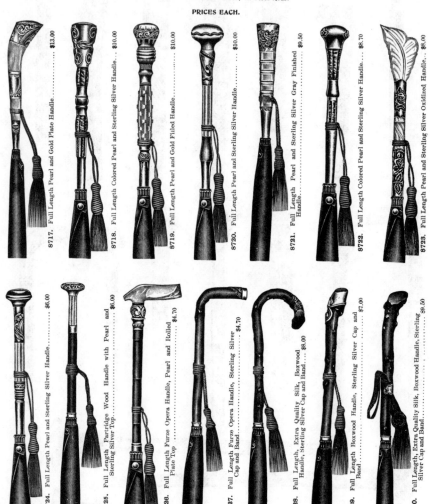

A wide variety of decorated handles is evident in this page of fine ladies' umbrellas of 1905 from the catalogue of Benj. Allen & Company, Chicago. Note the descriptions and wholesale prices of that year.

Lorgnettes.

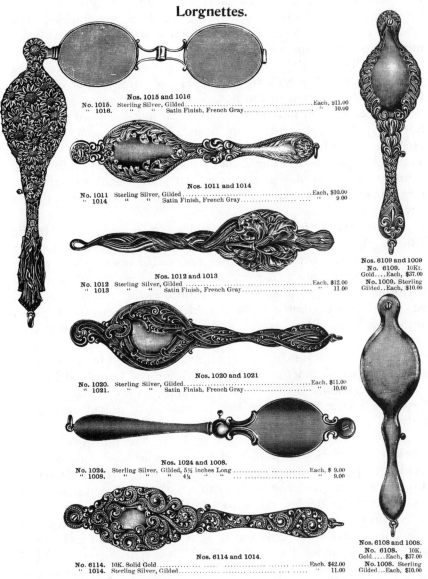

Nos. 1015 and 1016
No. 1015. Sterling Silver, Gilded...Each, $11.00
" 1016.   "   "   Satin Finish, French Gray...................." 10.00

Nos. 1011 and 1014
No. 1011 Sterling Silver, Gilded......................................Each, $10.00
" 1014   "   "   Satin Finish, French Gray................... " 9.00

Nos. 1012 and 1013
No. 1012 Sterling Silver, Gilded ....Each, $12.00
" 1013   "   "   Satin Finish, French Gray........................ " 11.00

Nos. 1020 and 1021
No. 1020. Sterling Silver, Gilded...Each, $11.00
" 1021.   "   "   Satin Finish, French Gray........................ " 10.00

Nos. 1024 and 1008.
No. 1024. Sterling Silver, Gilded, 5½ inches Long ....Each, $ 9.00
" 1008.   "   "   4¼   "   " .... " 9.00

Nos. 6114 and 1014.
No. 6114. 10K. Solid Gold............... .... Each, $42.00
" 1014.   Sterling Silver, Gilded............................ .... " 11.00

Nos. 6109 and 1009
No. 6109. 10Kt.
Gold....Each, $37.00
No. 1009. Sterling
Gilded..Each, $10.00

Nos. 6108 and 1008.
No. 6108.   10K.
Gold....Each, $37.00
No.1008. Sterling
Gilded...Each, $10.00

Lorgnettes with lavishly embellished handles were quite the fashion three-quarters of a century ago. A group of them with their original wholesale prices are pictured here in a page from the fine 1905 catalogue of Benj. Allen & Company, of Chicago.

It seems somewhat of a pity that colorful ladies' parasols do not abound today as they once did to brighten the streets and boulevards. But then, the ladies of this age do not have much time for leisurely strolling, and the sidewalk traffic in the large communities has reached the point where too many opened parasols could prove a menace to the streams of passersby.

You'll have to do some conscientious searching to assemble a good collection of interesting umbrellas and parasols; but once you find yourself attracted to the hunt, there may be no stopping you.

Chances are you haven't thought of the possibility of collecting fine early twentieth-century or nineteenth-century opera glasses. Here, too, is a field almost wide open. Besides, you don't have to attend the opera to use them; they come in mighty handy if you're a bird watcher. If you prefer to spy on your neighbors, however, forget opera glasses and get yourself a good telescope—and a good lawyer.

French- and German-made opera glasses were widely used in the United States in the nineteenth century. Particularly popular were glasses with white pearl tubes, and in the opera houses of the late nineteenth century, these were visible all over the place during performances. They were considered quite stylish and in fine taste. Also used were decorated 14-karat gold barrels, frequently engraved with designs of flowers, vines, and butterflies. Glasses of this type often had pearl eye-pieces.

Another type was made with barrels covered with black morocco, sometimes plain, sometimes with gilt trimmings. Of special interest to collectors should be the embossed aluminum opera glasses which were in evidence early in the 1890's. Some of these had shell-inlaid tops.

Featured in an 1892 catalogue of B. F. Norris, Alister & Co., wholesale jewelers, was a pair of striped pearl opera glasses with beaded nickel trimmings. Light and dark pearl stripes alternated around the barrels. Some glasses came with detachable handles. A pair of Lemaire smoke and white pearl glasses with a long detachable pearl handle and a plush carrying bag was offered at the wholesale price of $44 in 1892 by the B. F. Norris, Alister firm. Its other glasses ranged at wholesale from $7.50 for a pair covered in black morocco to $42 for a pair with 16-karat gold barrels. Those of aluminum with shell inlaid tops were priced at $28.50 to $32.

Those who could afford them usually purchased high-quality opera glasses, because inferior ones proved most unsatisfactory in viewing a performance. The difference was made primarily by the glass, and the ideal pair was one that opened up a large field, well lighted, without reflecting prismatic colors or causing a sensation of strain. Rays of light passing through a piece of glass whose two surfaces were not on a plane with each other were separated into the primary colors. In addition, such glasses often distorted the outlines of objects viewed through them. Lenses combining two kinds of glass cemented together and known as achromatic lenses were best.

Fine Lemaire gilt, pearl and morocco opera glasses of the nineteenth century and an opera glass holder.

Oskamp, Nolting & Co., of Cincinnati, in its 1902 "The 20th Century Jewelry Catalogue" offered both cheap and expensive glasses with low-quality pearl-barrel glasses wholesaling for as little as $4.80. Fine-quality pearl glasses with pearl handle ran as high as $41.30. "Dresden" opera glasses were made in various colors and were ornamented with jewels. They cost $23.80 a pair wholesale in 1902.

Thousands of pairs of rather plain leather-covered opera glasses have been produced through the years. Many of these were of high quality and served their purpose equally as well as those with pearl and other types of barrels: they are just not quite as appealing from the collecting standpoint.

Some opera glass holders were sold separately. The cheapest were made of celluloid with rolled plate mountings. Those of white or Oriental pearl were costlier. Also offered separately were cases and bags. The plush bags came in assorted colors to match opera gowns. Some had pockets for handles; others featured metal-trimmed compartments at the top. Simple morocco cases were available early in the century at only a few dollars each.

Bags also were made of velvet, silk, and chamois leather. Some of the early silk ones were decorated with attractive colored flowers.

There were small folding opera glasses that could be carried in one's pocket, because they were flat when closed. Some of these had a gold chain carrying handle. Small "vest pocket" glasses also were made.

Among the well-known manufacturers of fine opera glasses were Le Maire, Carl Zeiss, and Marchand. Some of the best Zeiss glasses were priced at more than $50 a pair in the mid-1920's.

Should you find yourself interested in opera glasses, you'll probably also be interested in lorgnettes and quizzing glasses. The former —eyeglasses mounted on a long handle and through which dowagers and others once appeared (quite erroneously, I'm sure) to be looking down (or up) their noses at individuals of lesser importance— are not in widespread use today, but they were sold in some quantities 65 or 75 years ago. There were ornate ones boasting sterling silver or goldplated handles, sometimes decorated in chaste patterns. These glasses could be folded flat against their handle. Perhaps the most intriguing lorgnettes from the collector's standpoint are those with rather rococo designs on their handles, most of which had a metal ring at the end for a cord attachment.

A quizzing glass was a single eyepiece, either with a metal rim or rimless, for close-up examination of objects through one eye. The rimmed ones normally had a small handle or a loop by which they could be held or fastened to the person. Those without rims had a small hole in the edge of the glass through which a cord could be attached.

The viewing devices mentioned suggest a group of allied items, including binoculars and field glasses, telescopes, and others, that you can collect if you wish.

A few pairs of opera glasses of early vintage have been offered for sale in recent months. Similar types, however, have varied in asking price from $7.50 to $35. Their trade names, construction, and condition should have a specific bearing on their value. However, since there are apparently very few, if indeed any ardent collectors of them as yet, you should be able to find these glasses at quite reasonable prices.

Almost no one seems to be paying much attention yet to ladies' handbags and purses of an earlier day except for a few museums that utilize them as costume accessories in their early costume displays. These bags and purses were made in great variety, and some of them are likely to be stashed away in the bottom of long-forgotten trunks and boxes in the attics, basements, or even garages.

There is not an abundance of very early purses and handbags around, because they, like so many other personal accessories, were frequently discarded after they had been used for a while or when styles changed.

You'll occasionally find handbags depicted in fashion prints published by some early women's magazines but not very many. Trade catalogues compose the best reference sources for those of 60 to 90 years ago. You may have difficulty locating handbags of cloth that are still in good condition, but those of metal were not subject to damage by moths and their pesky kin.

Quite stylish in the 1890's were purses of silver mesh with silver or silverplated decorated tops. Many of these were carried by chain handles or a large metal ring in the center of the chain handle. The B. F. Norris, Alister & Co. 1892 catalogue shows one in which a metal flower replaces the ring in the center of the handle chain.

So-called chatelaine top bags and purses were made of sterling silver mesh around 1900. The chatelaine tops of many were gold-plated and set with brilliants or other fancy stones. The tops alone could be bought in 1900 at wholesale prices of 46 cents to $2. The purses for the most part were attractive and not gaudy.

Sold separately were sterling purse chains, which enabled one to attach the purse to the person. They measured as much as five feet in length but the links were doubled in the fashion of locket chains for use.

A rather large number of the 1900 purses are back in style today, so you can wear your "antique" and have it too. This is particularly true of the leather ones in oblong shapes. Popular about 70 years ago were those made of seal and walrus leather, featuring snap catches, and inner pockets or compartments with a removable coin purse, or card case. These were lined with silk or other materials. There were also hand purses of calf and other leathers with embossed designs, called "carved" designs in advertisements. Small alligator skin purses had their following then as they do now.

In 1907, the House of Quality, Chicago, offered chatelaine purses of German silver with white kid linings at wholesale prices of $6.20 to $20. The same company tendered leather bags of seal, goat skin, morocco, and other leathers in a wholesale price range of $2.85 to $18.80. Seal finger purses were priced at $3.60 to $11.25. In that same year, Otto Young & Co. featured sterling silver purses with etched rococo designs on the sides at $12.50 to $16.50 wholesale. One or two of these would add considerable interest to any collection of purses and bags.

Beaded bags were popular for a good many years, beginning about 1912. Made of fancy beads arranged in various designs, they usually had beaded fringes at the bottom and linings of cloth or chamois. Also collectible are small leather hand purses with silver mounts and silver name plates.

For those unable to afford the more costly sterling silver purses, plated ones were provided, some with a fairly heavy plate of nickel silver. Small, oblong ones were designated as "vanity bags and purses."

Mesh bags of silver, plated on nickel silver, literally swarmed back into popularity during and immediately following World War I. The more expensive ones had such "extras" as sapphire knobs; and those who had money "to burn" invested in mesh bags of 14-karat green gold with jeweled knobs that sold at $650 to $800. You can pick up some early bags now at a fraction of their original cost.

The hand fan has just about been outmoded by air conditioning, but it once was a feminine adjunct nearly as important as the kerchief. Fans date back many centuries; primitive ones were made of such things as palm leaves and large feathers. Through the years fans have been fashioned of wood, fibers plaited together, paper, leather, ivory, metals, cloth, and other materials.

Eighteenth-century fans are greatly prized; some were decorated by noted painters and constitute works of art. The folding fan had been devised originally in the Orient, credit usually being given to the Japanese. Folding fans were in widespread use in France, the major center of their manufacture, late in the sixteenth-century being made of vellum with ivory blades.

However, court fans and other scarce and early ones are seldom available now to those who must count their pennies, so I will

Ladies' bags of earlier years were produced in scores of shapes, sizes, and materials, just as they are today. Here are some of them. Top row: sterling silver bags (the first has a chased frame and the one at extreme right has a fancy stone in its chatelaine top) of 1900. Second row: imported beaded bags of 1914. Bottom: three silver purses of 1892; a German silver chain bag of 1908 (above), and (below right) an opera glass bag of plush, dated 1892.

Two folding opera glasses (plus one shown opened and in use), and a plush opera glass bag for a handled glass are shown on the top row. From left, second row: a black velvet opera glass bag and one of silk, dated 1905, and a 1907 Marchand folding handle pearl opera glass. Third row: A chamois opera glass bag of 1905 with a mirror on the bottom; and 1892 vest pocket opera glass, and a 1907 gold-filled lorgnette. At bottom left is a silver mesh bag with a silk lining and at right, a "Goldine" English-finish bag of mesh. Both bags date about 1914.

Feathers were popular in headdress of the late nineteenth century, as evidenced in the illustrations on the top row from Harper's Bazaar of 1895. *(Reproduced through courtesy of* Harper's Bazaar*). Hundreds of inexpensive nineteenth and early twentieth century fans are around for collectors. On the second row from left are an 1892 opera fan, a 1900 hand-painted fan trimmed with lace and painted in colors and silver relief, and an 1896 hand-decorated fan with sticks of solid olive wood. Third row from left: an 1891 ostrich feather fan, and two Japanese folding fans. Japanese folding fans of early twentieth century also are on bottom row.*

eschew the temptation to embroider their history on the pages of
this book. Those interested in historical development may be able
to locate a copy of a most informative volume on the subject entitled *A Book about Fans: The History of Fans and Fan-Painting,*
written by M. A. Flory and originally published in 1895, or of an
earlier book, *History of the Fan,* written anonymously by Emily A.
Hall and published in Providence, Rhode Island, in 1886. Other
references on the history of the fan will be found in the Selected
Bibliography at the end of this book.

Note the prominence given fans in these fashion illustrations from
Peterson's National Ladies Magazine *in 1882.*

There are now available for collectors thousands of nineteenth-
and early twentieth-century fans worth preserving if for no other
reason than that many types of them are not likely to be made
again. These range from the ostrich feather fans which saw widespread use in the 1890's and early 1900's to straw and paper advertising fans once given away by merchants as a gesture of good will or
to promote the sale of their wares. These, of course, would be dis-
dained by such institutions as the Bargello Museum in Florence,
Italy, which numbers among its treasures the *flabellum* of Tournos,
once used in the celebration of the Mass (to keep flies from the
Eucharist) and reported to be possibly the earliest extant fan; but
they need not be shunned by those of today's collectors who believe, as I do, that there are scores of useful, interesting, and even
quaint objects made and used by our grandfathers and great-grand-

fathers that should be rescued from the disorderly ravages of time.

A large number of good quality fans used in this country last century were made in Germany; some featured rather massive designs. Delicate and attractive fans were produced by the Chinese and the Japanese.

Our opera fans were patterned largely after those made in France, were usually oval in shape, and had several ribs. They did not open out like other fans to the full extent but presented the appearance of a bunch of delicate feathers. They were made in colors, including blue and pink in addition to cream white.

Ostrich feather fans were quite fashionable in the 1880's and 1890's and made excellent gifts for birthdays, weddings, and other special occasions. The more commonplace were made with stick mounts of wood, bone or celluloid. They were offered in black, white, pink, or blue.

Simple but rather attractive down feather fans costing 25 cents to about a dollar were good sellers at the turn of this century. The cheap ones were mounted on wooden sticks and were frequently decorated with ribbon bows. Fans made of taffeta silk with loop edges of lace at the top and bottom were also inexpensive. A good many of this type were adorned with rows of spangles. The sticks frequently imitated carved ebony.

In 1905, the Cash Buyers Union First National Co-operative Society offered for only 24 cents a fan which it described as follows:

"This beautiful fan is made of glazed Japanese silk. Trimmed at top with English valenciennes lace 1½ inches wide. Has highly decorated silver embossed sticks, hand-painted decorations. Size of fan 8 inches."

Hand-painted silk fans from Japan were available early in this century by the thousands at retail prices of less than 50 cents. Some of the designs imitated those on fans of earlier centuries. The Japanese also exported better quality fans to retail at around $1.50. Some of these fans are so attractive and interesting as to offer solid visual evidence that the collectors need not limit their acquisitions to those made of expensive materials or requiring extensive labor to produce. Many souvenir fans, for example, were made of paper leaves and bamboo sticks, but a number of these preserve illustrations of historic buildings and scenes which once were a part of America and, in their own way, are akin to the historic plates once made abundantly in the Staffordshire potteries of England. Some such fans were issued in connection with expositions, fairs and anniversary observances by states and regions, and they should be preserved.

Among the most interesting (and, originally, the cheapest) of all fans were paper and straw ones manufactured in large quantities for business establishments to advertise their wares. These sought to boost the sales of everything from hats to soft drinks. Business firms often gave large quantities of these to churches, where perhaps they were used by members of the congregation to fan away some of the steam generated by hell-fire-and-brimstone sermons. Others were presented in quantity to fraternal lodges and various types of other organizations that met so frequently in sweltering lodge halls and rooms. A great many of these can be dated by the items they advertise; a large percentage of them also bear imprinted dates. Large quantities of cheap fans were produced for manufacturers, who, in turn, made them available to retail outlets for publicizing their products, leaving a space on which individual store names could be printed.

Particularly desirable are fans advertising fashions of earlier days or products which no longer are being made, and souvenir fans commemorating historic events. Some were made of strong paper and have lasted well through the years.

Speaking of souvenir fans, one type popular late last century was a folding paper fan used in lieu of an autograph album at parties and other events. The ladies requested celebrities and other guests at these affairs to autograph their fans. These were tucked away at home and kept, sometimes for many years, as mementoes of pleasant or memorable occasions.

Open straw fans with scenes or figures painted on them were popular in the 1880's and 1890's. More expensive were those of lined satin, decorated. Scenes on some fans dating back to the latter part of last century or the early years of this one were lithographed by commercial firms in this country and sent to Japan for hand painting and assembly. The finished products were then returned to the United States, where they encountered a ready sale. The Orientals also made fans of rice paper, intriguingly decorated and sometimes bearing inscriptions. A large number of decorated fans were printed from wooden blocks which had been engraved.

In some homes of earlier years there were so many fans that they were sometimes used for wall decoration. A collection of fans today may be utilized in the same way.

It is said that fans once were carried in certain ways to imply specific meanings and that by their use young ladies could convey messages to their swains and others. For example, the lass who wanted to tell her boy friend that she loved him but could not summon the words would draw her fan across her cheek instead. In her delightful book *Victorian Antiques*, Thelma Shull gives the "Language of the Fan" as registered in the United States Patent Office in 1879.

Many richly decorated German fans were imported into this country late last century, and choice ones may be found among these, some signed by their artists. Others were imported from Paris, Madrid, and Vienna.

Labelled "The New Styles for Spring Bonnets," this illustration appeared in Peterson's Magazine *in 1877 and shows some of the popular hat trimmings of that day.*

Quite desirable fans will be found today at prices of from about $3 to $50 and more; but many are still available at less than $5. Handpainted ones with ivory sticks are advertised at $8 to $15.

Uunquestionably, hundreds of thousands of women's hats adorned with trimmings which should have been salvaged have gone into the refuse heaps in past years. This subject arises at just this point, because feather fans serve as a reminder of the fancy feathers of all types, including ostrich plumes, which were utilized in decorating the lady's bonnet of years ago. Also used, of course, were a multitude of fancy ribbons, paper and war flowers and fruits, and assorted gadgets.

If you think some of the hats being worn by the ladies today are elaborate or extravagant or outrageous or beautiful, take a look at some of those worn by their grandmothers and great-grandmothers. You will find plenty of these in the fashion pages of women's magazines of years gone by. They may astonish or horrify or arouse envy within you; but what is most surprising is that the creative mil-

LES MODES PARISIENNES PETERSON'S MAGAZINE SEPTEMBER, 1891.

Parisian styles popular in the United States in 1891 included para-sols as accessories as indicated in this illustration from Peterson's Ladies National Magazine.

liners of today have not utilized in their creations some of the interesting hat accessories of the past. Or have they? At any rate, should you come across the hats of your late nineteenth-century ancestors, give them more than a casual glance and you may receive an inspiration in return. You can preserve the more interesting examples intact if you wish, or you can remove some of their more intriguing accouterments and utilize them in fashioning your own bonnet. About the only decorative accessory I have not thus far encountered on a woman's hat is a sweet potato, and I'm sure I'll come across one of those any day now.

The year 1913 was heralded as the "greatest season for ostrich plumes in 32 years." The comment was that of fashion authorities, who were bound and determined to put these plumes in their millinery creations. In its 1913 catalogue, Simpson Crawford Co., of New York City, said:

"When this page was written the Ostrich Plume market was all aflutter; manufacturers, wholesalers, jobbers and mail order houses were aware that they were at the dawn of an extraordinary year, and began sending orders post and cable haste.

"But Simpson Crawford Company had already prepared. Our Paris Bureau had long ago quietly informed us of the coming accentuated trend of fashion, and when others were beginning to buy, we had already bought! . . .

"Good plumes are like diamonds. They are treasured possessions, wise investments. A good Feather will last for years and may be used season after season, and it is always good style."

This company then proceeded to offer French Ostrich Plumes at prices of $1.98 to $7.98, depending on their length, which varied from 15 to 21 inches. Each added inch cost you a dollar. Interestingly enough, these "French" plumes came from Australia. The name derived from the type of curl the feather had been given. There was the French curl and the English curl but apparently no Australian curl.

Simpson Crawford was right in predicting that the feathers could be used season after season; they were still being featured in catalogues of the 1920's, which also proffered for hats coque feathers in dark iridescent shades, "Glycerized" feather fancies, coney pompons, silk floral wreaths, and metallic berry wreaths.

There is a great miscellany of millinery trimmings awaiting the collector—or ladies who enjoy making their own hats—ranging from aigrettes to bunches of muslin poppies. You can probably pick many of these up for little or nothing, and it could pay you to search around in your neighbors' attics, judiciously, of course, and with permission.

Three-quarters of a century ago manufacturers produced a host of small glass jars which ladies used in their dressing rooms for everything from beauty patches to vaseline. These were of many sizes, in numerous shapes and of various types of glass. A collection of these could be just the thing for ladies with apartments or small homes that have only a limited amount of space for display of collectible objects.

Bottle collecting has been the rage for the past few years. Those who have been overlooking these interesting little jars have been missing a good bet. They were made in pressed glass, good crystal, cut glass, and milk-white glass.

In addition, there were little containers—round, square and oblong—of sterling and plated silver and other metals, and these can be added to a collection for variety. They were designed primarily for holding creams and pomades. Both those of metal and those of glass quite often featured metal tops with rococo and other types of decoration. Jars with their original tops are more desirable than those without.

The dresser jars varied from an inch to several inches in height,

Some idea of the diversity of sizes and shapes of small glass jars and bottles of 1900 is indicated here. These were used to hold such things as powder, cold cream, salves and ointments, tooth brushes and other beauty aids. All have sterling silver tops and originally wholesaled at prices ranging from 50 cents to $3.50. All shown on the first two rows are of cut glass except the two at left on the second row, which are of crystal. All those below are crystal except the third from left on the third row and the small one directly beneath it, which are cut. The two jars on the right on the second row have amethysts in their tops. On the bottom two rows are bonbon boxes or bonbonnieres of sterling silver and plated silver. Those on the bottom row date 1892 and those directly above, 1900.

the tallest, perhaps, being designed as tooth brush containers. The more expensive had settings of amethysts or other stones in their silver tops, but many of these were available for less than $2 each at retail around 1900. We will exclude from this discussion the larger puff jars and hair receivers, which are discussed in my book *The Coming Collecting Boom.*

The glass containers were also used for such articles as tooth powder, talcum, salves and ointments of various kinds, cold cream, and soap.

During World War I, containers for similar uses but made of celluloid appeared on the market in sizeable quantities. You can collect some of these if you wish, but they lack the interest and value of those of glass and metal. Also produced were pomade and similar jars of imitation tortoise shell.

In a different category but of special interest are bonbonnières, which in the late nineteenth-century were also called bon bon or mint boxes. Their use dates back to the eighteenth-century when they were made of precious metals or fine enamels and were used to hold bon bons or dry sweetmeats or little pastilles for sweetening the breath. Frequently round but sometimes in other shapes, they were so small that they could be carried quite easily on the person.

These bonbonnières were made in fancy designs in both sterling and plated silver late last century, many being handsomely engraved. Silverplated ones could be purchased for a very few dollars, though those of sterling came higher. One was offered in 1892 in the shape of a butterfly. There was another in the shape of a heart which had the phrase "Sweets to the sweet" engraved on its cover. In addition to mints, cloves and other herbs were sometimes carried in them.

These most attractive little containers have passed their heyday, and more's the pity. Were they still in widespread use, we might have fewer television commercials in which the employee rushes up to his employer, exclaiming: "Boss, I hate to tell you this—but you have bad breath!"

And now that we have suggested a few items that may be of special interest to the ladies, let's consider in the next chapter some of the collectibles which should prove of prime interest to gentlemen.

[8]

For the Gentlemen:
a Choice Miscellany

Occasionally you will find a husband who strongly dis-
approves of his wife's collecting tendencies. Most husbands today,
however, have joined their wives in the fray. It is by no means rare
to find men who collect pattern glass, dainty porcelain, souvenir
spoons and an array of other objects whose strongest appeal, one
would think, is to the ladies. Normally, however, there are more
vigorous categories of collectibles whose primary appeal is to the
male. These include such things as guns, automobiliana, fire-fight-
ing memorabilia, and furniture.

This chapter will discuss some of the other collectibles of more
recent years which should have a strong masculine appeal. You'll
find still others, such as business collectibles, sports mementoes, and
matchsafes, described in other chapters of this book.

Early occupational shaving mugs have been collected for a long
time, and much has been written about them. One fine book on the
subject for those interested in values is *Price List of Occupational
and Society Emblems Shaving Mugs* by that astute student of the
American past W. Porter Ware, of Sewanee, Tennessee. The book
was published in 1949 by Lightner Publishing Corporation, Chicago.
Why not, however, start thinking also about the preservation of
other types of shaving mugs as well as such adjuncts of the art of
whisker-stripping as straight razors, shaving stands, fancy brushes,
and strops?

Razors of one type or another date back to antiquity. The relatively modern United States invention of the safety razor has just
about outmoded the use of the straight blade of the nineteenth- and
early twentieth-centuries except in barber shops. But late last cen-

tury the straight razor was used by nearly all males who could bear
to part with their whiskers, and they were produced by the hundreds
of thousands. More than a few of the keen-cutting blades were
housed in decorated handles of sterling or silver plate.

One American manufacturer, the J. R. Torrey Company, of
Worcester, Massachusetts, made substantial and highly efficient
straight razors which provided stiff competition (one is tempted
to say keen competition) for the fine ones imported into this country from England. We also imported early in this century large
quantities of German and Swedish razors with handles of rubber,
aluminum and other metals, bone, celluloid, bamboo, ivory, and
wood. But Torrey even exported many of its razors to Europe during the 1890's. Their domestic price at the time was about $1.75.

The wholesale house of Benj. Allen & Co., Chicago, sold its own
special razors with its name imprinted on the concave-ground blades.
Handles of hard rubber or of imitation ivory were favorites, and
the wholesale price was $36 a dozen.

Perhaps the major appeal of the old straight razors for collectors
will be their decorated handles. One particularly fascinating razor
made in Sweden and sold widely in the United States had a handle
of aluminum on one side of which was engraved a train of the 1914
period and with an engraving on the other side of a "prairie
schooner" with mountains in the background. This wholesaled for
$3.50. It was made by the Swedish firm of Eric Anton Berg.

Handles of other razors were decorated with scrolls, leaves and
vines, mermaids, beading, rope twists, crocuses, hunting scenes, and
other views. Handles inlaid with pearl are choice.

Safety razors were being shown along with the straight ones in
early twentieth-century catalogues, prominent among their names
being Gillette, Penn, Ever Ready, Sharp-Shavr and Simplicity. The
Geo. W. Korn Razor Manufacturing Company, of Little Valley,
New York, made "The Real" safety razor with a long steel blade
similar to the straight razor blade encased in a safety guard. The
guard could be removed if one preferred to use the blade in the
manner of the regular straight razor. "The Real" boasted celluloid
handles in various colors. The very early models of safety razors
also may be collected.

Intriguing decorated metal shaving mugs and cups were turned
out by the carload early in the present century, and there are still
many more of these around than there are of occupational mugs.
Adventurous collectors will seek them now, looking to the day
when they will become exceedingly scarce. Undoubtedly, many
thousands have been discarded in the past few decades.

As this century began quadruple-silverplated mugs were favorites and were made in a variety of shapes. Some were gold-lined.

Collectible shaving stands and razors of the 1908–1917 period. The stands on the top row are silverplated and engraved. All date 1914. The one at extreme left was made by E. G. Webster & Sons and the others by Homan Mfg. Co. On the second row are two Real safety razors of 1914, made by Geo. W. Korn Razor Mfg. Co., Little Valley, New York. Imported Swedish straight razors are shown on the next two rows. At bottom from left are the 1908 Gillette and Ever-Ready safety razors, and the 1917 Ever-Ready.

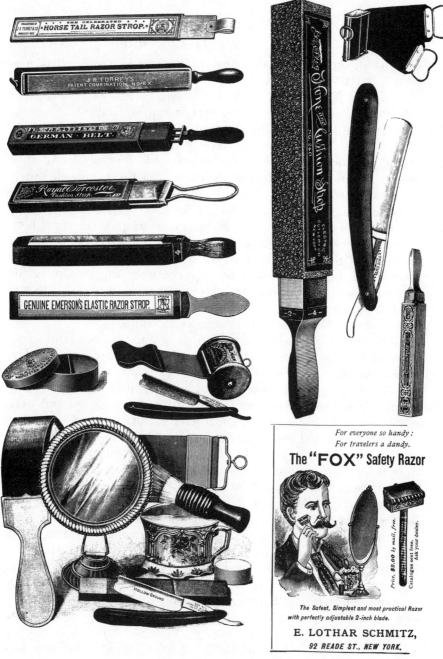

A group of the well-known *J. R. Torrey* razor strops are shown at the left. They are all dated 1900. An automatic stropper of 1917 may be seen at the top right, and below are the Electric Cutlery Company's razor and combination strop and hone of 1889. Another Torrey strop and hone combination is seen just below on the right. Below the Torrey strops on the left are a box of Torrey strop dressing and a Pullman strop with an English razor. Bottom left is a complete shaving outfit of 1900. Bottom right reproduces an advertisement of 1892 for the Fox safety razor.

Rococo-type embossed decorations predominated, and the great majority were handled. These handles, too, were fashioned in interesting variety. There were some less ornate mugs whose exteriors were fluted and with beaded borders at top and bottom.

A large number of mugs were made with porcelain cups and sterling rims. There was one type with a trough-like receptacle attached to the cup in which the brush could be placed. Another type had a small ledge attached to the top of the handle in which the brush could be laid when not in use.

Other mugs stood on oval-footed bases or on small-shaped legs or feet. Some featured opal glass mugs inside pierced metal containers. There were amusing mugs adorned with scenes and lettering. One of these depicted a man with razor in hand fleeing from a bulldog which had yanked out a piece from the bottom of his dressing gown. It was lettered "A close shave." Embossed decorations of various flowers were highly popular in the early part of this century. These ranged from roses to tulips.

Shaving sets consisting of a plated mug and a brush (and sometimes of a razor and strop as well) made fine Christmas, birthday, and anniversary gifts for the man of the house. These could be bought in inexpensive boxes in 1910 for as little as two or three dollars. The better cases were lined with satin or sateen and were made of wood covered with a leatherette fabric.

Nineteenth- and early twentieth-century shaving stands with attached mirrors and mugs also are of interest. Silverplated stands were turned out with extension rods, to the top of which a mirror was attached. Many of the latter were "swing" mirrors held on a semi-circular metal frame fastened to the top of the extension rod, but in the case of some smaller stands the frame holding the mirror was attached directly to the base of the shaving cup or mug. Also, very small stands were made without a mirror but with an extension handle on the mug. This held the brush. Most extension rods also had a clamp to which the brush could be attached. One type of stand not only held a shaving mug but was fitted with additional vase-shaped receptacles for soap, talcum powder, and mouth wash.

A wide variety of these shaving stands marked "Homan Mfg. Co." may be found. Some of these are footed or have wide circular bases. The better mirrors were of beveled plate glass, usually oval in shape.

The height of the stands varied considerably—from about 6 inches to more than 17 inches; so did the size of the mugs or cups. The majority of the mugs had removable liners of glass or porcelain.

In its 1912 catalogue, Albert Brothers, of Cincinnati, contended that although the shaving stands of the type being described had "sprung into great popularity," the market abounded in examples of inferior design and workmanship. This company then showed examples of what it claimed represented superior design and workmanship, commenting:

"The mirror backs are all engine turned and engraved in the newest and best styles; all the sets are provided with removable opal glass linings; and the shapes and general makeup of the various patterns are neat and attractive . . . All of these sets are furnished with 6 inch bevel mirrors, a size amply large for convenient shaving."

Wholesale prices of the sets offered by Albert Brothers ranged from $7.50 to $14.50.

Wallenstein, Mayer & Company, of Cincinnati, offered in 1918 a line of shaving stands with the shaving cups set in solid mahogany bases, complete with a name plate. The bases had metal mounts and feet. It also advertised a stand with a wooden instead of a metal post to which the mirror was attached. Near the bottom of this post were brackets for holding the soap dish and a tumbler. The same company provided stands with pierced silverplated round trays at the base for holding both the soap cup and a variety of other toilet articles.

The diversity of the stands presents a challenge to the collector: how many different types will he be able to find?

Shaving brushes are of interest primarily for their decorated handles, some of which were made of sterling and others of plated metal. Fine brushes with sterling handles exquisitely engraved were not for the hoi polloi: some cost as much as $40 or $50. Generally speaking, brushes with wooden handles are of minor interest, but those with horn ferrules offer possibilities.

Shaving was a chore in the days of our grandfathers and great-grandfathers. The blade had to be honed frequently to keep its cutting edge keen or one could end up with a badly mauled face. Many interesting razor strops were manufactured with novel handles or loops by which they could be hung. The J. R. Torrey Company made a combination four-sided hone and strop. The hone was on one side and leather of different sharpening qualities on the other three. You could buy one of these in 1891 for about $2.75. The Electric Cutlery Company made a somewhat similar combination. Self-coiling strops with silverplated cases and shields will be of prime interest. Both cases and shields were often ornately decorated.

Plain straight razors have been listed recently in the advertising columns of some of the collector periodicals at prices of a dollar or two each. Those with decorated plated handles should be worth

The collectible silverplated shaving mugs on the top two rows are
dated 1892. Some of the cups are gold-lined. Below are two silverplated
shaving stands with accessories of 1914. At right are three additional
shaving mugs dated from 1892 to 1902.

These shaving collectibles include a group of interestingly decorated silverplated-handle brushes of 1905, a set consisting of shaving cup and brush in a fancy paper-lined box (top right); a mustache brush of 1892; a pad of shaving papers enclosed in a seal grain leather container with sterling silver trimmings (bottom left); a group of straight razors of the 1905 period, and (lower center) a 1902 Star safety razor and a 1908 Sharp-Shavr safety razor.

Shaving accessories of 1900 with sterling silver handles as offered by Otto Young & Co., Chicago. The complete boxed set shown at bottom right included a brush in a sterling silver case, razor with sterling handle, and a silver mounted celluloid comb. The handsome razor at top wholesaled for $8.50 and the brushes for $1 to $1.50.

more. They probably will be as soon as the interest of collectors is aroused.

An advertising shaving mug picturing a man and woman using the same telephone and dated 1907 was tendered not long ago at $25, but many other types can undoubtedly be bought for a very few dollars. Shaving stands will probably start at about $5 for the plainer types with the ornate ones fetching more.

In an allied category are mustache combs and brushes, the most interesting of which have decorated handles. Combs were made that folded up into decorated silver cases, which sometimes had a loop at one end by which they could be hung. Other combs had cases of ivory or tortoise shell. Mustache brushes resembled ordinary hair brushes except that they were smaller.

A check of the major collector periodicals over the past several months discloses that some of the shaving accessories discussed herein are now attracting buyers. Here are some typical items advertised and the prices asked to serve for your guidance:

Straight razor with Wood & Butcher Sheffield blade, $1.50; straight razor, make unidentified, in original box, $2; straight razor of German make with celluloid handle in original wooden box, $3.50; J. R. Torrey straight razor with rubber handle, $2; razor strops, make unidentified, $3 each.

Large shaving mug with gold band decorations and handle, $5; Masonic shaving mug with name, $18; silverplated shaving mug, $5; assorted scuttle mugs, $5 to $12.50; Odd Fellows mug decorated with gold links and name, $17.50; pottery mug with soap divider, decorated, $14.50; silverplated mug with glass insert, $10. Finer ornate mugs are priced higher.

Silverplated shaving stand with matching brush, adjustable mirror, and opal glass bowl, $10.50; shaving mirror stand in chrome-plated brass with soap dish and brush, $12.50. Other similar late nineteenth- and early twentieth-century shaving stands are worth $7.50 to $25. Earlier stands are higher, often ranging to around $300 for early nineteenth-century ones.

Collectors have sought out cigar clippers, tobacco jars, pipes, and numerous other smoking accessories, but few thus far have turned to cigar and cigarette holders. A surprise could be in store here. A Meerschaum cigar holder that was advertised in 1907 had an amber mouthpiece with a stag ornament on top. A similar one was adorned with a horse, and others also were produced with attached ornaments of one kind or another.

There were early cigar holders with 14-karat gold-filled mountings or gold-filled bands. Some had Meerschaum bowls in various shapes, including one that curved sharply upward in the manner of some pipe stems. Other cigar holders were fashioned completely of amber except for a gold-filled or silver band at the extremity.

An exciting item to stumble across would be an early sterling collapsible cigarette holder with its accompanying case. These holders were designed to be carried in the vest pocket and were sold in 1918 at prices of $7 or $8. In the same year, sterling silver cigarette holders with mouthpieces were available at prices of $3 to $4.

Popular at the turn of the century were sterling-banded cigar holders housed in plush-lined cases and selling for about $5 each. One of these was in the shape of a pipe with a gold-filled mounting. It came complete with a plush leather case for $8. There were also combination pipe and cigar holders with amber mouthpieces and gold-filled mountings. Corn cob cigar holders with bone bits were offered as novelties in 1905 by the Cash Buyers Union First National Co-operative Society at 4 cents each! Or you could purchase a briar holder with a horn bit for a nickel.

During World War I, Marshall Field & Company offered a line of attractive cigar and cigarette holders in cases at prices from $3 to $9. These holders measured 2 to 3½ inches in length, and most of them were decorated with gold-filled bands or mountings.

Some of the earlier cigar and cigarette lighters are moving into the category of twentieth-century collectibles. About the time of the First World War, lighters were offered that provided a flame by drawing a striker across sparking metal. One of this type, called the Wonderlighter, was attached to a brass ashtray. The wholesale price was $2.50.

By the late 1920's, a variety of small lighters had been developed to utilize an inflammable liquid fuel. A group of these was designed as combination desk lighters and paperweights. Some cases were made of nickel silver or plated gold, and others of imitation jade, onyx, agate or other imitation stone substances, or were covered with leather.

Electic lighters were in use in the early 1930's. They plugged in to electric outlets. One type had coils which heated up when the lighter was turned upside down. The current was shut off when it was placed right side up.

Pocket lighters of numerous types began to appear abundantly in the 1930's and were the forerunners of many types in use now. The collector may also want to see what he can find in the way of the early clamp-on types of automobile lighters.

Historical flasks of glass have provided a delight for a fairly large group of collectors over a period of years, but largely neglected thus far have been the metal "hip flasks" which became popular with the young bucks, hunters and others in the latter part of last century and continued in use right on up through the Prohibition Era. Many thousands of electroplated metal flasks were turned out between 1880 and 1932. These can be picked up at prices far below those prevailing for the earlier historical flasks. Moreover, they can provide a perfectly intriguing collection.

Pocket flasks have been made in a wide variety of shapes, in several sizes, and with an almost astonishing diversity of exterior decorations during the past 90 years. The discussion about them that follows has nothing whatsoever to do with the morality or immorality, the advisability or inadvisability of alcoholic indulgence. It merely recognizes its existence and relates to the possibilities of salvaging and preserving some interesting relics of the fairly recent American past.

So-called hip flasks were made of both metal and glass. Perhaps the machine-made bottles should merit less attention than the metal containers; but since everybody and his brother, as we used to say, seem to be collecting bottles these days, the glass ones certainly won't be overlooked. Nevertheless, the flasks in metal cases had at least one major advantage when in use: they resisted breakage when one sat down briskly upon a hard surface with a flask in his hip pocket, which has long been a favorite toting place. There were, of course, small flat flasks which were sometimes carried in an inside coat pocket and were brought out and put to use when one was faced with snake bite, a cold rain, depression, joy, or ennui.

Handsome silver flasks appealed to the more affluent of our ancestors, but these were far exceeded in total numbers by electroplated ones. The silver flasks were frequently sedately engraved, but many of the plated ones flaunted outlandish rococo designs or were adorned lavishly with depictions of flowers. Others were lettered with phrases intended to amuse—and almost any phrase could amuse one after a few slugs of corn whiskey. In shape, they varied from oval to round, square, and oblong. (Flasks made of flint enamel in the shape of books were produced early last century and are delightful collectors' objects.)

A flask that undoubtedly had an appeal for young men of the early 1900's bore on one surface an illustration of two farmers, one bending over a fence rail and the other behind him with a board paddle. This flask was lettered "Have a smile with me."

A pint-sized plated flask issued in 1910 was lettered: "Drink of the dew of ruddy morn; Bacchus once blew from the rye and corn." A round flask of the same year was adorned with an illustration of a fine seated dog.

Of interest are flasks with collapsible cups. One of these advertised in 1892 was engraved around its surface with flowers and leaves. Its wholesale price was $5.50. Another of the same period, styled "Louis XV," had its exterior swirled with fluting.

In 1900, Otto Young offered a round flask with a capacity of six

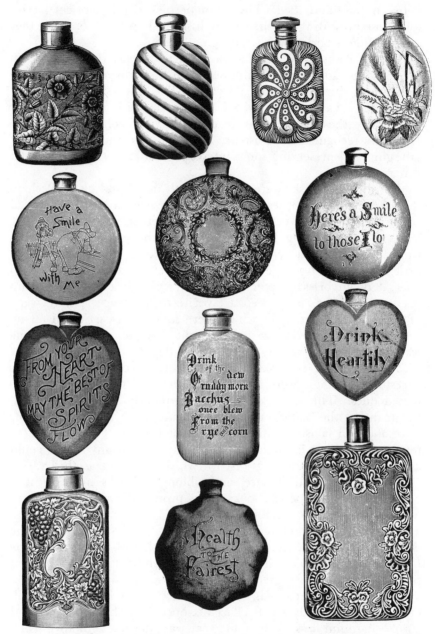

Sterling silver and silverplated hip flasks dated from 1892 to 1914. These varied in capacity and shape. All are worth salvaging.

ounces on which was engraved the phrase, "Here's a Smile to those I love." Others were made with name plates for engraving. A tiny but handsome square flask with a capacity of just one ounce was

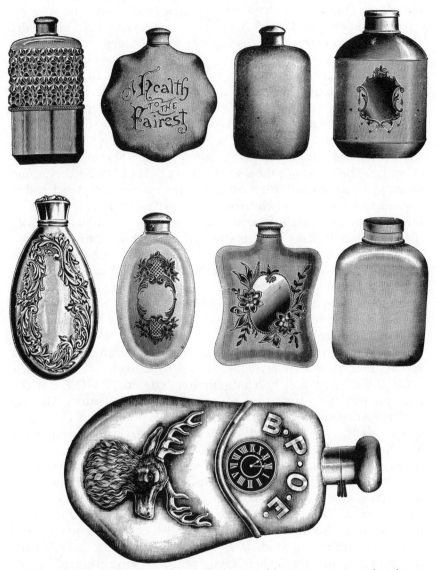

The sterling and silverplated flasks on this page were made about the turn of the century. The first two on the top row had a capacity of eight ounces each, the third six ounces, and the fourth ten ounces. Capacity of those on the middle row from left was three, six, and eight ounces (last two). The two on extreme right on both rows had collapsible cup tops. At bottom is a fine Elks' flask of 1905 with an enameled dial.

available in 1900 from this same company at a wholesale price of $13.34. It was made of sterling silver, embossed with flowers around the edges. One in oval shape with a capacity of three ounces, similarly embossed and also of sterling, was priced at $11, wholesale. Other flasks were available in capacities of six, eight and one-half and ten ounces.

In 1914, heart-shaped flasks were popular. One of these was lettered, "From your Heart may the best of Spirits flow." Another bore the words "Drink Heartily." Homan Manufacturing Co. made an odd-shaped plated flask lettered "Health to the Fairest."

For those fond of nightcaps before retiring, many "dram" flasks were produced. John Round & Son, Ltd., of Sheffield, England, offered a wide variety of these in the latter part of last century, some of cut glass, some combining cut glass tops with electroplated nickel silver, and some made of electroplate on Britannia metal. Of special interest are those made in odd shapes such as pyramidal, or those that had a small drinking cup attached to the base. Other containers also called "dram" flasks actually were made in capacities of one-fourth, one-half, and three-fourths of a pint and in full pint size.

Still other flasks of plated silver with glass liners were covered with morocco leather; some had morocco-covered top halves with the bottom half serving as a removable cup. These types also were made in sterling.

Special fraternal flasks will sometimes be found and will add special interest to a collection. The 1905 catalogue of Benj. Allen & Co. shows an extremely handsome one lettered "B.P.O.E." at the top and with an illustration of an elk's head at bottom. In the center is a depiction of a clock with the hands pointing to 11 o'clock. The clock dial was enameled. Made of sterling, this one wholesaled for the rather substantial sum of $24.

In the 1920's a group of sleek flasks of sterling appeared with capacities of one-half a pint to a pint. Some were produced in hammered silver and others with restrained designs. One brand was known as "Kap-Kup." These flasks were equipped with a cup inserted in the bottom and with screw-down caps and curved backs to prevent the pocket from bulging. These were not intended for the impecunious buyer, their retail prices ranging from $30.65 to $94.50.

Flasks may be displayed in a variety of ways—in a cabinet, arranged along shelves, or even attached to the walls.

Still another field that may be of interest to many men embraces such things as embossed and pictorial poker chips and dice, and decorated playing card cases.

Poker chips have been turned out with all sorts of embossed designs on their flat surfaces. Tower Manufacturing & Novelty Com-

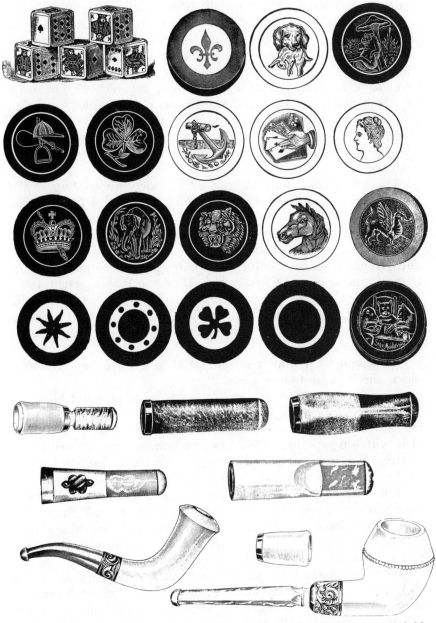

Poker dice of 1908 and a group of engraved, embossed, and inlaid poker chips of the same period, together with some early twentieth century cigar holders and a combination pipe and cigar holder combined.

pany, of New York City, illustrated a diversity of these in its 1903 catalogue of stationery and novelty items. The designs included golf clubs, bowling pins and balls, spread eagles, swans, anchors, playing cards, clover leaves, owls, bicycles, dragons, tigers, stars, classic heads, and one set even featured a depiction of a "Rough Rider" astride a galloping steed and brandishing a sword. They were made in diameters of $1\frac{1}{4}$, $1\frac{3}{8}$, and $1\frac{1}{2}$ inches. The same company offered engraved and inlaid poker chips in 1908, featuring depictions of shamrocks, horses' heads, elephants, caps, whips, dogs' heads, crowns, sunbursts, and frogs. One set depicted two cats playing poker with a monkey and was lettered at the bottom "Stop monkeying."

The inlaid chips were the highest in price, wholesaling at $20 a thousand, as compared with only $5.60 a thousand for composition chips.

Tower further provided pictorial dice. One set of poker dice came in sets of five, containing illustrations of ordinary playing cards, from the ace to the nine-spot. They came with square corners, round corners, or were octahedron in shape, having eight faces. They were made of ivory, imitation ivory, bone, and celluloid. Transparent dice which could not be "loaded" without showing the alterations are said to have been popular in games played with strangers.

(In a somewhat similar category and collectible are early dominoes, checkers, and chess pieces.)

Several experts have written authoritative articles and books on collecting playing cards, but I have found little available about playing card cases. These, however, have been made in silver and silver plate with hinged tops and elaborate decorations and are well worth seeking. So are silver game counters, one type of which was made in the shape of a shamrock with a dial and bell attachment.

The collecting of law enforcement and police goods of earlier days is likely to appeal to the masculine interest—and particularly to those who have been associated in any way with law enforcement.

Collectible objects in this broad field range from lanterns and badges to nightsticks and restraining devices.

Police organizations as largely constituted today are said to have originated in England in the early part of the nineteenth century, although some type of organized force for maintaining order and enforcing laws was utilized in most civilizations over a period of centuries. The police system in the United States was originally patterned after that in England but soon underwent changes which today make it a typically American institution.

Of interest to collectors will be all types of badges, insignia and

The playing card cases shown on the top two rows were all made of grain leather except for the one at right on the top row, which was of deerskin leather. They were offered in 1905 at wholesale prices of from $1.25 to $2.70, complete with a pack of playing cards. Below at left are two "collapsion" cups with handles in leather cases, which would have been ideal for traveling use with the half-pint leather-covered flask, which is dated 1905. On the right below are a table lighter called the "Wonderlighter," with attached ashtray, and a meerschaum cigar holder of 1918.

other identifying emblems, including uniforms and uniform buttons. A collection of buttons or of badges from various police departments and sheriffs' offices around the country would afford an attractive display. Some of these insignia are illustrated in this chapter.

Clubs and nightsticks of various types have been utilized through the years. Some early clubs or nightsticks, or billets, (sometimes called "billies") were made of rosewood with fluted handles to assure a firm grip. Flexible clubs were made of sole leather over a firm core and often had braided handles and a carrying strap. Early catalogues picture billets designated as "Manhattan," because they had been adopted as regulation pocket billets by the New York City Police Department.

One type of billet featured a piece of plain black leather over a coiled steel spring core; others had a steel spring core covered with braided leather. These packed a substantial wallop.

There were several variations of handcuffs, including "twisters," "nippers," and "chain nippers." These were usually made of nickel plated over forged steel. Various types of conventional handcuffs were made. One had a double lock—one self-locking and the other locked with a key. The same key unlocked both by turning it twice in the same direction.

Leg irons with balls and chains were once far more widely used than they are today. These sold at so much per pound of weight, the balls weighing from 12 to 50 pounds. They were attached by a stout chain to a locking cuff which fitted around the leg at the ankle. Leg irons resembling handcuffs but with a much longer chain were made, one cuff being locked around each leg.

Available at one time for police use were brass knuckles or "knucks," which fitted on to one's knuckles, but the use of these has been more associated of late with rowdies and thugs.

Bullseye lanterns were carried by policemen and night watchmen in the nineteenth century before the widespread advent of lighted streets. These will be found at what are still considered "reasonable prices."

Of great interest, not only to collectors of police goods but also to toy collectors, are the early cast-iron replicas of police patrol wagons. In view of the swiftly rising prices of all early cast-iron toys now, it seems almost incredible that police patrol wagons of cast iron, measuring 21½ inches in overall length and consisting of two-wheeled horses, a patrol wagon and seven policemen, wholesaled in 1906 at $22 a dozen sets!

Other objects for which to look include early jail keys, alarms of various types, including the rattles or clackers, and whistles; belts

Law enforcement mementoes can be fun to collect. Here is a group of law enforcement (and other) badges of nickel silver; an 1891 bull's-eye lantern; police nippers, a twister, and billets (or billies); a ball and chain of 1908, and a fine toy police wagon featured by Belknap Hardware and Manufacturing Company in 1906.

and buckles; helmets, caps; paraphernalia used in prisoner identification, and, if you can find them, police dockets or ledgers.

Instead of merely collecting police and sheriff's badges, you may
be interested in collecting identification badges in general. There

*Collectibles of law enforcement include police, marshal, constable
(and other) badges of German silver; a slung (not sling) shot, club, and
knucks (on the third row); a group of billies at left, and a group of
leg irons, handcuffs, and nippers. These date early in this century.*

are thousands of these available in many types. Such badges were made for newspaper reporters, hotel and railroad porters, conductors, bell boys, baggage men, constables, marshals, city councilmen, firemen, private detectives, elevator operators, night watchmen, members of insurance patrols, station masters, cab drivers, and others.

Some police items have been advertised for sale recently, and the following will give you a rough idea of the wide range of prices asked:

Pair of leg irons with heavy 20-inch-long chain, $8.50; pair of handcuffs similar to those used on the conspirators in the Lincoln assassination, $34.50; handcuffs made by the Mamatuck Mfg. Co., Waterbury, Connecticut, and dated 1904, $4.50; primitive handcuffs, $9.50; English handcuffs, $12.50; thumbcuffs, $9.95; early clacker alarm, $7.75; another clacker, $9.50; alarm rattle of about 1860. $12.50; Dietz "Police Regulator" lantern with bullseye lens, $6.75; lantern with cone-shaped top and whale oil burner, $12.50; brass billet, $5; early wooden police club from Kansas City, $4.50; badge of around 1840 period in shape of star and stamped "sterling silver," $8.50; sunburst badge, $3.75; police helmet, $15; and early Western jail keys, $1.50 to $7.

Knives of one sort or another date back, of course, to primitive times, the earliest of them having been crudely fashioned from flint or stone. Later the stone knives assumed a gracefulness of form, indicating considerable skill on the part of our very early forebears. Knives have been made through the centuries for dozens of different purposes, and it may not be generally recognized that the folding knife actually dates back to the ancient Romans. Spring or clasp knives were being widely used more than a couple of centuries ago.

Decorated pocket knives (including the larger jack knife) of more recent vintage might be of special appeal to the male collector. Intriguing pocket knives with handles of silver or other metals, bone, ivory and several other substances were made in tremendous quantities in the last half of the nineteenth century and are still fairly plentiful. There were some beguiling knives produced early in this century that should have a strong appeal to collectors. These ranged from miniature single-blade knives that could be worn as charms to large affairs with several blades of varying sizes or with blades plus such adjuncts as bottle openers, screw drivers, and manicure blades. There also are available folding combination fruit knives and nut picks.

As this century began, at least one manufacturer made a small hunting knife (8½ inches long when opened) with a genuine deer's foot for a handle. The blade folded into the unique handle. The knife could be purchased for a dollar in 1901.

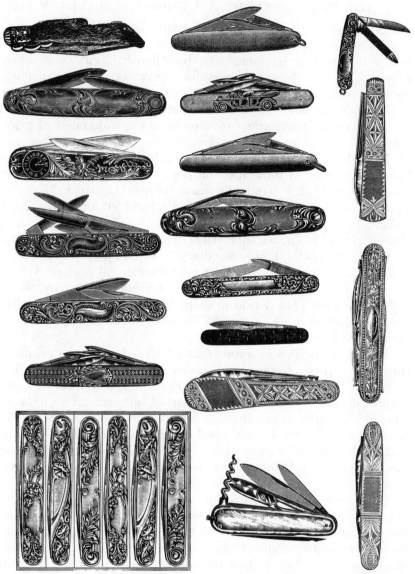

A group of interesting folding knives. Reading from top to bottom, left: a knife with a genuine deer's foot handle, dated 1901; knife with a patent spring opener, 1905; Elk's knife with enameled dial, 1905; knife with two blades and scissors, 1905; two-blade knife with silver handle, 1905; four-bladed knife with sterling handle, 1914; and an assortment of six sterling-handled pocket knives, which wholesaled for $10.35 in 1914. Center: gold-handled knife; novel sterling silver-handled knife with embossed touring car design, 1914; knife with three blades and a file in plain sterling handle, 1914; sterling-handled knife with two blades, 1914; two 1892 small knives in silver handles; a folding fruit knife and nut pick, 1892, and a 1907 combination. Right: a 1905 lady's knife and file, and three 1892 fruit knife-and-pick combinations.

There are available combination knives featuring a knife blade, corkscrew, nail file, and button hook. Others had such accessories housed in the handle as scissors and metal toothpicks.

Pearl-handled pocket knives were great favorites early in this century, supplanting to some extent the silver-handled knives that were quite popular in the waning years of last century. A 1908 jobber's catalogue shows combination pearl-handled knives whole-saling for $82.50 a dozen, though less elaborate combinations were available for as little as $34.50 a dozen. Simpler pearl-handled knives with a couple of blades wholesaled for only $19.50 a dozen (and small ladies' pearl-handled ones were offered at 12 for $10.75).

There were also small, folding budding, pruning, grape, corn, and chiropodist's, and other types of special knives. These types can add variety to a collection of small folding knives.

The sterling silver handles of many pocket knives were often elaborately engraved, frequently with floral motifs. Some cases were made of inlaid enamel in colors. There were pocket knives into whose cases or handles knife blades and accessories folded from two sides. There also were knife handles with solid gold sides, some of these containing a signet center on which one could have one's name or initials engraved.

Fine miniature folding knives were made to be attached to one end of a silver or gold-filled chain and many were sold as combinations with the chain. A novelty about the time of World War 1 was a one-blade knife housed in a gold-filled handle together with a pencil and a file. One brand of this type wholesaled at $4.50. Also attached to chains were small cigar knives which folded into gold-plated handles.

Stag-horn-handled knives have been popular over a period of many years. Otto Young & Company, of Chicago, wholesaled this type with two fine steel blades in 1907 for as little as 84 cents with better ones priced at $1.50.

Small and almost dainty penknives were made for ladies, and some were fashioned which could be secured and concealed by milady's garter, apparently as a safeguard against unwelcome advances. One of these with a pearl handle and dated about the middle of last century was offered recently for $18.50.

Numerous knives in addition to the pocket type are collectible, of course, but we'll leave them for other writers to discuss.

In case you're interested in current values, here are a few miscellaneous knife prices advertised during the past year:

Civil War period pocket knife with bone handle in the shape of a large figure "7," and marked on the blade "American Manu," $7.50; silver knife with a blade and pick, $6.50; two-blade knife in abalone handle, $1.50; bone-handled corn knife, $6.50; sailor's

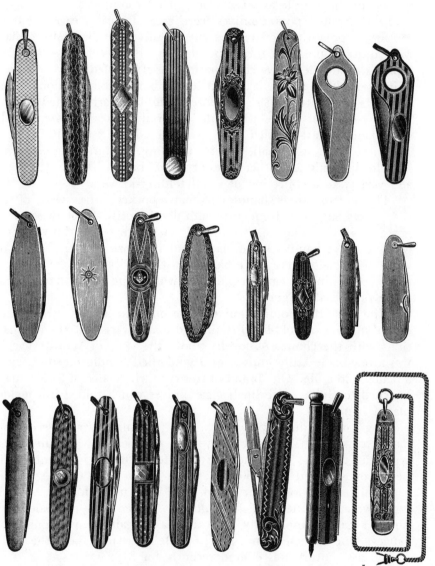

*Knives on this page were advertised about the time of the entry of
the United States into World War I. They boasted gold-filled or goldplated handles. The seventh object on the top row is a combination
cigar cutter and knife. At the extreme right on the bottom row is an
engraved knife and Waldemar chain combination.*

pocket knife of Civil War period, $8.50; scarce pocket knife of 1820-50 period stamped on blade "For Whalers," $15; a similar one with a wide ivory handle, considerably worn, $7.50; and a pocket knife with a wooden handle and silver mountings, $2.

Those interested in collecting knives will find much about those made in the United States in Harold L. Peterson's book *American Knives* (Charles Scribner's Sons).

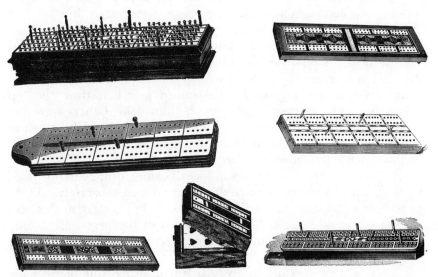

Early twentieth century cribbage scoring boards. Top, an "English Pull-up," and an inlaid board. Center, a "City Club" board made of two pieces of highly polished wood, and a board with a sliding bottom. Below, an inlaid board; a folding board, and a board with a white wood body and polished nickleplated top.

Finally, we come to the subject of cribbage—a game that continued in popularity among millions the world over for about 300 years until it was largely supplanted by bridge and canasta. We will not consider the various ramifications of the game here. Some old-timers still play it, we understand, and it's now usually a two-handed contest, although a three- or four-handed game also can be played. It is not the 52-card deck with which we will concern ourselves here but with the cribbage score board on which the players pegged their scores during the game.

The cribbage board is an interesting device, and it was turned out in a variety of forms through the years. The counting board was usually made of wood, the more interesting ones having been constructed of inlaid woods and sometimes of inlaid ivory or celluloid. The board contained four parallel rows of holes, each row containing 30 holes, plus one extra hole in the center of each end, or a total of 122 holes altogether. There also were two pins or pegs for each player. These fitted into the board's holes. As the players made points, they moved their back peg forward, indicating the points made and also the total score. Some boards came with pegs fastened tight to a metal spring inside the board box. These pegs could be pulled up and moved on the board but could not be removed completely from it and, therefore, were rarely lost.

A good many boards had a wooden body and a metal top, frequently nickel-plated, and contained a compartment for cards and for the pegs. A board might range in size from 2 inches wide by $8\frac{1}{4}$ inches long to $4\frac{1}{2}$ inches by $16\frac{1}{2}$ inches. Some of the boards were made of two pieces of wood joined together; thus, the top might be bird's-eye maple and the bottom oak. Others were designed in the form of a folding box. Such a box might measure $3\frac{1}{2}$ by 5 inches when closed. Some boards had sliding bottoms with compartments for cards and pegs.

Although many of the scoring boards came equipped with pegs, some did not, and the pegs could be purchased separately. These pegs were wholesaled to retailers in gross packages early in this century at prices of $1.30 to $1.60 a gross. Half the pegs were of one color and the other half of a different color, red and white being favorites.

There were some quite fancy boards with supporting boxes made of nickel silver in rococo designs. During the first decade of this century cribbage scoring boards wholesaled generally at prices ranging from about $1.20 to more than $60 a dozen. Many inexpensive flat boards without pegs were made in Germany. The highest-priced board offered by Tower Manufacturing and Novelty Company in its 1903 catalogue was an "English Pull-up" with the pegs fastened to a metal spring. The board measured 4 by $11\frac{1}{4}$ inches in size and wholesaled for $5. The same company offered a board of cast solid brass, either nickel- or gold-plated and polished, with a pin box on the bottom and game counters on the top at $21.60 a dozen.

Because cribbage boards were produced in so many designs and were fashioned of such varied materials, one can make an interesting collection of them as a reminder of more leisurely days. The illustrations accompanying this chapter will indicate their variety.

[9]

To the Boiling Pot
the Flies Come Not

☛ Homemakers of the 1800's believed in the proverb with which this chapter is headed. They also believed that an idle person was the devil's playmate and that doing nothing was doing ill. Therefore, they kept busy, if not improving each shining hour, at least keeping it adequately occupied. That was why home crafts of many types flourished and bills for home furnishings and accessories did not soar nearly so high as they often do these days.

There are hundreds of examples of home handicraft of less than a century ago begging to be salvaged, and even treasured. All sorts of materials and implements to help not only the housewife but also the young folk to emulate the way of the ant and be wise were proffered and bought in the 1880's, the 1890's and the early 1900's. China painting was a favorite spare-time occupation for ladies of the house. It was engaged in by both those with talent and those without. One result, of course, is that there are around today some pretty wretched examples of hand-painted china. But there also are available some excellent examples, and interest in these is beginning to percolate.

A number of well-known pottery and porcelain manufacturers produced white china for home decorators and others. Several periodicals of the late 1800's published how-to articles and designs for painting on china. Colors, brushes and other accessories for china painting were offered by numerous business establishments late last century and well into the present one.

Much of the whiteware for decoration came from Europe, some of it from the Haviland factories in Limoges, but a good bit also was turned out by several plants in the United States, including the

153

Jersey City Pottery, and Willets Manufacturing Company, of Trenton, New Jersey.

Some factories potted large quantities of whiteware to be decorated by artistic women in their homes and then sold at wholesale and retail as hand-painted china. The decorations on scores of pieces of this type were first-rate, but others were mediocre. Most work of this type was done on a piece-rate basis and provided an income for many gifted young women.

Some schools furnished instruction in china painting. The best-known family of china painters of the late nineteenth and the twentieth centuries was perhaps the Lycetts. The pioneer china painter of this family was Edward Lycett, who came from England to the United States just prior to the War between the States and who had obtained his apprenticeship in the famous Spode works in England. In 1865, Edward Lycett decorated a china service for President Lincoln. Several outstanding pieces he painted are now preserved in the Smithsonian Institution, and other fine examples are now in the possession of Mrs. Lydia Lycett White, of Atlanta, a member of the fourth generation of the Lycett family.

William Lycett, son of Edward, went to Atlanta and opened an art school. He also decorated numerous pieces of china, which fetch high prices today. His son Edward C. Lycett carried on the business after his father's death. Lydia Lycett married one of her father's employees, William A. White, another talented china decorator.

A most informative account of the work of the Lycett family was written by Wylly Folk St. John and published in *The Atlanta Journal and Constitution Magazine* for February 12, 1967. Much of the background for that was obtained from Mrs. White. Mrs. St. John reported that the gold formula the Lycett family has used for more than a century was a secret family formula but that one of its basic ingredients was pure gold.

Another enlightening article about the Lycetts was written by Mary Akers and was published in *Georgia Magazine*'s April-May, 1964, issue. An earlier account was written by the ceramics authority Dr. Edwin Atlee Barber.

In a scholarly article, "American Hand-painted China," in the April, 1967, issue of *Spinning Wheel,* Katharine Morrison McClinton lists among the companies producing china for hand painting Ott & Brewer, the Ceramic Art Company (which subsequently became the Lenox China Company), the American Art China Company, the Columbian Art Pottery Company, Knowles, Taylor and Knowles, and others.

Decorated in great quantities by homemakers were pieces such as plates, platters, vases, cups and saucers, and berry bowls. Hand-painted pieces done by professionals also included chocolate and tea pots, olive dishes, sugar and cream sets, puff boxes, hair receivers, lemonade jugs, salad bowls, sugar shakers, salt and pepper sets, candlesticks, hairpin boxes, cologne bottles, hatpin holders, ringtrees, and complete dresser sets.

Various materials for china and glass painting were offered in an 1894 catalogue of Artists' Materials published by A. Sartorius & Co., of New York City. It included such things as ready-mixed gold, silver, and bronze paints and rubbing powders, vitrifiable oil colors for overglaze painting, and brushes.

This company's introduction of some new colors for china painting under the name "Vitro Moist Water Colors" was heralded in the *Art Amateur* for May, 1895. These colors, it was reported, possessed special properties for tinting.

There were a number of instruction books on china painting available for those interested in the latter part of last century. Among them were *A Manual for China Painters,* by Mrs. N. diR. Monachesi; *How to Apply Matt, Bronze, Lacroix and Dresden Colors and Gold to China,* by Miss A. H. Osgood; *Suggestions to China Painters,* by Louise McLoughlin; *Pottery Decoration under the Glaze,* by the same author; *Practical Lessons in Painting on China, Etc.,* by Madame La Baronne Delamardelle and M. F. Goupil; *China Painting,* by August Klimke; and *Practical Hints for Amateurs in Porcelain Painting,* by F. Stanhope Hill.

Several dealers in artists' materials issued catalogues in which china-painting paraphernalia was offered between 1890 and 1900. Among these, Favor, Ruhl & Company, New York City, advertised Dresden china medallions for decorating at prices of 40 cents to $28.80 per dozen, depending on size. They were produced in oval, round and oblong shapes. The same company provided both composition and porcelain plaques for painters.

One of the best-known suppliers of artists' china was Thayer & Chandler, of Chicago, which offered large quantities of porcelain imported from European potteries. The company gilded and fired some of this in its own workshop. Among the whiteware for decorating that Thayer & Chandler advertised in an early twentieth-century catalogue were large stocks of Bavarian china (set of six cups and saucers for $2.60; Bohemian china vases at six for $3; 10-inch cake plate of Bavarian china for 85 cents); Derby dinner sets; Belleek china made by Lenox; Royal Satsuma; and varieties of inexpensive individual pieces at 25 cents up, including demitasse cups and saucers, muffin dishes, egg cups, vases, sugar bowls and cream pitchers, tea trays, tureens, cheese and cookie plates, fruit bowls and baskets, nut bowls, spoon trays, compotes, bon-bon dishes and boxes, salt and pepper shakers, mayonnaise sets, grape juice mugs, brush and comb trays, jewel boxes, and others. It even offered a white china-case boudoir clock for painting, complete with a movement for $3.50. Chas. Field Haviland's Limoges-made 16-inch whiteware platters were available at only $2.55.

Special china painters' palettes were sold in tin boxes with covers to prevent dust from specking the colors. For the serious china painter there were portable kilns fired by gas. Favor, Ruhl & Company offered Wilke's portable kilns in six sizes at prices of $25 to $75. These enabled artists to fire quantities of decorated porcelain and earthenware. F. Weber & Company, of Philadelphia, St. Louis, and Baltimore, offered several brands of kilns, including the Ideal, Revelation, Fitch's, and Wilke's. The least expensive model started at $30. The same company sold Dresden porcelain cuff buttons and studs for painting.

In 1891, even *The Youth's Companion* offered a china-painting outfit as a premium for one new subscription and $1.50 additional. It consisted of 13 china colors, a brush, a square shader, an outliner, a palette knife, a bottle of turpentine, bottle of mixing oil, a ground glass slab, a sheet of tracing paper, and a manual of instructions for beginners. You could buy the same outfit for $3 cash.

Some of the decorated porcelain objects you are likely to encounter in antique shops today were painted by housewives, and others by independent professional china painters, who bought their own supplies of whiteware and sold the finished articles either from their own studios or through retail outlets. You will have to be the judge of the artistic merits of what you may encounter.

In addition to the white porcelain for home decoration, some companies manufactured china with a design outline in the form of a transfer print; the outline was intended to be filled in with color. Some work of this type was done by regular factory employees, and a number of establishments sold large quantities of this hand-painted porcelain. Several wholesalers' and distributors' catalogues of the early twentieth century contain illustrations of such wares.

Some of the finest hand-painted porcelain of modern times was produced by the Pickard china decorating factory, established in Chicago in 1894 by Wilder A. Pickard and which continues today in Antioch, Illinois, as Pickard, Incorporated. The company was an outgrowth of a studio which Mr. Pickard opened in Edgerton, Wisconsin, a year earlier for the commercial production of hand-painted china, which was then in high vogue. Mr. Pickard employed several outstanding amateurs, many of whom had been trained at the Art Institute in Chicago.

The company's first location was set up in an old building that stood on what is now the edge of the loop shopping center in Chicago, and Mr. Pickard added ceramic artists of distinction from all

Jam jar in "Strawberry" design hand-painted for Pickard by the artist William Yescheck about 1898 (left) and chocolate pot in "Deserted Garden" design by John Nessy (about 1910). These lovely Pickard china pieces are in the collection of Mrs. Dorothy Pickard Platt.

over Europe to his staff. They were permitted great freedom in working out their individual decorative ideas. The Pickard hand-painted wares were so popular that larger space was soon needed, and in 1904 a special structure was built in the Ravenswood district, then on the outskirts of the city. The new building provided outside light for every artist on the staff. Among the prominent artists who worked for Pickard in the earlier years were John Nessy, William Yeschek, and Edward Challinor.

Wilder Pickard's son Austin joined his father in the company in 1925. Up until 1930, the company obtained its blanks primarily from Haviland and other companies in Limoges, France, although smaller quantities were bought from other porcelain factories. In the spring of 1930, however, the company decided it would be advantageous to develop a line of china of its own manufacture, and an experimental laboratory was added. Development work was carried on here for six years, and literally hundreds of clays were tested for properties of color and strength in the finished ware. In 1936, the breakthrough came: the laboratories perfected a type of china that met the high standards the company had set. Special character-

Hand-painted Pickard china dessert plate in "Currants" design by the artist Leon, executed about 1895 and now in the collection of Mrs. Dorothy Pickard Platt.

Beautiful hand-painted Pickard china dessert plate in "Lilies" design by the artist Schoner, executed about 1898. (From the collection of Mrs. Dorothy Pickard Platt.)

Hand-painted Pickard cake plate with peacock and etched gold design executed by Edward S. Challinor about 1919 and now in the collection of Mrs. Dorothy Pickard Platt.

istics included a delicate lightness in weight, a high degree of translucency, a fine ivory color, and strength and durability. The combination of china clays, ball clay, feldspar, kaolin, and flint with the mineral dolomite was responsible for the beauty and strength of the new Pickard china.

Test production of the new china of the bone or feldspar type was begun in 1937, and a plant was built in nearby Antioch while decorating work continued at the old factory in Chicago. Delivery of the Pickard-made and Pickard-decorated china to stores began in 1938. In 1940 a large addition was made to the test plant in Antioch, and another structure was erected and the decorating operations moved there the following spring. Growth has continued since that time.

The Pickard designs included informal monotone and gaily colored florals, formal designs in gold, and stylized decorations. Popular patterns around the time of World War II included Garland, Fantasy, Diana Green, and gold Rocail. The company's Botany pattern offered 12 different floral studies inspired by old botanical prints.

American hand-painted china of 1914. The decoration of the lemon-
ade jug on the third row from top and that of the tall jug and chocolate
pot below was called "Alhambra." The tankard at bottom left was
14 inches tall. These wares were offered by the A. C. Becken Company,
of Chicago.

Because the earlier blanks were obtained from other factories, you will frequently find European factory marks on these wares. The earliest pieces were desserts and tea sets. The company now utilizes a sitting lion with one paw on a shield as its trademark.

Henry A. Pickard, Jr., grandson of the founder, currently heads the business. Hand-painting has not been done for a good many years, but the company is continuing to produce beautiful china in new shapes and patterns with emphasis on the highest craftsmanship. The early hand-painted pieces are fetching increasingly high prices on the collectors' market. Mrs. Dorothy Pickard Platt, daughter of the company's founder and aunt of the current president, has an outstanding collection of the early Pickard pieces.

Striking among the new Pickard creations are its lines of gold china and platinum accent with the pieces hand cast in individual molds and with a number of additional hand operations performed by skilled workers.

One of the first books of instruction in painting china for amateurs may have been *A Guide to Porcelain Painting* by Sidney T. Whiteford, published in London by George Rowney & Company about 1880. I recently acquired a copy of this which bore no publication date. In his Preface, however, the author said:

"Whilst nearly every branch of Pictorial and Decorative art has been made the subject of numerous handbooks, it is believed that no manual of instructions in the art of painting on Pottery and Porcelain has hitherto appeared."

The author proceeds to give instructions for both painting over the glaze and painting under the glaze, the latter, of course, being a much more complicated process. The little book is illustrated with designs for painting on porcelain and pottery, several of them printed in color. As a further help, the author appended a list of works relating to the manufacture and decoration of pottery and porcelain, and there are 20 pages of illustrated advertisements of art materials which were offered for sale by Messrs. George Rowney & Company, of London—the same firm that published the book.

Several mail order houses early in this century offered quantities of good quality hand-painted china articles. In its 1907 catalogue, Otto Young & Company, of Chicago, illustrated ten pages of fancy plates, plaques, pin and comb trays, berry bowls, salad dishes, bread trays, vases, chop plates, cake plates, chocolate pots, pitchers, olive dishes, sugar and cream sets, cups and saucers, puff boxes, and hair receivers. Wholesale prices of the plates in $8\frac{1}{2}$-inch diameters ranged from $1.25 to $3.12. Tall hand-painted pitchers ranged up to $16.50, but chocolate pots were priced at $5.75 to $9. Individual cups and saucers were priced at $2 to $3.50, and you can sometimes find these at about those same prices at some shops and flea markets.

Shown here are pieces of American hand-painted art china produced prior to the first World War. Decorations of the first and fourth vases on the top row were called "Egyptian" type. Gold was used to decorate the second vase from left and the three plates on the third row. In addition, you will see the use of chrysanthemums, violets, tulips, poppies, roses, and cornflowers in the decoration of other plates and the tall vase at right on the top row. Some of these hand-decorated plates are selling today for as little as they cost more than half a century ago—about $5 to $10.

Large quantities of acid-etched china were turned out early in this century for encrusted gold decoration to be done by artistically-inclined ladies at home. Here are some pieces of it, showing a part of the variety in which it was produced. A good bit of the china you encounter in smaller antiques shops today may have had that worn gold on it originally applied in someone's home, and not at a porcelain factory.

Interesting lines of hand-painted china also were offered by A. C. Becken Company, wholesale jewelers of Chicago, in its 1914 catalogue. Many of these pieces were heavily decorated in gold.

A home craft that took a large part of the country by storm in the late nineteenth century and continued in popularity well into the present century was pyrography, sometimes referred to as painting with a hot poker. The "artist," in effect, heated a poker or similar sharp-pointed instrument until it was red hot, then proceeded to burn designs into wood.

The art of pyrography was being practiced early in the 1800's but it attained its greatest popularity toward the end of the century when manufacturers began turning out pyrographic implements, articles to be decorated, and designs to be copied. Women's magazines started publishing articles about the craft of burning designs in wood in the early 1900's, thus imparting the "know-how" to thousands of females who saw in it a fruitful and interesting way to indulge their leisure.

In the February, 1905, issue of *The Modern Priscilla* appeared an article entitled "Some Designs in Pyrography" by Harriet Cushman Wilkie. By that time the fireplace poker had yielded to pointed instruments especially designed for this work. Thayer & Chandler, mentioned earlier in connection with artists' china, became a specialist in pyrographic equipment. The company issued several catalogues over the years devoted exclusively to this subject. I have in my possession a fine one of 72 pages, undated but apparently published around the year 1900. Other catalogues of pyrographic supplies were issued by Frost & Adams, of Boston; Edward Malley Company, of New Haven, and F. Weber & Company, of St. Louis.

Available from such companies was a pyrographic implement consisting of a platinum point in a cork handle. The point was kept hot by pumping gas to its tip. Pyrography's basic materials toward the latter part of last century had been extended to include leather in addition to wood, and the platinum points for working these materials were fashioned in a variety of shapes. Some were designed to be used for general utility work, some for background and flat work, and some specifically for working leather.

A typical pyrographic outfit consisted of a cork handle and platinum point; a large rubber bulb with attached tubing; an alcohol lamp; a metal union cork; a bottle with a glass stopper and a wire hook; a bottle of stain and one of varnish; a piece or two of practice wood, and a set of instructions. One could purchase a simple outfit, boxed, for as little as $2 as this century opened; better ones were priced at $5 to $10.

One also could purchase separately such adjuncts as stains, varnishes, waxes, points, staining brushes, cork handles, and other accessories. An almost fabulous array of articles stamped with designs and intended for pyrographic decoration was available when this century opened. Among the favorites were picture frames, trinket and other types of boxes, book ends, bowls, plaques, towel racks, necktie boards, and serving trays. Literally hundreds of other stamped designs, however, were also offered. These included mirrors, tankards, various kinds of brushes, stationery holders, napkin rings, calendars, thermometers, paper knives, candle holders, music cabinets, fireplace screens, magazine stands, clocks, stools, chairs, tea tables, and even communion plates. Leather and plush articles offered for the pyrographic addict included table centerpieces, cushion cover fronts, and table and piano scarfs.

Thayer & Chandler acquired exclusive rights to reproduce for pyrographic decoration on wood drawings by the noted illustrator Charles Dana Gibson, whose "Gibson Girls" also were reproduced

Some of the objects available for home decoration early in the twentieth century are shown here. On the top row are some of the articles offered in colored glass. Table, bridge, and chair lamp shades are on the next two rows below. On the fourth row is a group of wooden plaques with color prints for gesso polychrome work, and at bottom are parchment bed and dresser lamp shades and lanterns for Oriental lacquer.

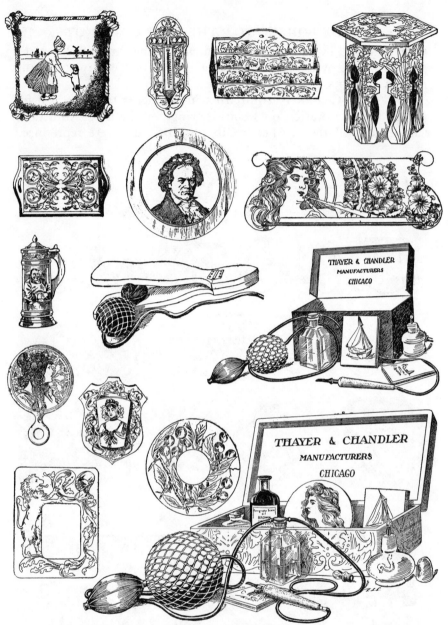

The diversity of articles decorated by the art of pyrography some years ago was almost astonishing. These articles could be purchased either pattern-stamped or plain. Those shown here were offered by the well-known firm of Thayer & Chandler, Chicago. On the top row, left to right, are a cushion cover, thermometer, wooden letter rack, and a tabourette. Second row, from left: a comb and brush tray, medallion of basswood, and a basswood necktie or towel rack. Third row: a wooden stein, an illustration showing a foot attachment for the bulb used with the pyrographic outfit, and Thayer & Chandler's No. 92 outfit, which originally sold complete for only $2. Another larger outfit is shown below. Other articles illustrated include a hand mirror, broom holder, and two basswood panels.

on porcelain plates by the Royal Doulton Company in England. Gibson Girl designs became a favorite with thousands of pyrographic decorators, and they appeared in profusion on photo frames, hand mirrors, calendars, and other objects.

Bowls, paper knives, match stands, and thermometers were often decorated with designs of flowers, vines, leaves, and fruit. Animals, Dutch scenes, Gibson Girls, and outdoors scenes were favorites for decorating ovals and panels to be hung on the walls of one's home.

The Modern Priscilla listed as the most popular objects for pyrographic decoration in 1905, frames, paper cutters, broom holders, napkin rings, cigar trays, letter racks, pen trays, and panels and plaques, in that order.

Wooden objects to be decorated could be purchased in the early 1900's for about a quarter up. Good hand mirrors with beveled glass were priced at $1.25 to $1.40, and a large music cabinet, stamped with a design, was available from Thayer & Chandler for $10. A similar cabinet decorated sold for $40. A child's rocking chair, with design stamped on, was available at $4.75 and a lady's sewing table at $6. Basswood hall chairs, stamped, were on sale in 1900 at less than what the lumber alone would cost now—$2.85 to $3.75.

A very large percentage of the articles done by pyrography years ago have little artistic value, and many persons do not think highly of them at all. However, they represent examples of what our grandparents and great-grandparents did to while away the time, and they do constitute a part of our past. That's why I think the best of them should be preserved. Some of the smaller articles will even serve for nostalgic decoration in the home.

Another home craft for ladies of the 1880's and 1890's was that of creating objects of crepe paper, or tissue paper. It was easy for those with skilled hands and a bit of imagination to fashion a wide range of decorative items from crepe paper and a coil of wire. Thousands of ladies worked at home, turning out lamp shades, fans, picture frames, wall panels, boxes, baskets, candle shades, doll clothing, glove and handkerchief cases, napkins, whisk broom holders, lamp screens, wall pockets, wedding cake boxes, and vases.

In the late 1880's crepe paper decorative outfits were sold. A typical one contained a dozen rolls of crepe paper (18 inches wide) in various colors; a coil of covered wire; a sheet of dark green tissue paper for covering stems, and several other sheets of different colors of tissue paper; bands for covering shades; half a dozen sheets of Bristol board; a couple of cabinet picture frames; a shade card of crepe paper; several brass rings; a thermometer; a calendar pad, and a sheet or manual of instructions. Some small outfits cost less than a dollar; those with more accessories were a little higher.

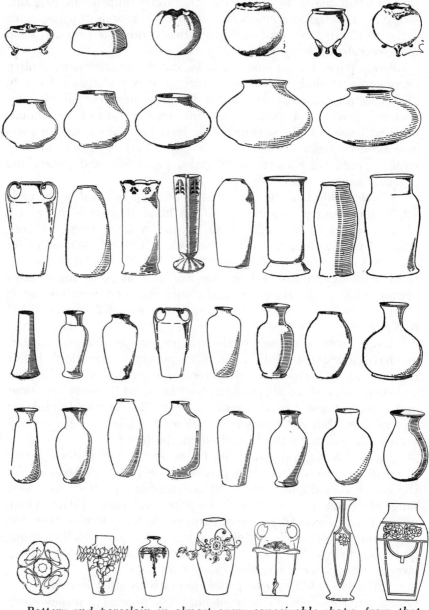

Pottery and porcelain in almost every conceivable shape—from that of rose bowls to urns—was utilized earlier in this century by ladies who burned with a desire to lavish their decorative talents upon them. Here are just a few of the forms in which the undecorated china was made. The pieces on the bottom row were especially designed for Oriental lacquer decoration. The art of home pottery decoration is being revived today.

Home crafts flourished late last century and early in this one as is evidenced by such outfits and examples as pictured here. Top, left to right: "Vienna Leatherette" articles of 1891, a lady's circular shawl made from materials available in 1902, and a "Priscilla and John Alden" pillow in tinted embroidery of 1905. The boys and men of the household used the outfit for tapping boots and shoes shown at left on second row a good many years ago. At right of this is a doll made from a spool and pipe. At left on the third row is a drawing of a youngster working with an outfit for making gold-wire jewelry (with an example at left just below). In the center is the Todd Adjustable Loom (1902), and to the right are a home-made pen-wiper and book mark. Home-made articles at bottom include a chamois container for eyeglasses, two pin cushions, and another pen wiper.

Many a feminine hand was kept busy in the late nineteenth century with such materials as these. At top are articles made of celluloid as is the decorated waste basket at left below. Decorated art pillow covers are shown to the right of the waste basket, and next is Tabby Cat, printed in colors on cloth and sold for a dime in 1893. Third row: an 1891 rug being made on a frame, and an embroidery outfit. Bottom: a plaiting machine, home basketry work, and an oil painting outfit for beginners.

As a premium, a crepe paper outfit was no exception for *The Youth's Companion*, which had offered thousands of other objects during the years in its efforts to broaden its list of subscribers. Commenting on the crepe paper art in 1889, this magazine said:

"The beauty of these Crepe Tissue Articles are [sic] impossible of realization before seeing. A lady's boudoir can be made by this means to look like fairyland; lifelike vines and flowers twined around the picture frames and mirrors; natty ornaments upon the dresser and mantel; attractive frames and pockets on the wall, and dainty touches everywhere."

To aid beginners in this art, some companies sold finished models, including those of flowers. Artificial flowers of crepe paper were great fun to make, and their composition required a bit of skill. Special outfits for making crepe paper flowers were also sold, costing about a dollar. They contained assortments of leaves, petals, buds, rubber stems, sprays, moss, wire, culots, and, of course, a number of sheets of tissue paper.

Dennison Manufacturing Company, founded in Brunswick, Maine, in 1844 with the factory subsequently established in South Framingham, Massachusetts, was a major manufacturer of specialties for wrapping and display; and this company naturally promoted the crepe paper art. Late last century it offered 105 samples of its English tissue with a 32-page booklet of directions and patterns for making flowers and other articles in exchange for two two-cent stamps. The samples and booklet were available from this firm's offices in Boston, New York, Philadelphia, Chicago, Cincinnati, or St. Louis.

Few of these fragile crepe paper objects have survived the wear and tear of the passing years, apparently, but one may occasionally find them stored away in old trunks and boxes.

Without question, the exercise of feminine artistic talents was just as widespread last century as it is today. Probably it was even more in evidence, because the ladies of several generations ago were reluctant to disport themselves publicly at such endeavors as golfing, canasta, government affairs, integration projects, and similar feminine sports which have become so popular in the late 1960's. They would have been horrified—at least outwardly—by such pastimes as miniskirt parades, go-go dancing, and bikini expositions. These breakthroughs came later, thanks to the zeal of Susan B. Anthony, Julia Ward Howe, Lucy Stone, and other valiant pioneers in the field of women's rights, and their successors. Our grandmothers and great-grandmothers, therefore, devoted much of their leisure to gossip and artistic handicrafts.

Painting of all types was popular. In addition to painting china,

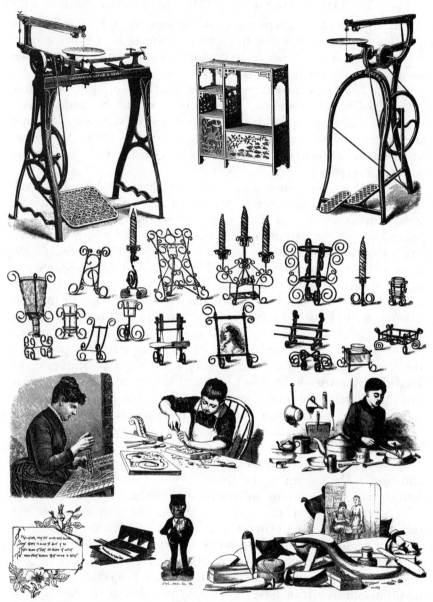

Ambitious youngsters of the late 1800's used the Companion lathe and saw at top left and the Rogers scroll saw at right to make such articles as the scrolled wooden piece shown between them in their leisure time. Examples of Florentine bent iron work are shown below. On the third row are the Griffin rug machine of 1888, youngster using an outfit of six carving tools, and a tinker's outfit. Bottom: a greeting and souvenir card outfit and one of the typical cards made with it, a Palmer Cox Brownie figure made on printed cloth by the Arnold Print Works (12 Brownies on one yard of cloth, 20 cents), and an outfit for tapping boots and shoes.

our female forebears painted crayon portraits from photographs, designs on needlework, and Christmas gifts. They gilded candelabra, gas fixtures, and furniture, and even lettered their own greeting cards. *The Farm and Fireside* in one of its issues in 1899 made this observation:

"When fashion exhausts all other modes of embellishing fabrics, and wearies of the exactness of machine-made decorations, she demands the invention of individual artists and the originality of design coming directly from a skilful hand. When this occurs in the great cities, a ripple of influence extends to the most remote country places.

"It is reported that one of the great ladies of New York is wearing a wonderful painted mantle, and at once we begin to paint on silks and satins with the intention of beautifying our garments. The mantle I have mentioned is described as made of grosgrain silk of a cream tint, cut dolman-shape. It is painted all over with bunches of dim flowers; the colors are clear but with such soft outlines that the whole has a soft indistinctness which makes a charming effect both at a distance and when closely examined. . . .

"When we read about these novelties, our thoughts turn to our paint boxes, and we wonder what possibilities lie in our talents."

The article proceeds to discuss certain items of dress which can be painted and the author adds:

"If I were asked to mention the greatest faults of the decorative paintings to be seen in the homes of amateurs, I should say, first, stiffness of drawing. To avoid this a person must imitate only the best models."

For just such endeavors, the Kensington Art Painting outfit was offered in the 1890's to amateur painters who could part with a dollar. It consisted of a variety of parchment stamping patterns, stamping powder, a pad, six tubes of oil color paints, a brush, four Kensington art painting pens, a felt banner stamped and ready for painting, and, naturally, a book of instructions.

There were gilding outfits for those who felt impelled to gild things other than the lily, and there were inexpensive outfits that contained designs for special occasion cards. Also of interest years ago were assortments of undecorated small objects that could be painted at home and utilized as Christmas gifts. Some periodicals published instructional articles in pre-Christmas issues dealing with a variety of simple and inexpensive gifts that could be made at home. These included chamois eye-glass holders, key and button-hook racks, pocket pincushions, paint brush holders, pen wipers, mending pockets, pipe stands, miniature étageres, and paperweights.

Popular were outfits for basketry work, most of which came complete with instructions, and also outfits for framing pictures.

Available too were novelty embroidery outfits and those for rococo art work in crochet. Untold hours were spent by the ladies in embroidering stamped designs on pillow covers. For small girls just beginning to sew there were animals and other objects printed in colors on cloth. They were cut out, sewn and stuffed. The Arnold Print Works printed Palmer Cox's famous "Brownies" on cloth to be cut out and stuffed. Shepard, Norwell & Company, of Boston, also offered a line of these novelty prints. Incidentally, some of these cut-out-sew-and-stuff prints are being reproduced today. My wife recently cut out, sewed, and stuffed a 13-inch-high tabby cat (originally patented in 1892) and presented it to me as an example of her deftness with the needle and the shears. When my own genuine, live tabby cat first encountered it unexpectedly, he bristled furiously and prepared for a fray.

Some housewives of the last century used "rug machines" to make their own rugs at home. These took some of the drudgery out of the hand work. "Machine" is really a misnomer; these were actually nickelplated devices or implements to be held in the hand and operated to work either yarn or rags. They represented an improvement over the simpler rug hooks. They sold for $1 to $1.50, and they certainly can be included in any collection of home craft implements. Other companies provided designs of animals or flowers printed or stamped on heavy burlap for use in home rug-making. The printed or stamped burlap, usually measuring about 2 by 3 feet in dimensions, was used as the foundation for the rug and was filled in with rags, worsted, yarn, carpet filling or other material arranged in narrow strips and drawn through the foundation from the underside by means of a hook. Rugs of this type were frequently made on an oblong wooden frame resembling a table with legs.

A variety of plating devices and hand looms for producing fancy work at home were advertised around 1900. One type of adjustable hand loom was invented about that time by a Mrs. Martha P. Todd, a Minneapolis school teacher, and was exhibited at the Pan American Exposition. It could be used in the production of such things as draperies, table covers, bureau and table mats, book covers, shopping bags, handkerchief and glove cases, and opera glass bags.

Celluloid work also was of prime interest in the 1890's. It was advertised as "a simple, beautiful and profitable art" and "a means by which young ladies can keep themselves supplied with pocket money." Complete celluloid work packaged supplies were available. They included a large sheet of colored celluloid, working designs and patterns, ribbon to match the celluloid, sachet tablets, a needle, a punch, and, often, such simple items for decorative purposes as thermometers and calendar pads.

The sheet celluloid was formed in whatever shape was desired

Home crafts of the 1880's. Left to right, top: The Royal china paint-ing outfit and the Murillo water color set. Second row: The Companion crayon portrait outfit and materials for Kensington art painting. Third row: the Companion crepe paper outfit and a rose creation of crepe paper. Fourth row: crochet work collar, materials for rococo art crochet work, and a rug machine. Bottom row: two gilding outfits and materials for fancy work to be done at home. These intriguing illustrations are from The Youth's Companion *of last century.*

and was then decorated with ribbon or painted with water or oil colors. Ordinary shears were used to cut the celluloid, and the punch was used for making holes through which the binding ribbon was pulled. The ribbon was formed into bows and tassels. Celluloid articles were sometimes decorated with decalcomania transfer pictures, which also were used in decorating a great miscellany of other objects in the late nineteenth-century home.

Among the articles made from celluloid and decorated were photograph cases, wall pockets and various types of catch-alls, calendars, letter racks, whisk broom holders, book marks, bon-bon boxes, napkin rings, veil holders, fancy boxes and trays for dresser use, needle books, and postal card cases.

Similar articles were made of leatherette tied with ribbons and bronzed. Gilding sets for decorating these were produced by many companies.

"Florentine Bent Iron Work" was heralded as a new home industry in 1894. This afforded a spare-time occupation for both male and female, adult and juvenile. Cold-rolled steel ribbons were used for fashioning (by bending and otherwise manipulating) such articles as candelabra, photo holders or frames, pen holders, ink bottle racks, flower pot stands, vase holders, tooth brush and toothpick holders, and card receivers. Complete outfits for such work included, in addition to the steel ribbon, a spool of wire, pair of nose pliers, a cutting file, lacquer, steel binders, designs, and instructions. The steel used was soft and pliable and could be twisted or bent into numerous shapes. Many simple articles could be made in less than an hour.

Fashioning gold-wire jewelry was another home pastime. A pair of pliers was used to twist gold-plated wire into fancy hairpins, brooches, tidy pins, and name pins. Youngsters often made such objects as gifts or sold them at bazaars and fairs.

There were not nearly so many home or away-from-home attractions for boys and girls 75 years ago as there are today, neither Disneyland nor television having been invented. Home crafts, therefore, flourished among the youngsters, who found they could put their spare time to intriguing and profitable use.

The Youth's Companion over a period of some years featured footpower lathes and scroll saws as premiums, and hundreds of these found their way into homes, where they were utilized by teen-age boys in particular in making various small pieces of furniture and decorative objects which were either used in the home or sold to understanding neighbors.

The lathes and saws were sturdy affairs, operated by foot treadles and equipped with dust blowers. The lathes could be used to turn pieces of wood up to 16 inches in length. Also provided with these machines were turning tools, saw blades, belt hooks, and other accessories. Many young men became rather proficient artisans by learning to use these devices.

To enable young people to be of greater assistance around the home, some manufacturers made tinkers' outfits for the repair of such commodities as tea kettles, pots and pans, graters, measures, and the like. Others produced equipment for tapping boots and shoes, for metal working, wood carving, and other crafts and occupations. There were even outfits for what was known as "hammer-ech brass work," which consisted of covering soft wood with a thin brass sheet and then hammering a design upon it. Hammered brass work is still being done today by amateurs as well as professionals. Favorite hammered brass articles of an earlier day included lamp bases and shades, jardinieres and fern dishes, candle shades, and broom holders.

Although decorating glass was less popular than decorating white china, some of this was done, too, earlier in the century. Scores of clear and colored glass articles were available for home decoration, using lacquers. Firing was not necessary. Objects sold for such a purpose included cream and sugar sets, bon bon dishes, a variety of candy jars with tops, candlesticks, cigar jars, cracker and cheese dishes, perfume bottles, console sets, and plates. Most of these were available in either amber or green glass. The glass objects were quite inexpensive. Colored glass candy jars could be bought early in the century in a price range of from 55 cents to $1.35. Colored glass plates sold for as little as 30 cents each, and tea cups and saucers for 48 cents.

Many of the pieces decorated at home made fine special occasion gifts. Some such pieces now turn up in antique shops, the lacquer often worn.

Fabric paint was made for decorating numerous articles of fabric from scarfs to handkerchiefs and shawls, and tracing patterns also were available. Art furniture for lacquer decoration was sold in great abundance. Much of this was made of three-ply wood and was shipped knocked down for easy assembly after arrival. It included such pieces as utility shelves, magazine baskets, book stands and troughs, wall brackets, foot stools, wall cabinets, umbrella stands, tables, china cabinets, clock cases, and telephone stands. Colored transfer pictures were available for use in decorating many of these objects. They were fairly simple to use. One coated the face of the transfer with transfer varnish and left it for about half an hour until the varnish became tacky. The transfer was then placed, varnished side down, on the article to be decorated and was rubbed hard with

Home crafts flourished as luxuriantly as the bay tree early in this century, and there was never a need for idle hands. Here are just a few of the things offered to housewives, homemakers and others to decorate in their spare time. Top row: telephone screens. Second row: two book troughs, two book ends, and a group of cigarette stands. Third row: two door stops, a hat stand, phone plaque, another cigarette stand, and a curtain tieback and three sizes of candlesticks. Fourth row: another group of book ends and a yarn holder known as "Handy Mandy." Bottom row: a fireplace screen on each end and a Japanese screen in the center. The screens came ready for lacquer decoration. These items were among hundreds sold for home decoration by Thayer & Chandler, of Chicago.

a rubber roller or a dry cloth. The paper was soaked with tepid water for a few minutes and was then slid off. One could moisten a soft cloth with turpentine to which a little gasoline had been added and rub it over the design to remove the excess varnish. When dry, the design was polished or varnished over. Thayer & Chandler, among other firms, offered parchment shades, lanterns, torchieres, and numerous novelty objects for lacquer decorating.

Some of these earlier home crafts are experiencing a revival right now, and undoubtedly some of the objects you will encounter in both gift and antiques shops were decorated by amateurs in their homes. The artistic impulse is a strong one, even—alas!—in the untalented.

This chapter has been primarily an introduction to some of the home crafts which helped keep our ancestors out of mischief. You can have fun researching others by looking through old catalogues, magazines, and books.

Not too many of the objects fashioned or decorated at home are of substantial value today, but many are worth preserving to serve as reminders of how our forebears spent their leisure. The various tools and implements utilized in these crafts should be salvaged, too. A collection of articles made in homes of yesteryear or of the tools and accessories used in their production not only could compose a fascinating display but also might serve to point a moral about the constructive use of idle time. You really don't have to hang around street corners or watch boring television shows, you know.

Quantities of the decorated china made by the Lycetts and Pickard and discussed earlier in this chapter are selling today at prices well above their original levels. A Pickard teapot 8½ inches tall, decorated with panels of fruit on a gild ground and signed by the artist Yeseck, was recently offered by a dealer for $40. Prices asked in recent months for other hand-painted early Pickard pieces include these: plate, 8¾ inches in diameter, marked "J.P.L., France" (J. Pouyat, Limoges), and signed by the Pickard artist "Soli," $17.50; 11-inch plate with open gold handles, decorated with a garden scene by Challinor, $39; 9½-inch-diameter bowl, decorated with leaves and blackberries and signed by the artist, $37.50; 6-inch-tall pitcher signed by Nessy, $75; creamer and sugar bowl, decorated on gold background, $22.50; 8¼-inch plate with garden scene, $19; three-piece decorated tea set, decorated with flowers against gold, $60; 8-inch-tall vase with berries, fruit and blossoms, signed by the artist, $18; 8-inch-tall pitcher with gold leaves and berries, artist-signed, $21; and 9-inch teapot, sugar and creamer, signed "Hessler," $65.

[10]

The Sounds of Music

☞ I remember a night back in the Dark Ages when I was at work at home, setting down something less than deathless prose on yellow copy paper. It was about 10 o'clock, and I was distracted by sound emanating from my radio. When I heard the word "accordion" mentioned, I turned from the typewriter and began listening. The announcer was describing a contest in which first prize was a Hohner accordion. This instrument was to be awarded the individual writing the best letter of 200 words or less delineating the effectiveness of a specified method of learning to play the piano. (I have long since forgotten the name of this method; suffice it to say I had never heard of it before.)

Then and there I decided that if there were anything I had to have, it was a Hohner accordion. There was only one problem: the contest ended that night and all letters had to be postmarked by midnight. The post office was 15 miles from my home. Undaunted, I dashed off a letter praising the piano-playing methods of which I had never heard and managed to get it to the post office shortly before midnight. I returned home, sleepy but full of hope.

This story doesn't end the way you probably think it did. I actually won the accordion. It arrived one bright summer day about six weeks later, and I couldn't wait to begin playing it. But there was another hitch: I didn't know how to play an accordion. However, I decided that anyone who could play a piano could probably play an accordion. So I went out and bought a piano. Not only that, but I also bought a set of the lessons whose merits I had so lavishly praised in my prize-winning letter. I agreed to pay for the piano on the installment plan—at the rate of $5 a month if I recall accurately.

I don't want to drag out this story. I never did learn to play the piano, and, therefore, never learned to play the accordion. The music store from which I had bought the former repossessed it, and I entered into an agreement with a local artist of some distinction: I would swap him my accordion for one of his paintings. He took the accordion off with him, and I never received the painting.

I have let this be a lesson to me and have never purchased another musical instrument except mechanical ones. But I still regret never having learned to play the accordion, and I secretly covet almost every musical instrument I encounter—even those in catalogues. I guess I am just a frustrated musician at heart.

You might be astonished at the variety of musical instruments which have been made through the years. Many of those produced as recently as the late nineteenth-century have become collectors' items. It is the purpose of this chapter to discuss some of those and to mention some instruments which, apparently, are no longer being made.

One interesting mechanical contrivance was the Roller Organ. This was operated by means of a hand crank and played tunes that had been pinned to wooden or cork rolls, or rollers. The music was produced, generally speaking, by the action of a cylinder, usually made of hardwood, which was turned by a gear and which operated a bellows. When the crank was turned rapidly, the metal pins in the revolving roller opened metal spring valves and permitted them to close again. The opening of the valves enabled circulation of air through the reeds, producing musical tones. The reeds were riveted to plates.

Two brands of these Roller Organs were quite popular in the late nineteenth- and early twentieth-centuries. One was known as the Gem Roller Organ, and the other was the Concert Roller Organ. In an 1895 catalogue of A. E. Benary, of New York City, importer and manufacturer of musical instruments and accessories, the former was listed at $9 with three rollers of music, and the latter was priced $19 with five rollers. Extra rollers cost $3 a dozen. In 1905, the same brands were offered at only $3.25 and $7.60, respectively, by the Cash Buyers Union First National Co-operative Society, of Chicago. Extra rollers were priced at 18 cents each plus 6 cents for postage.

Scores of tunes were available on the rollers. These ranged from religious favorites to popular songs of the day. The 1906 listings included such titles as "Auld Lang Syne," "Ambrosia Hymn," "Break the News to Mother," "Creole Belles," "Duane Street," "Gathering Shells," "Manoah," "Rig-a-lig," "Whistling Rufus," and "Zigzag Clog."

The Concert Roller Organ differed from the Gem in that the

An American Conservatory Mandola of 1906 is shown at the top with a Regal Mandolin to its left. At top right is a professional xylophone of the same date and immediately below it a set of musical sleigh bells. Below the bells is an early twentieth-century street organ— a loud-toned pipe organ that played 10 airs—and to its left is a set of Orchestra Bells. Lyon & Healy Cathedral Church Chimes are shown at bottom left and next is a set of bamboo chimes. Parlor Bells are seen at bottom right.

former had its working parts totally encased and came with a sounding board attached. It was made of walnut while the Gem was made of imitation walnut wood.

These devices may have evolved from an hydraulic organ designed in the year 250 B.C. by a Greek engineer named Ctesibus, who left a written record of his invention. If they did, needless to say they underwent many simplifications first.

You'll be lucky if you can find a Gem in good condition with a few rollers now for less than $100, and you may have to pay more. The Concert comes considerably higher. Rollers will cost you $3 each.

The Roller Organs are really fascinating instruments, and anyone who can turn a crank can play them. That may be the reason I bought one for myself.

Hand pipe organs were much larger and costlier in the late nineteenth-century. A French Hand Organ of the console type in a decorated, inlaid rosewood case measuring 24½ inches high, 23 inches wide and 13 inches in depth, was offered in the latter part of last century by the Chicago Music Company for $235. The same company advertised a Hand Orchestrion (or Tent Organ) with wooden pipes, brass trumpets, tambourine bells and so on, for $265. It was housed in a mahogany case with a front sliding panel and stood 45 inches high. Instruments of this type, together with Hurdy-Gurdies (which evolved from a device called an Organistrum developed in the tenth-century or earlier) were made in such relatively small quanties, however, and cost such a substantial sum when available that I will not delve into detail about them here.

To return, however, to accordions (also spelled "accordeon"), many varieties of these were produced in some abundance last century. The accordion was developed in Austria. (A kissing cousin was the concertina, called Konzertina in Germany.) The accordions had keyboards consisting of from five to 50 keys. Although perfected in Austria, their principle is said to have been known sometime earlier by the Chinese.

Some accordions were extremely elaborate with ebonized frames and panels of fancy open fretwork. Some of the best known were produced by Hohner, a German company that specialized in "Vienna" and "Italian" models. The Oliver Ditson Company, of Boston, in its 1906 catalogue gave an explanation of the two spellings of the name in a comment which follows:

"Habit and custom are responsible for a great many curious things in this little round world of ours. Years ago the concern that published the first catalogue of Musical Merchandise in America made a blunder in spelling Accordeons. Every dictionary gives the spelling as Accordions but every Jobber, and to-day every Manu-facturer, spells the word Accordeons—all because of the blunder made by the first house to issue a catalogue and price-list describing these wonderfully popular instruments."

Whereupon, Oliver Ditson proceeded to perpetuate the spelling "Accordeons." Popular brands of these instruments in addition to those of Hohner included Paragon, Clarion, Pitzschler, Empress, Kalbe, Majestic, Lyra, Zenith, Arion, Cosmos, Gessner, and Gebr Ludwig. Oliver Ditson, incidentally, during the early years of this century carried samples of these instruments from every manu-facturer in Europe in addition to its own exclusive lines. Accordions were not manufacturered in any large quantities in the United States before the twentieth-century but were largely imported.

At the turn of this century, accordions ranged in price from only $1.25 (for one with six keys) to more than $65. Accordions, of course, are still being produced, and the best of them cost sub-stantially more than the highest-priced of 65 or 70 years ago.

Desirable from the collector's standpoint are early accordions with cases of fancy inlaid woods. Thousands of miniature accordions with a small number of keys were manufactured and are usually valued a good bit less than the full-sized ones.

Also popular late last century was an instrument known as the blow accordeon (or accordion), sometimes also called the flute accordeon. These were similar, in a way, to harmonicas. They uti-lized a mouthpiece, which was blown into, as well as keys. Hohner made a well-known brand called the Hohnerette, featuring ten bone keys. Prices of these ranged from less than a dollar to around $5 early in this century. About 1910, the firm of M. Hohner introduced a variation called the Hohnerola. Constructed with reeds like the blow accordions, it could be placed on a table in front of the player and then played almost like a piano. The wind required to sound the reeds was supplied by the player through a metallic tube at-tached to the instrument. It had nine brass organ pipes attached to the reeds to give pleasing musical effects. The Hohnerola was ac-companied by an instruction book, and melodies were produced by following figures on the keys in accordance with the instructions in this book. There were ten solo keys and two bass keys. This little in-strument sold for $7. The blow accordions were used primarily by amateur music makers.

The concertina was invented in 1829 by Sir Charles Wheatstone, the English physicist who also took out the first patent for a magnetic telegraph and first put into use the principle of stereoscopic view-ing. The concertina is normally polygonal in shape. It is played by holding it between the hands with the fingers dropping down on studs which raise valves, thus allowing air, which is supplied by a

Shown on the top row here are two German Pitzschler accordions of 1906 and on the second row are two Vienna accordions, the one at left being an Arion and that at right a Majestic brand. Shown below are several early twentieth-century concertinas with two small accordions of 1891 and 1902 at extreme right on the bottom two rows.

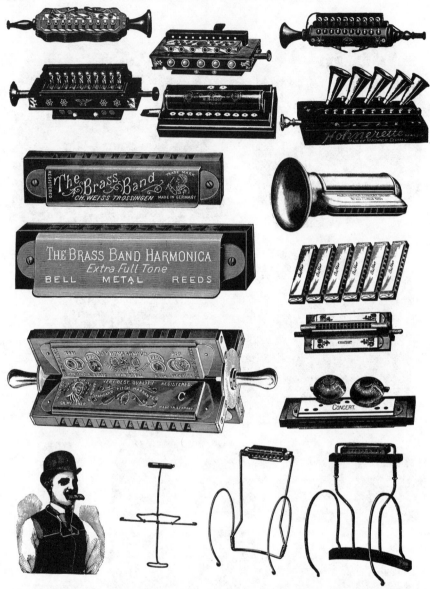

A fine group of Flute or Blow Accordeons is shown on the top two rows. At extreme right on the top row is the Clariphone and at extreme right on the second row, the Hohnerette. A Ch. Weiss mouth harmonica is at left on the third row, and a 1902 Melophone at right. On the fourth row are a simple harmonica of about 1895 and a group of 1891 harmonicas. Messner's "Big Four" Harmonica is at left on the fifth row. This four-sided instrument boasted four different keys. A similar one may be seen to its right just above it, and below this is a Bell, Tremolo and Concert Harmonica of 1891. Early twentieth-century harmonica holders are shown on the bottom row.

bellows, to act upon a series of metal tongues, which are similar to those of accordions. Many of these instruments were imported into the United States last century and early in this one from England and Germany. A large number were made of rosewood or imitation rosewood. In the late 1800's they could be bought at prices ranging from a little over a dollar to around $70. Most of the German concertinas sold for very low sums, fine English ones fetching higher prices. A well-known English manufacturer of concertinas was Lachenal & Co., headquartered in London.

Chances are that should you come across early ones, you'll have to have the bellows repaired.

Remember the Bandonion mentioned in the opening chapter? This was a sort of cross between an accordion and a concertina. It was popular in certain European countries but apparently only a limited number were sold in this country. The illustrations will give you an idea of what they looked like.

Early in the twentieth-century you could purchase a small Bandonion for $20 or less, but a full-sized one might cost $140 or more.

The banjo is said to be about the only musical instrument invented in America until at least fairly recent times, although it probably had ancestors abroad. Until about 1830, it was called the bonja. The banjo was used extensively in American minstrel shows and its use was popularized by our Negro musicians. Of late, however, the guitar seems to have replaced the banjo in favor with folk singers and other musical groups.

Primitive banjos were made of strings placed across such things as gourds and cheese boxes, but the instrument had become quite refined by the latter part of the nineteenth-century when it was in great demand, for use not only in playing popular music of the day but also for the performance of classical music. Of it, the famed Lyon & Healy, of Chicago, which is still in operation with quarters at Wabash Avenue at Jackson Boulevard, said in its 1906 catalogue:

"To those who have never had the pleasure of hearing the banjo in the hands of a skilled performer, let it be said that this instrument is capable of producing music of the highest order, and equal to a small orchestra."

Of the banjo as played by Frederick J. Bacon, one-time director of the Banjo Department of the Siegel-Myers Correspondence School of Music and the author of a course of lessons in playing the banjo, the same company wrote:

"The music brought from the banjo by Mr. Bacon is not the 'plinkety-plank' of by-gone days, but really the sweetest of tones."

Even so, the "plinkety-plank" music had its devotees, and a great deal of music was written to be played to a "plinkety-plank" rhythm. I am sort of partial to it myself; but, being a fellow who never even

learned to play the accordion, I lay no claim to being a judge of
music.

Almost astonishingly large numbers of banjos have been turned
out during the relatively short period of this instrument's existence.

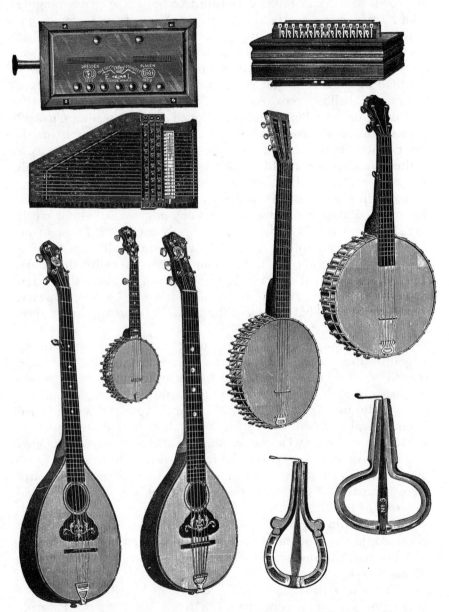

*Nineteenth-century musical instruments included the Flute Harmon-
ica (top left); Flutina (top right); Apollo Harp (second row); and
(left to right) Mandoline-Banjo, Piccolo-Banjo, Mandoline-Guitar, Guitar-Banjo, Banjorine, and two jews' harps.*

*An American Guitar (top left) is shown beside the "Hard Times"
Banjo of the 1890's, described as "the best cheap Banjo on earth." Top
right is a clear bore specialty cornet, Courtois model, of the same period,
and just below it is a Ballad Horn of German silver. To the left is a
harmonica pouch. Below are two organ stools of the 1890's, a Fanfare,
and, at extreme right, a Hand Orchestrion (or Tent Organ) with its
sliding panel removed to show the interior mechanism. This machine
had three cylinders and played 27 airs. It stood 45 inches high and was
31 inches wide. It dates around 1895.*

Although the great majority were of the same basic shape and construction, they have been manufactured under a wide variety of trade names, well known among these being Manhattan (made with spun German silver rims), Peerless, Bruno, Benary, Buckbee, Washburn, Kenwood, Rex, and Converse. The Converse was named after Frank B. Converse, who attained world renown as a banjoist and as a maufacturer of the instruments. In 1890's, Hamilton S. Gordon, Manufacturer, of New York City, acquired from Mr. Converse his patents and trade mark and thereafter made the Converse solid-arm banjos. This instrument was supported throughout its length by a solid arm and strengthening bar, consisting, therefore, of only one solid piece of shaped wood. In most other banjos of the time the arm and strengthening bar were made of two pieces of wood.

Various models of the Converse banjos bore such names as Gentlemen's Standard, Ladies' Regular, Professional Grand, and the Converse Orchestra Banjo.

Hamilton S. Gordon's catalogue issued about 1895 contained several pages of tribute to the Converse banjos from noted persons of that day. Among these was one from Billy Carter, who described himself as the "Ethiopian comedian and banjoist" and who signed himself "Yours banjoically." Carter wrote the company to this effect:

"I have never used any but the solid arm banjos, but the trouble has been to get them made. Now you have 'filled the bill full' and more than that, you have conferred a blessing on all who love and play the banjo, now and for all time to come. Spread the glad tidings."

In the 1890's banjos could be purchased for as little as $1.75! The best ones, however, sold at prices of $100 and more.

Similar in appearance to the banjo was the Banjorine, usually used as a tenor instrument when two or more banjos were played. It was tuned a bit higher than the banjo. The rims of these were large and the necks short with the fingerboard extending over the head. When the banjo was tuned in the key of A, the banjorine was tuned in the key of E. One company termed this instrument a Banjeaurine.

There also was a Banjorine Mandolin, designed for mandolin players who did concert playing. One company said that it could not be detected from a banjo by the general public since the quality of its tone was exactly that of a banjo. It had four strings, was tuned like a mandolin and was played with a pick.

The Banjorines were originally sold in a price range of $15 to $45, and the Banjorine Mandolin sold for $30.

Finally, there was the Guitar-Banjo. This, said the Chicago Music Company in a catalogue issued in the 1890's, was designed for "guitar players who, for a temporary change, or perhaps, for other reasons, desire to play the banjo and who lack the time or inclination to learn the system of Banjo playing." This instrument had the same scale as the guitar and was strung similarly. The necks were made with a long heel piece. Guitar-Banjos (one company called them Banjo Guitars) were priced at $5 up.

The mandolin used to be a favorite instrument for young swains to play for their lady loves. (I remember that my Mother had one, but I never learned to play it either.) This instrument belongs to the Lute family and is of Italian origin. It could be played either with the finger or with a plectrum, which is a two-syllabled name for a pick of wood, ivory, metal or other substance.

There were several varieties of mandolins, including the Neapolitan, Milanese, Spanish, and Turkish. These differed in the number of strings. Woods generally used in their manufacture in the nineteenth- and twentieth-centuries were maple, walnut, cedar, rosewood, and mahogany. Many mandolins had rings of colored wood inlaid around the sound hole, and the sound boards often featured inlay.

The mandolin was so popular some years ago that complete outfits were sold, consisting of a mandolin, case, an instruction course, fingerboard chart, and a tuning pipe. Prices of these started at only slightly more than $5. In 1906, Lyon & Healy offered a 50-lesson course free with the purchase of certain of its mandolins, and a 100-lesson course with the purchase of certain higher-priced ones.

The Washburn mandolin line was quite popular early in this century, and testimonials about its performance were obtained from such persons as Emma Calve, the noted French opera singer, and Giuseppe Campanari, the famous Italian cellist and baritone.

Other well-known brands of late nineteenth- and early twentieth-century mandolins were Regal, American Conservatory, Columbus, Jupiter, Gordon, National, Champion, Paragon, Bruno, Vernon, Gibbs, Neapolitan, Leland, and Martin. The firm of John F. Stratton, of New York City, manufacturer and importer of musical merchandise, sold its own mandolins under such names as Maud, Frida, Trilby, Lottie Collins, Davenport, Tempest, Mitchell, Lucia, Langtry, Neilson, Bernhardt, Norma, Thursby, Hank, Eames, and Melba.

When I was a child, there used to be a popular song entitled, as I recall it, "Paddlin' Madeline Home"; at least, those words were in the lyrics. I seem to remember that this was frequently played on a mandolin in a canoe. If the male occupant of the canoe was playing the Mandolin, it probably was Madeline who was doing the paddling.

Another stringed instrument, the bandurria, is of Spanish origin and somewhat resembles a guitar in general appearance. It had 12 strings which were plucked with a pick, and its use is said to have been popular in native Spanish mandolin clubs some years ago. The very earliest Bandurrias had from four to 12 strings.

The dulcimer goes back to antiquity and has been referred to as that "ancient box of strings," because it was encased in an oblong box. United States mountain families imported and played varieties of this instrument in years past. Dulcimers were available in this country in the early part of this century, but not many persons played them. They featured frames of rosewood or an imitation of it, or of spruce. C. Bruno & Son, of New York City, offered one of 39 strings and 26 notes, complete with hammers, a tuning key, and an instruction book at $40 in its 1910 catalogue.

Zithers, which evolved from a Greek instrument known as the cithara, were found in this country in more abundance than dulcimers. The zither consisted of a resonance box with a large circular sound hole close to the center, and strings, ranging in most models from 32 to 46 in number. The strings were tuned at one end of the box. This instrument was played with the fingers and a metal ring on the thumb of the right hand. Five of the strings were stretched over a fretted keyboard and were used to play the melody. There also was a viola zither, played by a bow.

In the early part of this century, the Washburn line of zithers sold at prices from $11.25 to $53.75, and the company would make special designs of them to order. There was a Columbia brand zither which cost as little as $3.25, about the same time, and the price included a cardboard case; but this instrument was not particularly choice. In 1895, A. E. Benary offered a fairly wide range of zithers at prices of 95 cents (for a little 15-stringed box) to $40 for one of Rosewood with an inlaid sound hole.

The Chicago Music House advertised a Bow Zither around 1895 for $8 in imitation rosewood and $12.75 in genuine rosewood with inlay. It featured a fine traditional zither at $80. Some zithers boasted machine heads of German silver. Variations of this instrument included Harp Zithers, Guitar Zithers, and Zitherns.

There also was the Piano Zither, a chord instrument with keys for striking, similar to a piano. These were available for a very few dollars, and some were sold by department stores early in this century.

A novelty item of the early twentieth-century was the musical door harp. These harp-shaped instruments were fastened on the inside of a door (usually in the dining room). When the door was opened, balls struck the instrument's strings, producing soft chords. The balls were suspended from pegs at the instrument's top. They could be bought for $10 or less, and the revival of such an instrument today might prove a happy circumstance for other frustrated musicians. Anyone who can open a door can play it.

There were several harp-type variations of zithers. These included Phonoharps, which were actually zithers with shields covering certain strings so that the pick or thumbpiece drawn across them would strike exposed strings, thereby producing chords. A similar inexpensive instrument was known as a Harmony Harp. Then there were the popular Apollo Harps, in which the strings were extended from the pinblock down and around the end of the harp and back to the other side of the same block. The manufacturer boasted that these devices would remain in tune indefinitely. Some of them were fitted with a keyed bridge to obtain beautiful dulcimer effects. Music houses were lavish in their praise of the Apollo Harps, one commenting:

"This Harp brings together every requirement for a perfect instrument, giving the possibility for any and every chord in every key, and opportunity for modulating from any key to another, equal to the piano or organ. Thus whatever is lacking in any other instrument to produce this grand result is found here and made perfect."

Then there were the Autoharps, an American invention. They were made in various sizes and with from 18 to 45 strings. Models included the Parlor Grand, Concert Grand, and others designated simply by factory numbers. Autoharps were patented by C. F. Zimmermann on May 9, 1882. Shortly thereafter they were marketed at prices ranging from $5 to about $250 for the Concert Grand, which featured 45 strings, six bars, 10 shifters, adjustable in three different positions and producing 72 chords. By the early years of the twentieth-century, the price of the Concert Grand had dropped to about $85. One company offering Autoharps claimed that they could be played by a six-year-old child. One could play it by a figure system, similar to those used today to play small organs and other instruments.

Another novelty-type stringed instrument developed in the late 1800's was the Harmonette, which closely resembled the Autoharp No. 1 and which had three bars and 18 strings. It, also, was played with a pick. You could buy one of these late last century for $2.50. Apparently only a limited number were turned out, and they appear to be quite scarce today.

Let's get away from the stringed instruments for a moment and talk about those small instruments which at one time abounded in every community and almost every household—harmonicas.

The harmonica and other members of this family of instruments were developed primarily in Germany. For some years their manufacture was confined to that country. These little instruments were Liliputian in size compared to many others, but they could be made

The Washburn Zither of 1906 is shown on the top row at left and at right is a Guitar Zither of Ebonized maple. Second row from left: an Arion Zither, a Bandonion, and an Autoharp, the "Favorite." Third row: an 1889 Harmonette-Autoharp, and a 1906 ocarina. Fourth row: an 1891 Ideal Harp, a Guitar Zither in maple of 1906, an 1891 Harp Zithern, and an 1889 Harp Harmonica. Bottom: the American Zither of 1893, an 1892 Autoharp, and (above) a 1902 Metallochord and (below) an 1891 Flute Accordeon.

to emit substantial sounds. Moreover, they were produced in an amazing variety of designs, constructions, and shapes.

John F. Stratton, of New York, invented and patented a new and improved type of mouth harmonica in March, 1890. In his patent specifications, Mr. Stratton stated:

"In mouth-harmonicas as heretofore constructed the sound after passing through the reeds passed directly to the outside through apertures formed in the rear of the covering-plates or in the top of the same. By this construction the player was compelled to use a large quantity of air to play the instrument successfully, as the sounds passed out of the instrument without being retarded in the least; and further, the tones produced were necessarily not very full and rich. By my construction . . . the player needs but a small amount of air to play the instrument successfully, and produces better and richer tones."

In brief, Mr. Stratton claimed to have invented a harmonica provided with a deflecting and resonating chamber having air outlets at the front.

Stratton's Patent Mouth harmonicas were sold under such trade names as Admiral, Dictator, Silver Queen, Silver King, and Emperor.

Hundreds of thousands of harmonicas of every type were turned out by the Hohner Harmonica Factory, founded by M. Hohner, Sr. In the late nineteenth-century this was the largest reed instrument factory in the world, producing seven million instruments a year in its plants in Germany.

In the early part of this century dealers were urged to promote the sale of these instruments by sponsoring the organization of Hohner Harmonica Bands. One such group organized was the Hohner Harmonica Band of the East Side Branch Y.M.C.A. of New York City, which gave concerts before many organizations.

In 1910, Hohner offered assortments of harmonicas designed to retail at prices of 25¢ to $1.

Other well-known harmonica manufacturers of 60 or 70 years ago included the German firms of F. A. Bohm, Gerbruder Ludwig, Ch. Weiss, C. H. Meinel, and A. Koch. Hohner made a line of harmonicas under John Philip Sousa's name, and each of these bore a facsimile signature of the famous conductor and composer. C. H. Messner & Cie in France made a harmonica line for the American market. The best-known early American manufacturer was the National Music String Company, which, in 1910, claimed that its Bell Brand harmonicas were the only mouth organs made in the United States. This was an inexpensive line, wholesaling for $1.90 a dozen.

Harmonica also is the name given earlier to a musical instrument made of a number of glasses of water which were "played" by touching them with a dampened finger. Well-filled glasses produced higher tones and the lower tones came from those with a smaller quantity of water; or glasses of different sizes could be used. The principle of producing tones in this manner is said to have been known a couple of centuries ago, but the glass harmonica is usually credited as having been invented by the prolific Benjamin Franklin in 1762.

Numerous variations of the reed harmonica were devised and produced under various names. One was the Hohner Hohnerphone, which, in effect, consisted of a small detachable brass horn and the normal harmonica mouthpiece. Muting of the sound could be produced by a slight movement of the hand over the mouth of the horn.

The Hohner Cartridge Harp was quite similar, the horn in this case being in the shape of a cartridge shell. Hohner, and others, made an harmonica with a bell attachment. One type had two bells in different tones manipulated by handles which were pressed to sound the bells.

There also was the Pipeolion, patented and manufactured by Ch. Weiss, of Germany. The reeds of this instrument were fastened on specially constructed brass reed plates inside a series of pipes. By blowing single reeds, the player could imitate a cornet, but when blown in harmonica chords, a pipe organ tone was obtained. Somewhat similar in appearance was Hohner's Trumpet Call, in which the reeds were connected with a wooden sound box into which the tone passed and then found an outlet through five brass miniature trumpet horns which protruded from the box.

Although the majority of simple harmonicas were fairly small in size and oblong in shape, others were square or round; some had four sides; some were made with attached handles at the end; and there were some that measured a foot and a half in length.

Some performers used to play more than one instrument at the same time (and some still do). To free the hands so as to enable a musician to play, say, a mandolin while blowing an harmonica, wire harmonica holders were made. Some of these fitted to the vest and others passed over the shoulders.

Little instruments known as jews-harps were once popular. These consisted of a steel tongue within an iron frame. The tongue was plucked while the instrument was held between the jaws, the tone being changed by varying the position of the mouth. These were inexpensive little gadgets and not professional instruments by any means, but there were a lot of them around at one time. Oliver Ditson Company said in one of its catalogues: "You can't make much music with a poor Jews-Harp." Actually, you couldn't make very much music with any kind, but you could make a considerable amount of sound. The simplest jews-harps sold for just a few cents apiece, but better ones with two tongues cost nearly a dollar early in this century. They ranged from about 1¾ to 4½ inches in length. These instruments were once known, says the *Encyclopedia Americana*, as "Jew's Trump," which might have been a corruption of the Dutch word *Jeudgtromp*, meaning child's trumpet. They are not of much interest to collectors, but if you're determined to put together a representative selection of musical instruments, you might as well throw one in.

Then there was the Metallaphone, which was a Glockenspiel. In substance, this was made of a number of bells originally, and later of a number of metallic bars enclosed within a frame or box. The contrivance was played by striking the tuned bars with small hammers. These instruments led to Marimba-Xylophones and xylophones. A variation was known as Celeste Song Bells, made by J. C. Deagan, Inc., which included in their construction and operation a small electric motor. The motor gave a tremolo to the tone produced when the bars were struck. Other variations included one known as the Turkish Tubephone, consisting of hollow brass tubes in a frame, also played with hammers. The xylophone, by the way, was an American invention, once called a "wood and straw piano," since it was made of a number of pieces of dry wood cut to different lengths laid on straw or some similar non-conducting substance. In the same family were Parisian Parlor Bells with plates of tempered steel. Early examples of all of these are worth collecting. You might even learn to play them.

Of course you are familiar with the Zobo. Or are you? This was little more than an improved Kazoo. The Kazoo made its appearance about 70 years ago and was a toy instrument for youngsters. It looked somewhat like a hollow cigar made of metal, nickel-plated, with a round metal opening extending upward at the top near the mouthpiece, which was blown into. It was said that anyone could play it without instructions, and that it could be blown to imitate the calls of birds and animals, bagpipes and snare drums. Band players could use it as a mouthpiece on brass or tin horns to produce music without having to finger keys.

Of this contrivance, Oliver Ditson Company remarked in its 1906 catalogue: "The small boy is miserable without a Kazoo, and the big boy is made miserable if he doesn't buy him one." This was correct. I pestered my own father until he bought me one; and, if I remember correctly, I hummed into the mouthpiece and some rather astonishing nasal-quality sounds were emitted. Kazoos could be bought at that time for about a quarter.

The Zobo was shaped like a horn, one type resembling a cornet without keys. This was called the Zobo Cornetto and sold for $5 a dozen wholesale. Other types of Zobos imitated in shape such full-fledged instruments as slide trombones, saxophones, and bass horns. The Zobo Cornetto cost only about a dollar, perhaps a little less; but the much higher quality Zobo Cornets sold for more than $20 each about the first of this century. Sonophone patented several types of Zobos on December 11, 1900. Skins were stretched across the mouthpieces or just inside them, which helped account for the nasal quality of the sound. You sometimes blew a hole in the skin and had to replace it with a new one, but it was said that the longer the same skin was used, the better the tone.

Vocophones were quite similar to the Zobos. One company made these in sets of eight little instruments of pasteboard, including a cornet, alto, tenor, baritone, bass, tuba, horn, and clarinet. The wholesale price of these sets was $10 in 1910. A larger four-piece set (cornet, baritone, bass, and slide trombone) in pasteboard sold at the same price.

Musical sleigh bells were interest early in the century and were used by some orchestras and military bands. The bars were made of steel, tuned. The bells were mounted on leather straps in frames or were housed in hardwood cases. The sets were made in two, two and one-half and three octaves. There were several other types of orchestra bells, one having been known as Parsifal Bells. These were used, incidentally, by bands conducted by the noted John Philip Sousa, who was somehow induced to write about them as follows:

"It is my desire, at the moment, to compliment you on the tone and quality of the set of Bells (Parsifal), used during my last tour. You have every reason to be proud of your skill in making such an artistic instrument. The octave harmonic which really makes each bar a double tone is such a relief, so satisfying, as compared with the old style of Band or Military Band Bells."

The Parsifal Bells and the musical sleigh bell sets in general were expensive, selling in 1906 at prices of from $60 to $200.

Musical cow bells, used in "musical burlesque," came in sets of eight to 16 bells and ranged in price from $21 to $43.75 a set.

Also in the family of musical bells (and xylophones) were instruments known as Parlor Bells, Arch Bells, and, of course, the fine Swiss hand bells, which are still being used. The Arch Bells were Swiss bells mounted on an arch and played by pulling a cord attached to the action on the inside of the bell. The action was of the check spring pattern, giving the performer full control of the beater. Each bell had a resonator mounted with it which more than doubled the volume of tone. Each bell, therefore, had a cord, an action, a damper, and a resonator. The bells were mounted in a double arch on a rack made of steel tubing, braced to prevent shaking while they were being played. The rack could be taken down and folded and the bells placed in an ordinary trunk. The complete set weighed about 90 pounds and cost around $350.

There also were early musical rattles, which were swung by a handle. They were fitted with resonators and were made in both one and two octaves, the latter containing 16 rattles and the former eight. The sound they made stopped as soon as the handles were released.

Some of the early toy pianos are of interest. Excellent ones were made by the A. Schoenhut Company, a firm that was established in Philadelphia less than a decade after the War Between the States by Albert Schoenhut, a German immigrant, whose forebears had been toymakers. It became one of the largest and best-known toy manufacturers in the United States, making a varied line of jointed wooden toys as well as numerous other types.

The toy pianos were manufactured in various sizes, the finest ones originally selling for as much as $30, although some very small ones once could be purchased for as little as 25 cents! Today, the Schoenhut pianos have been selling at prices of from around $7.50 to $75 or more, depending on quality and size. Some of the toy models were excellent replicas in miniature of the full-sized pianos. Many music dealers as well as toy shops offered the Schoenhut instruments. Early in this century, Oliver Ditson offered them in a price range of $1.40 to $30. The highest-priced model had a hinged lid, 37 chromatic keys, three panels at the top, and measured 25 x 24 x 13 inches in dimensions. It was made of rosewood. The toy piano stools sold separately from 50 cents to $1.15.

Before departing from pianos, full-sized early piano and organ stools are now in growing demand and at good prices. Some are being used as vanity table seats and for other purposes. Some quite elaborate stools were made late last century and early in this one, featuring turned and fluted legs and center pedestals, turned stretchers, and claw-and-ball feet. Many were turned out in solid hardwood finished in imitation walnut, ebony, mahogany, and rosewood. Height of the revolving seats was adjusted by means of a turn-screw. Many were ponderously late-Victorian in appearance and were extremely sturdy. Some were made with seat edges decorated by beading or fluting.

One type of stool was made with mohair padded seats and heavy grooved legs in a cyma curve with bulbous or vase-shaped pedestals. Some seats boasted skirts cut in cyma curves. There also were ottoman-type piano and organ benches with silk plush seats and scroll feet with pendants on the pedestals. Some of the stools also had pedestal pendants and finial knobs on the upper parts of the legs. Occasionally, you will find these stools with carvings on the knees of the legs. The claw feet frequently clasped glass balls. One popular stool in the opening years of this century featured rope

At top are three of the fine Schoenhut toy pianos of 1906 and two
toy piano stools to match are shown at the bottom right. The numbered
instruments are for a Kinder Symphony and are: 20, a Cuckoo; 28, a
Mirliton; 24, Quail; 20–46, trumpet of several notes; 58, hand bells;
60, Metalophone; 26, rattle; 32–34, trumpet; 30, Waldteufel; 100, 12-inch
drum; 56, sleigh bells, and 22, Nightingale. At the right of these are three
Vocaphones in the shape of a tenor horn, clarionet, and cornet.

molding on legs, stretchers and pedestal. Another was made with dolphin feet.

If you're at all interested in stools of this type, you shouldn't overlook the late nineteenth-century bench stools used by watchmakers, jewelers and others in their shops. These were quite similar in appearance to the piano stools, and some were produced with wire legs with an antique copper finish, resembling the heavy wire legs of early drug store soda fountain chairs. Some bench stools were made with backs of steel spring and an iron frame.

I had some doubt originally as to whether to include in this chapter a dissertation on parlor organs, turned out in such enormous quantities in the nineteenth-century and in quantities not much less early in the present one but have finally decided to yield to the temptation. The reason is that a number of persons have recently been buying these old organs and restoring them to playing condition. Being able to restore an organ seems to do something for one's ego.

Tall, elaborately ornamented parlor organs with decorations and decorative gadgets only a trifle less than horrifying were offered in 1910 by music and department stores at prices of less than $25 and up. And you could buy a "Kenwood Jr. Organ" for $13.50. Should you reside in an apartment and simply have to have an early organ, consider the junior size, since the jumbo size probably would occupy the larger part of your living room.

The "Kenwood Jr. Organ" featured four octaves, a case of golden oak, and turned reeds of solid brass. Its hardwood pedals were covered with patterned linoleum. The organ stood 36 inches high, was 11 inches deep and 30 inches long. Two models were available—one with the four octaves mentioned, or 49 notes and 49 reeds, and the other with five octaves and 61 notes and reeds. These were not cluttered with ornamentation as were the larger sizes.

The Cash Buyers Union First National Co-operative Society, Chicago, offered a wide range of Kenwood brand parlor organs in its 1905-1906 catalogue. The Majestic Grand model was guaranteed for 25 years and not only was advertised as dust-proof but also as mouse-proof, which undoubtedly was a great reassurance to those who resided in mouse-ridden homes. This instrument soared 87 inches high and measured two feet in depth and four feet in length. The top model, consisting of 292 reeds, 17 stops, two couplers, and two knee swells, in either an oak or walnut case, could have been yours at that time for only $59.25, plus shipping costs. Everything about it was ornate and extravagant, including several gargoyles thrown in for good measure.

A Cornish Parlor Organ of 1888 and a Companion Organ of 1885, the latter made as a premium for The Youth's Companion, *and four rather elaborately turned hardwood piano stools from the opening of this century.*

The seller made these modest claims for this organ:

"The case of this instrument is without doubt the grandest, handsomest, and most artistic design ever created, presents a magnificent appearance and will add grace, beauty and refinement to the most richly furnished parlor. . . . The top of the case is the most beautiful design ever created, presenting features of artistic, ornamental carving, such as have heretofore not been used in any organ case. Consists of two cabinets on either side, both fitted with oval glass doors, and at the back a French, beveled, plate-glass mirror; in the center you will find a large beveled plate-glass mirror, 11x14, supported by a shelf with turned spindles and railing. The cabinets on either side can be used as curio cabinets, or as a music or book case. The entire top rests on carved lion claws, and is characterized by a number of beautiful turned columns, scroll work and beaded molding. . . . At either side of the desk will be found an ornamental lamp shelf of special design. The key board is an attractive design of handsome carved wood and raised hand carving. The bottom of the case is the most solid, massive, three-panel construction, absolutely mouse-proof, resting on handsomely turned trusses. The pedals are covered with the best Brussels carpet, making in all the acme of solid construction, beautiful appearance and everlasting durability."

So you thought extravagant claims had been invented by our present-day advertising copywriters? We could continue with the description, since it occupies a large printed page in the catalogue. Nevertheless, if you like conversation pieces, you might like this organ—at least for a while. Eventually, you might beat your brains out trying to get rid of it. On the other hand, since there is no accounting for the whims of today's collectors, you just might be able to dispose of it for well above what you paid for it. It's fun to speculate about such things isn't it?

Pianos we won't discuss. Music boxes are in a category all their own, and you can read about them, if you wish, in one of my earlier books, *Treasure at Home* (A. S. Barnes and Company, Cranbury, New Jersey).

There are numerous other instruments that are collectible, and you might want to watch out for such things as early Flageolets, tambourines, castanets, various types of drums, guitars, Flutinas, novelty ocarinas, and a number of wind instruments.

Just one more note before concluding. If you possess a Stradivarius violin, please don't write me about it. I once wrote an article on violins and mentioned the magnificent instruments made by the great Italian instrument maker Antonio Stradivari in Cremona well over 200 years ago. Stradivari made a good many violins, and the originals are now of great value but apparently only a relatively

few are extant. There are, however, hundreds of thousands of reproductions bearing the name Stradivari or Stradivarius—some good,
some bad, some indifferent.

As a result of my article on violins, I received hundreds of letters from persons who said they owned a Stradivarius. Some of
them were marked "Made in Germany." Despite the geographical
changes in this globe on which we live during the past century or
so, Cremona is still in Italy, not Germany.

I would not know a genuine Stradivarius if I saw it; so, if you
think you have one (and the odds are greatly stacked against this
possibility), take it to a qualified appraiser of musical instruments,
who, for a reasonable fee, will tell you what you have.

Mechanical musical instruments, including player pianos, are
discussed in my book *New Horizons in Collecting: Cinderella Antiques* (A. S. Barnes and Company, Inc.)

Just for the fun of it (since these prices cannot serve as any
real guide to values) you might be interested in noting prices asked
recently for certain musical instruments of earlier years. They have
included these: Vocalion Pipe Organ and bench, $350; restored
hurdy gurdy, 40x29x60 inches in dimensions, playing 10 tunes on
one record, $800; Estey organ dated 1877, $175; Degan xylophone
with legs and case, $60; American mandolin harp patented 1894,
$15; Regent zither No. 5, patented 1893, in original case, $17.50;
Hartman Bros. & Reinhard Concert zither with original box, $20;
Columbia No. 3½ zither, lacking case, $15; Celestaphone, $15; small
hurdy gurdy, 14 x 13 x 9 inches in dimensions, $350; hurdy gurdy
that plays ten tunes, $750; Symphoniam Organette (made by Wil-
cox & White) with 40 paper rolls, needing some repairs, $100.

〖11〗

His Master's Voice - and Others

☞ Because the phonograph is not a musical instrument in the same sense as most of those discussed in the preceding chapter but is a device for reproducing sound, including music, it will be discussed separately here, though briefly.

For several years the very earliest models of phonographs have been collected by a relatively small group of individuals and by the musical museums; but some of the later models, now being rapidly relegated to the past by the wondrous high fidelity instruments, solicit at least a modicum of attention.

As most school children know, the phonograph as it was known in subsequent years was invented in 1877 by the multi-talented Thomas Alva Edison, who gave the world so many of today's necessities. He was granted a patent for his invention in 1878.

Edison's first model was a simple and far from perfect device. Essentially, it was composed of a somewhat awkward mouthpiece with a diaphragm. A metal point was attached to the middle of this piece. In addition, there was a tinfoil-covered cylinder on which the sound was recorded and subsequently played back. To record, sound was projected on the diaphragm through the mouthpiece, which, as it vibrated, cut a groove on the outer surface of the cylinder, which was rotated. The cylinder, which then became the record, was treated to harden it. That sound that had been recorded on it could be played back by returning the cylinder to the position it had occupied when the recording was made with the point of the needle precisely opposite the position it had when the recording started. Again the cylinder was rotated, and as the needle followed the grooves it had originally cut, the diaphragm again vibrated in response to the sound waves to cause the emission of the sound originally recorded.

That explanation isn't very scientific, but we do not intend to concern ourselves here with the technical aspects of the phonograph's construction and operation.

Edison was just thirty years of age when he built his first successful model. It became a sensation. Eighteen years later, after having added various improvements of one kind or another, he made a major change by discarding the tinfoil-covered cylinders and using instead cylinders made of wax and hollow inside.

In the spring of 1878, the Edison Speaking Phonograph Company was organized, and Edison was paid what at that time was a handsome sum for his patent, plus a share of the profits of the new company.

So much interest in the new "talking machines" was generated throughout the country that other individuals and companies entered the phonograph field. These included the Volta Graphophone Company (of which Alexander Graham Bell, inventor of the telephone, was a principal) ; the North American Phonograph Company (which bought the Edison phonograph patents in this country) ; the American Graphophone Company; Columbia Phonograph Company; and numerous others.

The history of the progress of the phonograph and of the various companies and the products they made or handled is an extremely complicated one and is related with great authority by Oliver Read and Walter L. Welch in their exhaustive book, *From Tin Foil to Stereo,* first published in 1959 by Howard W. Sams & Co., Inc., and the Bobbs-Merrill Company, Inc., of Indianapolis and New York. This book is recommended to all interested in the numerous ramifications of the phonograph's development through the years.

Suffice it to say here that before the end of the nineteenth century, "talking machine" interest was soaring. Names given to some of the machines included phonograph, phonograph-graphophone, graphophone, and gramophone. Claims and counterclaims by numerous individuals and firms accompanied the progress of the machines for years after the first successful ones were placed on the market. Interchangeable cylinders which could be played on machines of different makes were developed, and, in the 1890's a radically new type of machine employing a disc instead of a cylinder made its appearance. The discs were made of hard rubber and were the forerunners of the type used today. It is interesting to note that the early talking machines were considered business devices rather than instruments to provide entertainment and that the earliest models were leased instead of being sold outright.

Incidentally, the coin-operated phonograph is no "johnny-come-lately" in this business. Coin machines were made in the last decade of the nineteenth century.

Major firms in the phonograph business in the early years of its existence included, in addition to those already named, the Edison Phonograph Company and the Edison Phonograph Works, the National Phonograph Company (also formed by Edison), the Columbia Graphophone Company, U. S. Gramophone Company, Berliner Gramophone Company, National Gramophone Company, American Talking Machine Company, Universal Talking Machine Company, Consoldiated Talking Machine Company, Victor Talking Machine Company, and others.

The standard discs that revolved at a speed of 78 revolutions per minute have been replaced now by those with speeds of $33\frac{1}{3}$ and 45 rpm's, and the earlier 78 rpm discs are slowly beginning to be collected. So many of them were made through the years, however, that the majority are now worth a good bit less than the price for which they originally sold. Certain records are worth more, and the early cylinders are all collectible unless they have been warped so they will not play.

Edison's first phonograph may now be seen in the Edison Museum in West Orange, New Jersey. He also produced a different model in 1877 with a crank handle on one end and a small horn through which the sound was amplified. The first phonograph is almost priceless and only a couple of hundred machines of the second model were produced so that these are scarce and quite valuable.

Subsequently, Edison made numerous other models as did other companies, particularly Columbia Phonograph Company, Duplex Phonograph Company, and Victor. The last-named made famous its symbol of a seated dog listening to a recording with the phrase "His Master's Voice" accompanying the illustration. Its machines featured an internal horn early in this century.

Various other companies produced some inexpensive phonographs of simple types in the late nineteenth and early twentieth centuries. These featured names such as Zonophone, Lyric, and Busy Bee.

Some of the simpler early phonographs (Columbia called its machines "Graphophones") originally sold for $5 up. In the opening years of this century several companies offered talking machines as "rewards" to persons who sold specified quantities of their products. In 1904, Acme Chemical Company, of New York City, offered a rather simple model of the Columbia Graphophone with an aluminum reproducer to persons selling 36 packages of Perfection Bluing. Three years later, Bluine Manufacturing Company, of Concord

This device is said to have been the first disk talking machine (Gramophone). It was exhibited in 1888. (Photo through courtesy of RCA Sales Corporation.)

Junction, Massachusetts, offered a cylinder talking machine, make unspecified, to individuals selling 40 packages of Bluine at 10 cents a package and remitting the $4 to the company. Logan Day Company, Chicago, offered a crude machine, the Concert, made on a box, in exchange for the sale of 24 Iris Crystal, Japanese Agate, and Swastika Luck Cross hat pins at 10 cents each. The machine played Columbia records.

The Youth's Companion, in 1900, offered a $15 Zonophone in exchange for seven new subscriptions. It described this machine as "an improved Gramophone, over which it possesses many advantages." As a special inducement, the magazine offered also to throw in without charge special records to the value of $3.

A simple Graphophone that played cylinder records was offered in 1904 by the Safe Jewelry Company, New York City, in exchange for the sale of $3.60 worth of its "handsome, fast-selling Fancy Articles," which were not further described except to characterize them as "not trash but costly goods that sell, having merit and value."

Interestingly enough, some of these early devices are avidly sought by collectors now and bring substantial prices. Some of them are shown in the illustrations accompanying this chapter.

Don't make the mistake of believing that a phonograph is quite

A Talking Machine That Talks Talk⟶

BERLINER GRAMOPHONE

LATEST AND MOST REMARKABLE INVENTION OF EMILE BERLINER.
SIMPLE BEYOND BELIEF.

NO COMPLICATED MECHANISM. NOTHING TO GET OUT OF ORDER. NO ADJUSTMENTS.
A CHILD CAN OPERATE IT. THE "RECORDS" PRACTICALLY
INDESTRUCTIBLE.

Gramophone does not imitate, but actually reproduces with lifelike fidelity, purity of tone, distinctness of articulation, all the varying modulations of pitch, quality, and volume of the human voice in speech or song, the music of band, orchestra, solo instruments of every conceivable kind, in fact, everything within the range of sound. Its repertoire is limitless, and its possessor has at his command, at merely nominal cost, all of the latest songs, operatic airs, instrumental solos, and choral selections, as rendered by the most popular artists. Thus the device remains forever new.

It's expensive to hire an artist to come to your home and play for you, or a famous singer to sing for you, but if you have a Gramophone you can buy a "record" of that artist's playing, or that singer's singing for fifty cents, and you can listen to it and entertain your friends with it as often as you please.

The Gramophone is intended solely for the entertainment of the home circle or for public exhibition. Its "records" are in the form of discs of practically indestructible material, can be safely sent through the mails, will last indefinitely.

Reproductions for the Gramophone are given forth through a horn or amplifier, and are loud enough and distinct enough to be plainly heard in a large public place of entertainment.

GRAMOPHONE OUTFIT COMPLETE, INCLUDING AMPLIFYING TRUMPET, CASE FOR MACHINE AND TWO SELECTIONS, $15.00. EXTRA SELECTIONS 50c. EACH.

We will, on receipt of price, send it express prepaid, to any point in the United States east of the Rocky Mountains.

NATIONAL GRAMOPHONE CO., 874 Broadway, N. Y.
FRANK SEAMAN, Proprietor.

FOR SALE BY ALL MUSIC DEALERS.

An 1896 advertisement, showing the Berliner Gramophone. (Photo courtesy of RCA Sales Corporation)

valuable if it is old. On the contrary, although some early models are now worth far more than their original prices, thousands of others, which are still plentiful, are selling for less than they did when they appeared on the market. The value depends upon such factors as the type of machine and the model, its condition, and whether accessories of interest are included, such as reproducers

An early table model of the Victor Royal disk machine with horn.
(Photo through courtesy of RCA Sales Corporation)

and horn brackets. It is demand that really fixes the value. A model of the first machine to bear the Victor label may bring, in fine condition, up to around $2,000; but this is exceptional. Other desirable and scarce early machines are worth $100 to $250 in good condition. Machines in poor condition or with parts missing bring far less. The kind of reproducer and the size and type of horn also are factors in determining price. Machines with the Morning Glory horns are very desirable, and even more valuable are those with colored horns or horns bearing unusual designs.

Large sums were spent on advertising talking machines early in this century, particularly in behalf of the Edison models. Advertisements with illustrations showing the machines from magazines of 65 or 75 years ago help identify some of the models. As early as 1904, the International Correspondence School offered language courses on cylinder records to be played on Edison phonographs.

Trade name of early Edison models included the Home, which could be operated at two speeds and which would play both two-

MUSIC

SOUSA,

The March King, says:

"The Victor Talking Machine is all right."

John Philip Sousa

A Talking Machine so perfect as often to be mistaken for the original band, orchestra, or singer is what we claim for the "VICTOR." Consider for one moment what this means. If you believe it to be true, you should at once take steps to reap the personal benefit from this wonderful instrument. If you doubt it, we will take pleasure in forwarding you a "Victor" on approval. You will find the

VICTOR
Talking
Machine

in the homes of many music lovers, who have previously scorned the talking machine on account of its mechanical imperfections.

Send for New Catalogue.

The "Victor" and "Monarch" Gold Label Records are acknowledged by all to be the best talking machine records made.

Manufactured by ELDRIDGE R. JOHNSON,
19 South 12th Street, Philadelphia, Pa.

THE TALKING MACHINE CO., 107 Madison Street, Chicago.
EASTERN TALKING MACHINE CO., 177 Tremont Street, Boston, Mass.
WESTERN ELECTRIC CO., 933 Market Street, Philadelphia, Pa.
P. E. CONROY, 1115 Olive Street, St. Louis, Mo.
MAGUIRE & BAUCUS, 44 Pine Street, New York.
THE RUDOLPH WURLITZER CO., Cincinnati, O.
H. R. EISENBRANDT'S SONS, Baltimore, Md.
NATIONAL AUTOMATIC FIRE ALARM CO., New Orleans, La.
GRINNELL BROS., Detroit, Mich.
J. F. SCHMELZER & SONS ARMS CO., Kansas City, Mo.

This advertisement of 1901 for the Victor Talking Machine illustrates the famous dog trademark. (Illustration courtesy of the RCA Sales Corporation)

Evolution of
Victor's
Model XI
1910 - 1926
The most Popular Victrola

1,049,198 WERE MADE,
ALL CONSOLES EXCEPT 6,392

1917
$110.⁰⁰
List

1910
$100.⁰⁰
List

1912
$100.⁰⁰
List

1922
(No. 100)
$150.⁰⁰
List

1923
(No. 100)
$150.⁰⁰
List

* Catalog number changed from XI to 100

(Illustration through courtesy of RCA Sales Corporation)

and four-minute cylinder records; the Home with a carrying case
top that resembled a sewing machine case; the Standard, a somewhat
similar model but with a smaller horn; the Gem, with an unusual
bracket support for a large horn; and the Triumph, which featured
a bell-shaped horn.

Later Edison machines bore such names as Diamond Disc, Amberola, Concert, and others, and there was a line in period-type console cabinets bearing such designations as Jacobean, William and Mary, Louis XIV, Chippendale, Hepplewhite, and Sheraton.

Of special interest to collectors should be the early coin-operated Graphophones produced by Columbia in the early 1900's. These will now fetch $150-$250 or a bit more, depending on condition.

There are some fairly early small Victor Victrolas, which you may still find at prices of $50 or a bit under.

Many refinements were made in the appearance of the various table model machines as the twentieth century progressed until the handsome upright consoles appeared. Some of the companies issued catalogues, which are treasure houses of information about the various models and which, though eagerly sought, are becoming very scarce. Much information also will be found in early catalogues of general merchandise.

In its huge catalogue for 1905-1906, the First National Co-operative Society pictured 13 models of talking machines. Among those offered was the key-wind graphophone, made under patents of Edison, Bell, Tainter, and McDonald. The Parlor Graphophone, operated by a spring motor and complete with a reproducer and a long japanned horn, was available for only $4; or you could buy the same machine with a carrying case and 12 records for $10.75. The Columbia type AJ Graphophone, which played disc records and had a horn mounted on an unusual bracket, was priced by this company at $20. It played both 7- and 10-inch diameter records. The horn was 16 inches long and featured a polished brass bell. The Victor Royal was a similar machine but not quite as elaborate and sold for $5 less.

Shown in the same catalogue are the Victor Monarch and the Victor II, III, IV, and V models at prices ranging from $30 to $60. All of those models played discs.

This company also offered five models of the Talk-o-Phone—the Herbett, Brooke, Ennis, Clarke, and Sousa—at prices of from $15 to $49. These, also, played discs and had outside horns, which were attached to brackets and were detachable.

Japanned tin horns were available for the cylinder-playing Graphophones at prices of 30 cents to $7.50, and hammered brass horns cost 75 cents to $15. Prices of horns for the disc Graphophones ranged from $5 for one 22 inches long to $25 for one 56 inches long. Blank cylinders for making one's own sound records ranged from 20 to 75 cents each, shaved and boxed. Columbia cylinders pre-recorded could be obtained for 25 cents and the Columbia New Process 7-inch disc records for 50 cents. Grand Opera 14-inch disc records, however, cost $2 each. In those years the Victor records

On the top row from left are a crude 1908 Concert "talking machine,"
the Victor No. 3 with new tapering arm of 1905, and the improved
Victor No. 4 of 1905. Second row: Columbia cylinder Gramaphone No. 5
of 1908, and a toy phonograph of 1917 that played "Little Wonder" disc
records that sold for 10 cents each. Third row: a 1900 ZonoPhone; the
1904 Edison Home phonograph, and the 1905 improved Victor No. 5.
Bottom left is an illustration depicting a demonstration of the United
States Talking Machine of early in this century, and the Lyric Graphophone of an early twentieth century date.

Top (left) the Victor Gold Medal talking machine of 1905 (with the famous trade mark dog), and the Victor Royal, 1905. Second row: Victor Monarch Special, 1905, and Victor-Victrola XVI, 1908. This console model sold in Circassian walnut for $250. Below: the Vitanola of 1926; Victrola XVII of 1917, and another 1926 Vitanola.

in 7-inch size cost 50 cents, the 10-inch size sold for $1, and the 12-inch size for $1.50. American 10½-inch records were priced at a dollar, and the Zonophone records ranged from 75 cents for 9-inch diameters to $1 for the 10-inch ones.

In 1907, Lyon & Healy, of Chicago, reported that talking machines were the fastest-selling instruments in its catalogues. Talking machine manufacturers were producing 4,000 machines and 195,000 records a day! This company contended that the Victor was the best disc talking machine in the world and that the Edison was the best machine using cylinder records. As to which one might be preferred, the company said, "It is largely a matter of individual taste."

By 1911, an exceptionally handsome upright console Victor model, the Victrola XVI, was available at $200, and the Victrola XII, a table model, was selling at $125. A small model, the Victor Junior, was available that year, however, for only $10, and the Victor O for $17.50.

With the prices of the larger and more elaborate talking machines rising, a few companies attempted to capture a share of the market by producing less expensive machines. One of these, the Musiphone De Luxe, was offered in a Standard model in 1916 by the Standard Mail Order Company, of New York City, for $11.98. It had a 16-inch square cabinet with a mahogany finish and a tone arm that could play all brands of records in any size. By that year, among the well-known brands of records were Edison, Rex, and Pathe; and a new 5-inch record, Little Wonder, which played for 1¾ minutes, was being produced to sell for 10 cents.

Some mail order firms had their own "brands" of machines made for them. Among these was Curtis Miller & Company, of Chicago and Pittsburgh, which featured phonographs bearing its name, including a table model at $23.50 and upright consoles at $59.75 and $98.50 around 1920. In 1918, Sears, Roebuck had extremely attractive upright console models of its Silvertones for as low as $76. The Larkin Company was offering its Symphonolas in several models in the early 1920's, and, in 1926, Spear & Company, of Pittsburgh, had Vitanola consoles with a horn inside the cabinet for as low as $69.95.

A popular brand of phonograph during World War I was the Sonora, which was distributed by the Sonora Phonograph Sales Company, formerly the Sonora Chime Company, headquartered in New York City. This machine had been awarded the highest score for tone quality at the Panama Pacific International Exposition of 1915. The Sonora was not an inexpensive machine, prices ranging up to $1,000 in 1918 for the Supreme model.

Top left, an Edison phonograph of 1908, and, right, a Graphophone of similar appearance. Below left is a 1904 talking machine once offered as a premium for selling merchandise. At the right (below) is a similar one of 1904 (above) a Columbia Graphaphone of 1908.

On the top row from left are a 1922 Cecelian; a machine sold by Sears, Roebuck about 1920, and a 1910 Montgomery Ward machine. Second row: a 1922 Cecilian console, an early twentieth-century cylinder record cabinet, and a 1918 Monophone Style "B." Bottom: a 1910 Columbia Grafonola "Regent" model; a Symphonola of 1922, and a 1918 Monophone console style "D."

Phonograph record cabinets and cases. Top row, left to right: two cylinder cabinets offered in 1906 by Lyon & Healy, Chicago, with capacities of 125 and 150 records, respectively, and a 1905 Victor cabinet for holding both 10- and 12-inch discs. Center row: two Lyon & Healy disc cabinets of 1906, and a six-shelf Larkin cabinet of 1922. Bottom row: two additional 1922 cabinets offered as Larkin premiums, and 1906 Lyon & Healy machine and phonograph horn carrying cases.

Shown are corners of the Victor and the Edison sales rooms of Lyon & Healy, of Chicago, as they looked in 1906.

Well worth looking for are some of the early toy talking machines. Some of these were made by Victor, Columbia, and Berliner and were operated by hand power and, in excellent condition, they may fetch up to $100, possibly a little more, now.

Early this century the United States Talking Machine Company made an instrument in a square wooden case. It played vulcanized rubber discs and came equipped with two sets of ear tubes so that two persons might listen at the same time. The entire instrument weighed only 3½ pounds. A supply of these were closed out early in the century at just 98 cents each!

Recently, Edison Home models have been offered for sale at prices of from around $45 to more than $100, depending on type. Some of the Edison Standards fetch $75 to around $100. Edison Amberolas have been offered of late at prices of $40 to around $100. The Edison Concerts are scarce and desirable and may be found priced at $200 to $500.

As interest mounts in collecting early talking machines, the prices of these and other early Columbia and Victor models are likely to start ascending. But remember that thousands of later machines are still available for far lower sums.

Phonographs and records are advertised in most of the collector periodicals. Some dealers issue lists which will give you the best idea of current prices.

The illustrations accompanying this chapter will probably tell you more about the talking machines than the text has.

{12}

Those Fascinating Match Boxes

☞ The most interesting thing about matches is not that they set so many houses afire but that they led to the invention of the match box. Many articles have been written about match boxes (or match cases or safes, if you prefer), and it is not my intention to say very much about them here. Actually, match boxes probably do not belong in a series of essays devoted primarily to offbeat collectibles, but there are so many of these delightful containers around that the temptation to include a picture-chapter about them was too great to resist. Besides, in my foraging trips through old catalogues, magazines, and newspapers in search of illustrations for other objects discussed in this book, I came across scores of pictures of match boxes and holders so that it is likely that even many veteran collectors will find some pictured here that he or she has not yet come across. And some of these, obviously, may be assigned to an "offbeat" category. This, then, will be primarily a story in illustrations. *Better Homes & Gardens* published a short article of mine under the caption "Treasure Hunt—Match Safes and Hatpin Holders" in its November, 1966 issue, which discussed many of the intriguing old match safes in some detail, and I am indebted to the magazine for permission to include some similar brief background about these collectibles here.

The modern match was not invented until 1827 when friction matches of sorts first appeared on the market in England. This was nearly 160 years after phosphorous had been discovered in Germany by one of the many alchemists there who seemed to be eternally searching for inexpensive ways to produce gold. In the final quarter of the seventeenth century flames were produced by drawing sulphur-tipped wooden splinters across a bit of paper coated with phosphorous. In those days this was an expensive procedure because of the excessively high cost of phosphorous, so not many persons indulged in it. There are various ways of creating fire, but, contrary to popular opinion, you cannot do it by rubbing two Boy Scouts together. When I was a Boy Scout, I won a fire-making contest by rubbing sticks together quite rapidly, thus creating friction, and I do recall that the occasion was one of the proudest moments of my life. I believe it was the first contest of any kind I ever won.

Perhaps the most sensible match ever invented was one known as the Drunkard's match. It was chemically treated so that it would burn only half way up its shaft, or splint. Someday, I hope, someone will write an article on the self-lighting cigar, invented in Austria well over a century ago. However, this isn't a treatise on matches, so let's get back to match containers.

These containers date back to around the middle of the nineteenth century. The early ones were made of tin, iron, glass, or pottery, and were used primarily in kitchens to hold matches for lighting the stove, or logs in the fireplace. A number of our glass manufacturing plants made novelty holders of pressed glass in numerous patterns. Tin, iron, and pottery holders were produced by the thousands, and many of these had a nail hole at the top so they could be attached to the wall. Many small holders that could be used interchangeably for toothpicks or matches were designed to be placed on the table. Early in this century, hundreds of these were made in what we now know as Carnival glass, and others were made in so-called art glass of the late nineteenth century. Some individuals have fine collections of these small holders. Catalogues of manufacturers and wholesalers described them as "toothpick or match holders," clearly indicating they could be used for either purpose. I remember that my grandparents had several of these small containers in their home in North Carolina; and I recall, too, that my grandfather became aggravated on more than one occasion when he tried to strike a toothpick so that he could light his after-dinner cigar.

Beautiful handpainted match holders on goldplated feet were made by the C. F. Monroe Company, of Meriden, Connecticut, in its Wave Crest Ware, which was a painted opal glass. The white glass was blown in full-sized molds and subsequently decorated. In 1907, *The Youth's Companion* offered two of these Wave Crest match holders in exchange for one new subscription and 20 cents extra—or they could be purchased for a cash price of only $1 postpaid. Today, of course, they fetch a great deal more.

Highly desirable are cut glass match holders made in various patterns during the "Brilliant" period of our cut glass production (1880-1905). In 1900, these were listed in wholesalers' catalogues for as little as 40 cents each, and almost invariably each was described as a "pick or match holder." Most of these measured 2½ to 3 inches high, and some were footed.

Many thousands of match (or tooth pick) holders in scores of designs were made of plated silver in the late nineteenth and early twentieth centuries. In the early 1900's these wholesaled for as little as 60 cents up to more than $3 each. You will see some of these among the illustrations accompanying this chapter. An interesting one was made tipped forward on a footed base, apparently being supported by the spread wings of an eagle. It wholesaled for $3.20. Some featured repousse designs; others were engraved, and some were gold lined. Occasionally they were lettered, such as one which bore the words "let there be light." One in brass finish was made with a cast figure of a dog standing beside the match well. Another, in silver, had a goat at the front of the well. Still another was made in leaf form.

An interesting collection can be made of hanging match safes of iron fashioned in ornamental designs. Some of these had oblong basket-like troughs for the matches, and open-work decoration featured the fronts of many of these baskets. A keyhole-like opening at the top of the back permitted these to be hung on the wall. Although this type is worth several dollars on the collector market today, they wholesaled in 1901 at $1.70 to $2 a dozen. They measured 3½ to 4 inches in length and about the same in height.

The mechanical woodpecker match safe is not nearly so recent as many seem to think. It was offered at $4 a dozen wholesale in the 1884 catalogue of Sargent & Company, of New York and New Haven. In this contrivance, a metal woodpecker, mounted on a metal pin, picks up a match from the container in its beak.

The pocket match safe began appearing on the market in quantity early in this century (although boxes of this type had been made years before) and in a tremendous number of fanciful designs. It had been preceded, of course, by the snuff box and the tobacco box on which design artists had lavished their talents for many years. Most of these pocket safes have hinged tops, and a few of the finest were even made of gold. The most expensive—and scarcest—of such safes are adorned with jewels or bear designs in mother-of-pearl.

Many safes of this type were produced of sterling silver. Some of these which had concealed or trick windows were described in an interesting article, *The Match Box Story,* which Ray E. Wentworth wrote about his own outstanding collection in the October, 1965, issue of *Western Collector.* Many sterling silver safes were produced for the various fraternal organizations and bear their insignia. Others were made as commemorative items for major expositions and fairs. Still other safes were made of brass and plated

This mechanical bronzed match safe, a delightful collector's item, was offered in 1884 at $6 a dozen, wholesale. It remained popular for many years, and a cigarette box resembling it has been popular in recent years.

silver, and a large number of inexpensive ones were distributed by commercial firms as advertising pieces.

About the time of the First World War, thin metal safes for holding books of paper matches were put on the market. Inexpensive ones were made of nickel silver but those of sterling cost $5 or more each in 1918 when they were offered in profusion in wholesalers' catalogues. Some distributors offered the nickelplated safes in assorted designs with a dozen to the assortment at $4.

Handsome nickelplated match safes were advertised in the 1908 catalogue of Tower Manufacturing & Novelty Company, New York City, at $2 to $2.50 a dozen wholesale. The same firm had assortments of silverplated safes packed 12 to a carton at $6 a dozen.

Ornamental wall match safes were turned out in a great variety of shapes in the 1880's. One of these was in the design of an acorn mounted on a metal replica of a large oak leaf (a double oak leaf design also was available with two acorn holders attached). The "Game" pattern featured a metal bird and a rabbit hanging on each side of a metal pouch intended to look like leather. The pouch had two pockets for matches. The "Rustic" pattern featured a metal trough for matches surrounded by metal foliage. There also was

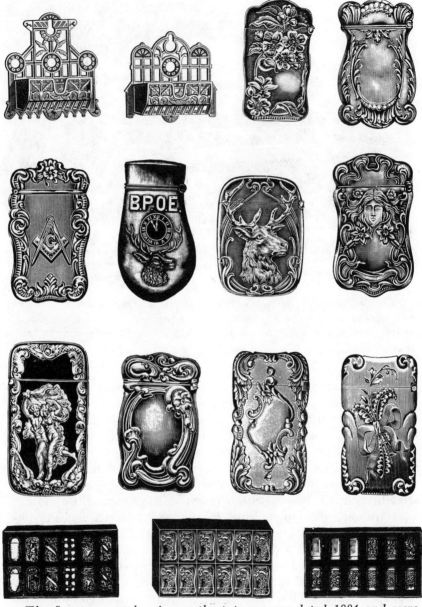

The first two match safes on the top row are dated 1884 and were made of bronzed metal. On the bottom row are shown three 1908 assortments in cartons. The others on the page are dated 1905 and were made of silverplated metal.

The match safes on the top row and the two at left on the second row were all advertised in 1884. The third one on the second row is dated 1900 and the fourth one 1906. The first two on the third row were offered in 1906, and the remainder on the page in 1908.

A group of 1900 cut glass match holders is shown on the top row. At left on the second row is a pair of Wave Crest match safes. The next two on this row are silverplated, dated 1892, and the last one is dated 1914. The others on this page were offered in the late nineteenth and early twentieth centuries and were sterling silver.

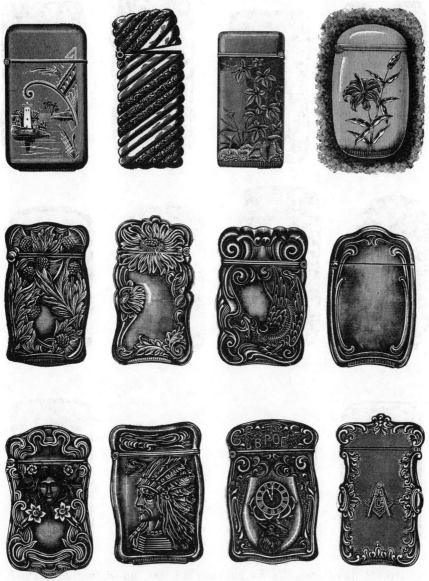

Sterling silver match boxes. Those on the top row date 1892 and in that year wholesaled at $7 to $7.50 each. The next three rows show boxes of 1906, which originally wholesaled at $2.85 to $5.65 each. The costliest was the B.P.O.E. box. The Masonic box was priced at $5, which was the same price as was asked for the Indian chief and the maiden swathed in flowers.

Ornate quadruple-silverplated match boxes, all dating to around 1900 except the two in the center on the bottom row which are dated 1892. The two boxes showing the United States flag are enameled. Of particular interest is the box on extreme right on the top row. This shows a hunting scene and the illustration should be turned sidewise to view it. The one second from left on the second row is covered with alligator hide. These boxes originally wholesaled at from 40 cents to $1.75 each.

These silverplated match boxes were all produced just prior to the outbreak in Europe of World War I and were being advertised in 1914. The one on the second row at extreme left is among the special boxes produced for fraternal organizations, this one having been made for members of the Benevolent and Protective Order of Elks. All are decorated with raised ornaments.

The match safes on the top three rows offered on this page were offered in 1900. All are of sterling silver except the first three on the third row from top, which are gold or gold-filled. Wholesale prices of the silver boxes ranged originally from $1.42 to $4.75. Highest priced was the 10-karat gold case at left on the third row. ($16 wholesale). The match safes on the bottom row are dated, left to right, 1914, 1905, 1905, and 1908.

These rather awkward looking match safes were made of brass, finished in gilt, silver or copper, and were offered in 1900 at wholesales prices of $10 to $18 per gross.

Silverplated match (or toothpick) holders of 1914.

1905 leather match box.

*Sterling silver match boxes offered in 1918 by Wallenstein, Mayer &
Co., of Cincinnati, are shown on the two top rows. The first three boxes
on the third row are of nickel silver and cost about half as much as did
those of sterling. The last box on the bottom row is solid gold and
wholesaled for $20 plain or $30 inset with a cut diamond.*

one designed simply as "Double," which had two match containers in the shape of urns against a background of metal flowers and vines.

An 1892 safe, which also could be utilized as a toothpick holder, was made with a metal replica of a goat attached to the round silver, goldlined holder. Other animals were fashioned as adjuncts of other types of safes.

Nor were rather risqué designs lacking on our late nineteenth century match safes. This is just one more link in a long chain of evidence to indicate that our ancestors were not as prudish as they often are accused of having been. Many of the risqué decorations undoubtedly were passed off as scenes from classical antiquity, which they most certainly were not. This is especially true of many of the bare-breasted females of vigorous proportions whose embossed contours graced the cases of more than a few silverplated safes.

Other cases were decorated with hunting scenes, milkmaids, snakes, faces (both grotesque and demure), Indian chiefs, flags, lions, dragons and other assorted animals (domestic, wild, and legendary), and dozens of different types of flowers.

Whether you specialize in safes of a particular material or play the field, you'll still find these interesting containers available in sufficient quantities to enable you to gather a good collection at modest cost.

Here are a few recently asked prices for various types:

Sterling silver pocket safe with diagonal bands and scrolls, $4.75; nickelplated Knights of Pythias pocket safe, $3.50; nickelplated pocket safe with raised oval buckle design, $2; ornate silverplated pocket safe with nude dancing group, $4.50; pine wood wall holder in shape of bucket with bail, $4.75; wooden wall holder painted white with ornate decorations, $15; Masonic pocket safe, silverplated, $3; hinged tin wall pocket safe, $4.75.

There are still a good many match safes around at low prices such as those above, but better-made ones, those with jewels, and scarcer models will cost more.

[13]

Watch the Birdie

Stereoscopes and stereoscopic views and Daguerreotypes and their cases have been collected for years, but early photographic cameras have thus far been relatively neglected. Yet these cameras preserved for us the world of yesterday and even treasured moments of joy and ecstasy in our own childhood.

The modern photographic camera is a fantastic device, having evolved through the years from its crude beginnings as the camera obscura—an optical instrument that dates back several centuries. This early precursor of today's cameras was a darkened chamber (sometimes even a room) into which light was admitted through a very small opening. The camera obscura was used for photographic purposes back in the latter years of the eighteenth century.

Photography as we now know it began its evolution early last century. A highlight in its progress was the development of the daguerreotype process made public in 1839. It resulted from the joint work of Joseph Nicéphore Niepce and Louis Jacques Mande Daguerre. Their achievement constitutes an intriguing story and has been told in other books.

It is not the purpose of this chapter to relate the history of photography. This story has been told in a number of excellent books, some of which you will find listed in the bibliography at the end of this volume. But we will describe quite briefly and illustrate some of our early cameras and accessories with the hope that some of you at least will be stimulated to an effort to rescue them from undeserved oblivion. Not only early cameras but fine early examples of the art of photography, including even tintypes, ambrotypes, and *cartes des visites* photographs, provide a rich field for exploration by individual collectors.

Many of our early simple cameras were boxlike affairs with a

237

pinhole or lens on one side and a piece of light-sensitive material on the other. Numerous box cameras were used in the nineteenth century and early in the present one, even though cameras of a more complicated type with bellows that permitted focusing had been developed last century. In fact, E. I. Horsman Company in its 1889 catalogue illustrated its No. 3 "Eclipse" photographic outfit, featuring a camera with bellows, stating that "any child of 12 years" could make a photograph with it. Perhaps twelve-year-old children of those days were more precocious than they are today.

Light-sensitive material in the form of rolls of film were being used in cameras in the latter part of the nineteenth century, and in 1894, Alfred C. Kemper, a manufacturer of Chicago, was advertising the "Kombi" camera—a true miniature, measuring only 1⅝ by 2 inches in dimensions and weighing 4 ounces. The "Kombi" took 25 pictures on a single loading and featured both instantaneous and time exposures. This camera retailed for $3.50 and the film for 20 cents a roll. The "Kombi" was made of metal with a silver-bronze finish and presented the appearance of a tiny oblong box.

The box camera with a lens on one side and a ground glass and holder for the light-sensitive material on the other was in fairly widespread use prior to 1888, when George Eastman, whose name is now known throughout the photographic world, marketed the first camera substituting roll film for plates.

The reflex camera popular today is by no means a recent invention. An Englishman named Thomas Sutton invented a camera of this type well over a century ago so that the image on the focusing screen could be seen right-side-up instead of upside-down as had been the case earlier. It was about a quarter of a century later, however, before the reflex camera was perfected as an instrument for amateurs.

The Kodak Company put its first pocket-size roll film camera on the market in 1891 and devised a folding camera not long thereafter. Highly popular as this century got under way was Kodak's famous Brownie camera. This one, certainly, could be used by a twelve-year-old child, and it was so inexpensive that it gave a great boost to the art of photography among amateurs all over the country.

Scores of different types and makes of cameras, ranging from the sub-miniature to the Polaroid with its almost instantaneous development of the finished print, have been marketed in recent years, but those that merit collectors' attention were the forerunners of these, some of which are shown in the illustrations accompanying this chapter. You will be surprised at how many old cameras you can pick up at prices of $15 and under. Close examination will reveal that many of those are fine instruments, made in earlier years by talented craftsmen who took great pride in their work.

So many different types of cameras have been produced that you want to specialize in specific types. Those who take this area of collecting seriously may wish to collect so-called "classic" cameras, or the first in a group or series that were produced by one specific plan. The "landmark" cameras are those that heralded new developments in the art of photography; and among these are even some fairly recent inventions. Of great interest and importance are the forerunners or originals of models that subsequently attained renown in the photographic world. One example might be a model of the first stereoscopic camera with a twin lens, which dates back more than a century. Or you may wish to limit your collecting to cameras that are fairly scarce or even rare, such as models produced for only a short period of time. Some years ago I sold for a dollar an exceedingly small "Expo" camera made in the shape of a watch. As I think back on this, I calculate that I must have been excessively ignorant and exceedingly hard up for money at the time! The "Expo" is a desirable camera for the collector.

Any photographic materials available from the early years of the daguerreotype (1839 and for several years thereafter) is of value. Fine early daguerreotypes may be worth $25 to $35 or a little more.

The same hold true for materials from the Talbotype period, which takes its name from William Henry Fox Talbot, an Englishman, who succeeded in the 1830's in perfecting a sensitized paper that was more effective than earlier papers and of fixing the image obtained by its use in the camera obscura. Subsequently, Talbot perfected a method for obtaining a positive photograph from a negative, and this is the process we now refer to as Talbotype, although the inventor himself called it Calotype.

The Daguerreotype was largely replaced following the invention of the Ambrotype by James Ambrose Cutting, because of the lower cost and easier processing of the Ambrotype, which was a positive picture made from a glass negative by combining the latter with a dark background. Fine examples of the Ambrotype are of value and probably will increase in worth.

Interest is now being evidenced in so-called *carte de visite,* which came into prominence shortly after the turn of the middle of last century with the invention of a camera with four lenses and a plate holder which could be moved and with which eight pictures could be taken in succession. The first *cartes des visite* were toned paper prints mounted on cardboard so they actually could be used as visiting cards, complete with a likeness of the visitor. They were exceedingly popular in their day, which was largely during the Civil War period, and they are well worth collecting and displaying. You will find some recent prices asked for these cards later in this chapter.

The so-called "cabinet photograph" became popular immediately after the War between the States. Measuring $4\frac{1}{2}$ by $6\frac{1}{2}$ inches in size, these photos depicted, full length, groups of individuals. Many of those surviving contain likenesses of persons who attained fame in their day. Like so many other early photographs, their interest also lies in the fact that they have preserved for us illustrations of the dress worn in the post-Civil War period.

You've undoubtedly heard of tintypes or ferrotypes. These were made over a period of many years, extending into the twentieth century. The ferrotype was a photograph taken on a sensitized sheet of enameled iron or tin, and the words ferrotype and tintype are used interchangeably. The use of japanned surfaces preceded the use of the iron or tin sheets. Not long ago, I purchased a miniature album filled with miniature-sized tintypes for a dollar; and I had probably been "living right" about that time. The value of early ferrotypes, particularly those depicting nineteenth-century costumes and well-known persons of the day, will undoubtedly grow as the supply dwindles in the years to come.

Perhaps a very brief discussion of a few of the numerous types of cameras of earlier years may interest you. Take the Harvard, for example. This was a small metal camera popular in the 1890's. It utilized negatives 4 by $2\frac{1}{2}$ inches in size and was offered, together with a tripod head and a few darkroom accessories, for $1.75 by *The Youth's Companion* in 1891. In offering it at this price, the magazine commented: "Were this camera to go through the regular channels of trade, it could not be sold for less than $3."

This same publication offered numerous other small cameras at what now seem fantastically low prices. Even the rather elaborate "Companion" camera, a bellows-type using plates $4\frac{1}{4}$ by $6\frac{1}{2}$ inches in size, was tendered, together with a tripod, a carrying case, and darkroom accessories, for only $15.

In 1891, *The Youth's Companion* also offered a tintype camera, "The Phoenix Gem," which took six pictures on each plate. After the plate had been developed and fixed, the pictures were cut apart with scissors, each individual picture measuring $1\frac{1}{4}$ inches square. The camera had six lenses and six chambers, and, of course, all six pictures were taken at one time. The publication offered this in exchange for one new subscriber plus $1 in cash, or it could be purchased outright for $2.75 with six plates, an album, 24 mounts, a glass graduate, a sheet of ruby fabric (for use in making a darkroom light), developing agents, and a manual of instructions.

Some of you may recall the roving photographers who, in earlier years, set up their tintype cameras on sidewalks in heavily traveled areas and took photographs of passersby they could interest. The finished tintypes were delivered to customers on the spot.

In addition to the famous "Brownie," other box cameras made

The folding Kodak as advertised in 1904.

The Kodak No. 1 camera, of 1888—the first roll camera for making 100 exposures 2½ inches in diameter on flexible roll film. This was built by the Eastman Dry Plate & Film Co. (George Eastman House Collection)

their appearance around the turn of the century, priced at $1 to $3. They were just about foolproof: if you could locate your image in the square glass finder, usually located at the top front of the box, and could press the shutter lever, you could take a picture. Some of these cameras used dry plates, others roll film.

Somewhat similar in appearance to the Brownie was the "Cyclone," which took pictures 3½ inches square but used a double plate-holder instead of roll film. In 1904, the No. 2 folding Brownie, described in advertisements as "Almost a Kodak," was retailing for $5. It boasted an automatic shutter with iris diaphragm stops, a Meniscus lens, an automatic focusing device, a reversible finder, and two tripod sockets. It used daylight film cartridges with six exposures and a picture size of 2¼ x 3¼ inches.

The Premo was another popular early twentieth-century camera manufactured by the Rochester Optical Division of Eastman Kodak Company. By 1910, this camera was being made in 50 styles and sizes. It utilized film packs, and both box and folding types were available.

Another early camera, the Hawkeye, was manufactured by the Blair Camera Company, of Boston, which also produced the Kamaret. Hawkeye models sold early in this century at $15 to $50 and used dry plates, or film rolls on which 25 to 100 pictures could be made without reloading.

Morse & Company, of Augusta, Maine, was offering its "Dollar Camera" in 1892, and the price included darkroom accessories. It took pictures 2½ inches square, utilizing plates.

Rochester Optical Company's Premier camera of 1893 was available in either box or folding type. Models were available which utilized glass plates, cut film, or roll film and which sold for $18.

These names represent only a very few early cameras which are now collectible. You will find literally dozens of others.

Those who decide to collect memorabilia of early photography will want to visit the George Eastman House of Photography, founded in Rochester, New York, in 1947. Maintained there is a permanent collection of photographs, motion pictures, apparatus, documents and books pertaining to photography. This museum also conducts research in the history of photography and cinematography, and supports a publication program.

The house was built in 1905, is located at 900 East Avenue, and was formerly the residence of George Eastman. When Mr. Eastman died in 1932, he left the house to the University of Rochester. In 1947, an independent organization, Trustees of the George Eastman House, Inc., was formed, and the house was opened as a photographic museum two years later.

Top row, left to right: 1895 Poco, 4 x 5 camera, Rochester Camera Mfg. Co.; Korona Series 1-A, Gundlach Optical Co., Rochester; Hawk-Eye Tourist model, 1898, Blair Camera Co., Boston; and No. 2 folding Brownie, 1907, Eastman Kodak Co., Rochester. Second row from left: Tronkonet, 1893, The Photo-Materials Co., Rochester; U.S. camera, 1887, U.S. Camera Co., New York City; Champion camera, 1887, The Schultze Photo Equipment Co., New York City; Premoette, 1907, Rochester Optical Co.; Premo, 1893, Rochester Optical Co. Third row: "Companion" camera No. 2, 1891 offered by The Youth's Companion; Scoville camera, 1889, Scoville Manufacturing Co.; Kombi, 1894, Alfred C. Kemper, Chicago. Bottom row: The Harvard, 1894, offered by The Youth's Companion; and another Harvard model, the Snap-Shot (2½ x 4 inch picture size), with accessories.

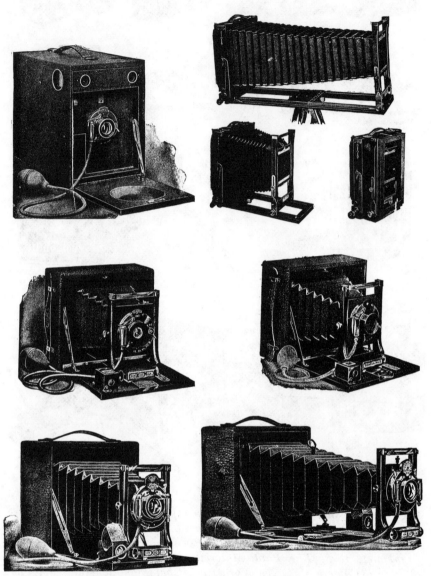

A group of cameras offered in 1905. Top from left: the Seneca 4 x 5 "Chief," and three Seneca view cameras (top and below). Second row: Seneca No. 1 and Seneca No. 3. Bottom: Seneca No. 7 and Seneca No. 8.

Visitors may see at the museum an extraordinary exhibit of the growth of photography from the earliest days to the present. Its Mees Gallery houses the scientific principles of photography and apparatus of every design and manufacture. The Brackett-Clark Gallery offers changing exhibitions of the great photographers of all time.

An 1892 advertisement of Morse & Co., Augusta, Maine.

One also will find there three permanent exhibitions: (1) The Art of Photography, a collection of 300 photographs from Daguerre to the present day; (2) Pictures for All, a collection of popular photography; and (3) The Science and Technology of Photography, which features visitor-operated devices explaining the principles of photography.

The George Eastman House collection of cameras, lenses, and photographic apparatus is reported to be the largest in the world. It also has a library of more than 8,000 books and pamphlets on photography. The House has offered traveling versions of its exhibitions for more than a decade.

There have been many famous photographers through the years. Among the distinguished names in the field are Alvin Langdon Coburn, Timothy H. O'Sullivan, Aaron Siskind, and Edward Steichen; but perhaps that of Mathew B. Brady, the noted Civil War photographer, is best known.

Born in 1823, Brady opened a photographic studio in New York City as a young man and achieved renown for his early photographic portraits, in which he utilized the daguerreotype process. Several years before the Civil War, he turned to the use of photographic plates, and after the war's outbreak, he was designated as the official Federal photographer. He and his corps of assistants went out to the battlefields around the country, taking an estimated 3,500 photographs. The majority of these were originally published in

1870 in *Brady's National Photographic Collection of War Views and Portraits of Representative Men*. The government bought more than 2,000 of the Brady photographic plates in 1875 and placed them in the War College.

If you're interested in learning more about Mathew B. Brady and the photographs of his time, you'll find some reference material listed in the Selected Bibliography of this book. Material about cameras also is listed.

Recently asked prices of cameras and allied photographic equipment include the following:

Eastman Brownie with leather bellows (roll film type), $10; Wollensack folding camera, patented 1901, with brass trim and plates, in original case, $25; Gundlach folding camera (bellows), made of mahogany, $15; No. 2 Kodak, about 1890, with manual and wooden carrying case, needing repairs, $7.50; Chicago Ferrotype Company camera, box-type, mounted on tripod, patented 1914, $15; Hawkeye plate-using camera, early 1900's, with carrying strap, $7.50; Eastman folding camera dated about 1909, $7.50; early twentieth century Kodak in carrying case, $12; darkroom kerosene lantern, $4.25; Conley camera with six plates and case, $12; Poco Cycle No. 3 camera (1903), with two film holders and roll film adapter, $8.50; Premo D. camera (Rochester Optical Company), $12.50.

Daguerreotypes: Union soldier, seated, some defects, $4.50; Union sailor, identified, $8.50; Union noncommissioned officer, standing, attired in kepi and frock coat, $6.50; full-length, Union soldier with tents in background, identity established, $7.50. Other daguerreotypes may be found in shops priced at about $3.50 up with rare ones fetching $15-$25 or more.

Cabinet photographs: *Police Gazette* photo of the actress Maggie Cline, $2; Lillian Russell, $2; actress Hattie Moore, $1.50; James J. Corbett in dress suit, $1.50; American Express Company agent in winter dress, about 1870, $4.50; Charles Dickens, $2.50; two Civil War soldiers, twins, $2.50.

Cartes des visite will start at $1 and go well up from there, depending on the individual picture, age of photo, and rarity. Here are some sample prices: President Rutherford B. Hayes, $1; Civil War Confederate General James J. Archer, $5; Stephen A. Douglas, $2; General George A. Custer, $22.50; General J. M. McNeil, of Missouri, with name of the photographer "Anthony" (New York City) on the reverse, $6.50; Kit Carson, $14.50; General P. T. G. Beauregard, $3.50; John Burns, civilian hero of Gettysburg, taken by Weaver Photo Gallery, $27.50; Alexander Ross, Lincoln's confidential agent in Canada, $17.50; Civil War general made from Brady's original negative, plus photos of five additional generals, $14.50.

Top row from left: Eastman's Autographic Kodak, 1914; a Premo box-type, 1917, and a folding Premo, also 1917. Second row: the Companion camera No. 1, 1892; the 1901 Harvard, and (below) a 1903 Star Premo. Bottom: a 1910 Premo film pack camera, and a 1907 Eastman Brownie.

Top row, from left: the "Tourists'" camera, 1900; the Argus 12-shot magazine camera, 1891; the Phoenix camera and accessories, 1891; and (just below the Phoenix) a Duplex darkroom lantern and paper and fixing-toning solution. Second row: the Harvard camera on tripod in an "action" illustration in 1891, and the Cyclone, 1892. Bottom: the Gem tin-type camera and outfit, 1891; the Hawk-Eye, 1891; a sketching camera, 1891, and (below) the Junior ruby darkroom lantern, 1894.

A 2¼ x 3¼ roll film size camera offered by a mail order house early in this century and not identified as to make but merely as "the brand-new product of a large, new factory that has thrown down the gauntlet to the Camera Trust." This camera retailed for $10.65.

E. I. Horsman's No. 3 "Eclipse" photographic outfit, which, in 1889, sold for $10 complete.

Top row from left: Chatauqua folding camera No. 5, early twentieth century; No. 2 folding Brownie, 1904; a 1908 folding Premo, and a folding camera offered by Sears, Roebuck and Company in 1904. Second row: an Eastman folding Kodak, 1895; an Eastman folding Kodet, 1895; and the Ingento magazine camera, 1905. Third row: The No. 4 folding pocket Ansco, 1905; the Ansco No. 2, 1905, and a folding camera offered in 1904 by Sears.

Ferrotypes: Civil War soldiers, $5 to $8.50 each; policeman in uniform, 1880, $4.50; Lincoln and Hamlin, $32; miscellaneous small tintypes, 50 cents each.

It may be of interest that a photograph by Lewis Carroll (Charles L. Dodgson) of his original Alice (Alice Liddell) sold some time ago at auction for $225.

In your peregrinations in search of photographic materials, watch out for the names of pioneers in the field, such as D. O. Hill, who has been called "the first Victorian photographer"; Alexander S. Wolcott, John W. Draper, Robert Cornelius, Thomas Wedgwood, Sir Humphrey Davy, Richard L. Maddox, George Eastman, and even some of the moderns, including Edward Steichen, Alfred Stieglitz, and Arnold Genthe.

Although many larger newspapers have modernized their "morgues" (reference libraries of clippings, pictures and allied materials), chances are that some early photographs will be found in some of these, as well as in the morgues of long-established magazines. A number of these may very well be classed as works of art. Early color photographs (the first of which is reported to have been made in 1877 by Louis du Hauron, although James C. Maxwell had given a demonstration of a process for making color photos in London 16 years earlier) should be treasured.

If you have early photographs to sell, try some of the historical societies.

[14]

The Cluttered Table

☞ The formal dining table in the middle- and upper-class Victorian home was delightfully cluttered. Epergnes, gorgeous berry bowls on silver or silverplated stands, and a host of other decorative accessories imparted an air of elegance. Serving pieces and other dining adjuncts no longer in use today once helped make dining a pleasure and an art. Let's consider some of these collectible dining adjuncts in this chapter—and may they, eventually, clutter your own table. You may be the happier for it.

What, for example, has happened to the condensed canned milk holder, once made in both porcelain and silverplated metal? These were used, precisely as their name indicates, to hold cans of condensed or evaporated milk. Nineteenth-century trade catalogues depict them, but they are now seldom around—despite the fact that condensed or evaporated milk is still widely used. Today's homemakers pour this milk from the can into a cream pitcher for use on the table so that the average guest thinks it's cream fresh from the dairy.

A wide variety of plain and ornately decorated condensed milk can holders "made to fit the regulation condensed milk can or glass" were offered in quadrupleplate in the latter part of last century by the Adelphi Silver Plate Company, of New York City. They consisted of container, a top with a knob (or finial), and an underplate to catch the drippings. Plain holders in "satin" finish wholesaled at prices of $3 to $3.75. Much more delightful were those with fancy repousse decorations at $4.25 to $5.25. Some holders had handles so they could be lifted more easily. A group is pictured in Catalogue No. 28 of Simpson, Hall, Miller & Co., of Wallingford, Connecticut. Some of the latter had two handles, and most were embossed with designs of flowers and scrolls. These were given such trade designations as "Umpire," "Thrasher," and "Weaving." Wholesale prices here ranged from $4.50 to $6.75.

Many beautifully decorated condensed milk holders of porcelain were manufactured by potteries in this country and abroad. I have some attractive ones produced in Limoges, France, by J. Pouyat. Not long ago, a Limoges holder was advertised at $12.50.

Another Victorian table favorite was the combination sugar stand and spoon rack. These were made of plated silver and also of glass in a silverplated stand. The sugar bowls came in both clear crystal and colored glass, ruby having been in much demand. Some of the plated bowls and the stands were footed; others rested on round bases. The spoons were held by brackets arranged around the out-side of the bowl or stand. Some of these combinations held six spoons, others a dozen. The combinations could be had with either conventional curved handles at the sides or with large bail-type handles. Adelphi Silver Plate Co. offered some delightful combinations with bird finials on the cover of the sugar bowl. Last century's prices ($4.50 to $7.50 wholesale) seem astonishingly cheap today. B. F. Norris, Alister offered one of these combination bowl-spoon holders in 1892 with a butterfly finial atop the bowl at a wholesale price of only $6.50. Otto Young & Co. had one in 1900 in a satin finish at a wholesale price of just $3. Why these convenient combinations have just about disappeared is difficult to appreciate.

Spoon trays in silver or silver plate were once popular too. They were sometimes referred to as spoon baskets. Plated spoon trays or baskets with gold linings abounded in the opening years of this century and had been in favor earlier. The trays resembled small oblong boats with handles, their length ranging from about $7\frac{1}{2}$ to $10\frac{1}{2}$ inches. Many of the baskets were footed, and both baskets and handles were frequently decorated with such things as beading, grapes, leaves, and flowers. Upright spoon holders resembled oval or round sugar bowls without tops. Some of these also were footed, and all the metal ones were handled. The bowl-type spooners were made in both metal and glass, and pattern glass ones of early vintage have been popular with pattern glass collectors.

In a category somewhat similar to the condensed milk and spoon holders were bottle holders made of metal and designed to hold such things at catsup and Worcestershire sauce bottles. Prior to World War II, Wallenstein, Mayer & Co., of Cincinnati, offered silver-plated bottle holders complete with full bottles of catsup or Worcestershire sauce at wholesale prices of $4.50 each. The silverplated holders were of pierced metal with a solid metal crest decoration. These holders kept the catsup and sauce from making messy rings on the tablecloth. The early ones are well worth seeking and can be used to advantage on the table today.

Caster (also spelled "castor") sets of various types have been

A group of elaborately decorated silverplated combination sugar stands and spoon holders of the late nineteenth century is shown on the top two rows. Below are two 1905 silverplated spoon trays.

collected over the years, but egg casters have been largely neglected. John Round & Son, Ltd., of England, made a variety of these sets (which it called "egg stands") in the latter part of the nineteenth century. The sets consisted of egg cups for boiled eggs (usually four to a set) electroplated on nickel silver on an electroplated handled and footed stand. A holder for the egg spoons was normally an integral part of the handle.

Silverplated pickle casters. Types of glass containers in these are, top row from left: cut crystal, decorated ruby, and decorated clear glass. Second row: clear pressed glass in imitation of cut, ruby, and clear crystal in imitation of cut. Bottom: engraved crystal, decorated ruby, and crystal, fluted.

A number of the stands—oval, square, or octagonal in shape—were lavishly ornamented. Handles were oval, square, round, or heart-shaped, and one pictured in a John Round catalogue has a satyr mask at the bottom of the handle.

Egg steamers with an alcohol lamp for use right at the dining table came into use later. Most such steamers could cook from one to six eggs at a time. The alcohol lamps were wickless and could be regulated to cook eggs as soft or as hard as desired. They were made of both nickelplated metal and copper. The eggs were placed in receptacles arranged around a small stand. The steamer was usually an oval-shaped vessel with a bottom compartment for the eggs and a removable top. The alcohol lamp was placed in a receptacle in the base of the stand. The steamers resembled the larger chafing dishes.

Small individual breakfast egg casters also were produced on stands as were breakfast sets consisting of two egg cups, a salt cup and pepper bottle on a tray.

Even though pickle casters have been collected for a long time, any red-blooded writer on collectibles ought to give them a plug, because you'll still find hundreds of these sets that are just about irresistible. In fact, one of the joys of the catalogue addict is viewing the illustrations of early pickle casters. These sets consisted of a glass jar set in a metal (usually silverplated) frame. Frames had oval or footed bases to which fairly tall handles were attached. The pickle jars had metal tops, most of which were decorated with finials.

Just as was the case with multiple-bottle breakfast or dinner casters (for holding condiments), the pickle caster frames were ornately decorated or ornamented, and handle shapes ranged from the exquisite to the grotesque. Some collectors, however, find their greatest interest is in the glass jars or containers. These were produced in clear crystal, cut glass, engraved glass, colored and shaded glass (ruby in particular), often decorated in enamel. Metal tongs, which hung on a bracket near the top of one side of the handle, completed the sets. Although the majority of pickle caster sets had only one glass container, double sets with two jars were produced in lesser quantity.

Lovely pickle casters with ruby glass thumbprint patterns in silverplated frames sold near the end of last century for as little as $3, wholesale. Today, they will fetch $50 or more in fine condition. In 1900, Otto Young & Co. was offering a caster set with a container of cut glass in a quadrupleplated fancy embossed frame for only $2.50. The same price was asked for one with a patterned ruby glass jar in a chased frame with a burnished base and cover.

Occasionally you may encounter one of these sets in which a

A group of late nineteenth-century silverplated condensed milk can holders is shown on the top two rows. Below are plated novelty tooth-pick holders of the same period.

pickle fork has been substituted for the tongs usually accompanying them. Smaller double pickle casters were made in England late in the nineteenth century with simpler frames, small handles in the center, and two small bottles. Frames also were available without the jars or bottles; "store bought" pickle or sauce bottles could be set in them.

Collectible table serving pieces shown here date late last century. Top row from left: a glass mustard or horseradish pot with glass finial; a silverplated "slop" bowl, an orange holder, and another slop. Second row: two silverplated "handy" or salad bowls decorated in repousse. Third row: another handy bowl; a horseradish pot in a burnished holder and with a bone spoon, and a mustard pot. Bottom: three celery stands of silver plate with decorated glass vessels.

Nineteenth-century novelty silverplated toothpick holders. Imaginations ran riot in the creation of these.

Various other types of caster sets also are collected. Take a look at the illustrations accompanying this chapter if you want to see just how appealing some of the pickle casters are.

Tilting sets for water, coffee and other beverages were quite the thing for formal occasions in upper-class homes last century and even early in this one. Many, made of quadrupleplated silver, were ex-

tremely ornate. The pitchers were attached to frames with bases
and tilted forward to pour. Frequently a metal container to catch
the "drippings" (and called a "slop") sat in the base of the frame.
The more expensive sets had goldlined slops, and others came complete with one or two goldlined goblets. The water (or coffee) pots
were frequently decorated by chasing. Some had covers with unusual finials. One of these was in the shape of a miniature man
leaning against a ball.

The pitchers or pots were lined with various materials, usually
porcelain or metal. Early in this century tilting sets for water were
called "water tilters." About the time this country entered the
Second World War, a tilting set in polished brass, 19½ inches tall,
was offered for $22 wholesale. The same pitcher without the tilting
stand could be had for $11.50.

Also in widespread use in the late nineteenth century were electroplated tea kettles on stands which held an alcohol lamp. Some
kettles were attached to their stands by chains. Coffee sets of this
type also were in use. John Round & Son made a "Five O'clock
Tea Service" consisting of a teapot on a stand and a creamer and
sugar bowl, all electroplated on Britannia metal, plus two china
plates.

If you encounter a fine tilting set whose silver is badly worn, you
can have it replated. Many articles of this type that have been replated are reported selling briskly in antique shops in one of the
Southern states noted as a resort area.

Have you ever seen a "folding biscuit box?" These were produced in numerous fanciful shapes, plated on nickel silver, by John
Round. They consisted of two compartments for biscuits attached
to a stand. When not in use, the two compartments could be folded
together for compactness. These boxes had carrying handles of
various shapes and sizes. Some of the biscuit boxes were made of
glass with metal tops and frames. Some also were decorated with
Medusa-like, dragon, or other animal heads. The folding boxes
were available in this country, too, though I have seen only a few
of them in early trade catalogues. Simpson, Hall, Miller & Co., of
Wallingford, Connecticut, offered them late last century at wholesale prices of $12 to $14 each, and they were called "nut or biscuit
bowls." They had pierced metal tops, were gold lined, and were
embossed.

Nut bowls were produced in great abundance and in a tremendous diversity of shapes. They should afford an excellent field for
collecting. They were made with flat bottoms, with feet and on
pedestal-type stands in compote form. Thousands of silverplated
ones were turned out through the years, some silver lined and others gold lined. Embossed decorations ran the gamut of fancy, rang-

These are all silverplated toothpick holders with the exception of the one at the extreme right on second row from top, which is of cut glass. The chick with a wishbone was a favorite design for many years.

Beverage table pieces of last century are shown here. Top row from left: fancy repousse coffee pot, tea pot, and ice pitcher. Second row: two urns. Bottom: tea pot with capacity of 2½ pints, a table kettle and stand, and a swing tea or coffee kettle. All are in silver plate except the kettle in the center of the bottom row, which has a brass finish.

ing from depictions of fruits and flowers to birds. One of the most delightful types imaginable was offered in 1893 by B. F. Norris, Alister & Co. The bowl itself was in the shape of a mammoth nut with half of one side of its shell removed. Its handle was in the form of a tree branch with leaf, and an inquisitive metal squirrel stood audaciously atop the upper half of the shell. The bowl was on a footed silverplated stand. A number of other nut bowls (which often were used interchangeably for fruit) also featured squirrel decorations; several of these had bowls in the shape of a realistic leaf.

Before leaving the subjects of nuts (of the fruit variety), give consideration to novel nutpicks, which you may spell as two words if you prefer, and also to nutcracks. Many silver and silverplated picks boasted novelty handles, a group of these having been made by Rogers & Bro., of Waterbury, Connecticut. One, designated as "Assyrian," featured the head of a lady, apparently Assyrian, at the handle top with a spiral shaft above the pick. Pearl-handled picks with silverplated mountings are choice. The rather plain silverplated and nickelplated picks are not of much interest.

Several types of novel nutcracks also were turned out in past years. One of these was the Harper "cracker," advertised in 1905 as "the only cracker made that keeps the hulls from falling on the floor!" Instructions were given for its use as follows: "Place the nut between the jaws from the under side, press handles together, and crack the nut, letting the hulls and kernels drop in the receptacle or hand. The jaws of this cracker are much wider than any other, and the nut resting against the plate brings it on a line with the jaws, hence the nut is cracked all over evenly, while with other crackers only part of the nut is cracked." The "plate" mentioned above refers to a metal ledge attached to the jaws of this crack. This crack together with six nickelplated picks wholesaled for only 65 cents in a leatherette case. A similar silverplated set cost $1.70.

Produced in even greater abundance than were nut bowls were syrup jugs. These were fashioned in more shapes and sizes than you can shake a stick at and are still plentiful. Hundreds of thousands have been made in quadrupleplated silver—tall, squat, oval, round. Handles were fabricated in numerous shapes as were the finials on the tops or lids. A great many syrup jars (or pitchers or jugs, as you prefer) were accompanied by underplates to catch any syrup that might otherwise drip on a neat tablecloth. Many syrup pitchers sat on flat bottoms; others were footed. The more chaste of the metal types were engraved with floral designs.

Glass syrups were made in plain crystal, pattern glass and were cut. The fine early cut glass syrup pitchers with their silverplated tops fetch handsome prices now as do most articles of cut glass made between about 1885 and around 1910.

Several plated cake baskets, a handsome water pitcher, and a cracker jar (bottom left).

Collectible creamers, sugar bowls and spoon holders. A "dessert" sugar of silver in the Louis XV style is shown on the third row at left at a matching creamer below. On the third row at right is a sugar bowl of decorated opal glass (called "opal buff bisque glass" by its manufacturer) with matching creamer below. Note the paw feet of the sugar and creamer on second row.

Table adjuncts of the nineteenth century include on top row from left: two biscuit (or cracker) jars of decorated porcelain with silverplated tops and bails, and two individual novelty salts. In the center are a porcelain handpainted pepper and salt set in a silverplated holder, and a silverplated sugar shaker. At bottom from left are an individual caster consisting of pepper, salt, napkin ring and butter plate; a breakfast caster with three decorated bottles, and a fine six-bottle caster set on a silverplated stand.

Two delightful nineteenth-century silverplated napkin rings are shown at top with a silver candelabrum and two silver candlesticks below. Along the third row are plated bon bon bowls and trays. On the bottom row from left are a silverplated wine cooler, ice tub, and a copper egg steamer with alcohol lamp. The egg steamer was made before World War I.

Late nineteenth-century cut glass table pieces. Top row, from left: a nappy or jelly dish with handle and two spoon trays. Second row: two foot-long celery dishes. Third row from left: three cream pitchers and a carafe or water bottle. Fourth row: an oil or vinegar bottle and two violet or flower balls. Bottom: a one-pint decanter and two jars which were used for either biscuits or marmalade.

*Silverplated butter dishes were made in a wide diversity of shapes
and designs last century.*

Fruit or berry bowls of glass in silverplated holders (some of which are known to collectors as "Brides' Baskets") are among the most delightful of table collectibles. Several nineteenth-century ones are shown here with a jelly dish at extreme left on the top row. The glass basket or bowl in the center at top is ivory inside and rose outside; that at extreme right is of colored decorated crystal. Another ivory and rose bowl is on the second row at left and a clear crystal bowl to its right. The bowl on the fanciful stand at bottom left is of imported decorated glass and that at right bottom is rose decorated inside. This last bowl was reported in the Louis XV style.

QUADRUPLE PLATE SILVERWARE.

NO. 465. TILTING SET, COMPLETE.

Satin, Bright Cut, Slop and Goblet Gold Lined.........................$33 00
No. 465. Plain Satin Gilt.. 30 50

NO. 167. CHASED TILTING SET, COMPLETE.

With Cup and Slop Bowl Gold Lined $42 00

Two elaborate tilting sets in quadrupleplated silver as shown on a page from the 1892 catalogue of B. F. Norris, Alister & Co. Note the prices at that time.

A group of late nineteenth-century silverplated syrup pitchers and two of cut glass. Note the female heads atop the finial and handle of the pitcher at the extreme right on the top row.

Late nineteenth- and early twentieth-century syrup jugs or pitchers with plates.

Silverplated nut bowls of late nineteenth century are shown on the top row and at left on the second row. A 1905 nut bowl is at right on the second row with additional ones on the third row and at bottom left. At right on the bottom is the Harper Nutcrack of 1905, described in the text.

Two silverplated nut bowls, 1893 vintage, are at top. Below from left ares 1908 catsup holder, 1908 Worcestershire sauce holder, and 1893 nutpicks. The pick at extreme left has a pearl handle; the others are by Rogers & Bro. On the bottom row are two late nineteenth-century combination fruit knives and nutpicks and a decorated nutcrack.

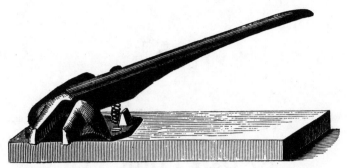

Nineteenth-century japanned nut crack.

Silverplated syrups in octagonal shapes were in favor from 1910 to 1914. They were burnished, engine turned, and engraved, primarily with leaf-type scrolls. Take a look at the illustrations of them in this chapter to obtain an idea of the numerous types available.

Toothpick holders have been written about almost fulsomely, and I have little to add to the knowledge already imparted about them. However, I have included illustrations of some fascinating ones in this chapter for your delectation.

Other miscellaneous table accessories once utilized in myriad homes and definitely collectible include silverplated and glass "slop" bowls, cake baskets, candelabra, epergnes, berry or fruit bowls (and a dozen other types of bowls including "handy bowls," which were used for everything from salad to fruit), celery dishes and jars, toast racks, ice pitchers, butter dishes, sugar bowls and creamers, mustard pots, horse radish holders, bon bon bowls and dishes, cheese and cracker sets, lemon dishes, and salt and pepper shakers. Some of these have been written about before, but we show you a good many examples in this chapter to whet your collecting appetite.

[15]

From Metallic Stylus
to Ball Point Pen

☞ We have traveled a long way in time from the era of hieroglyphics. This progress makes all the more dismaying our efforts to decipher the handwriting of so many of our fellows today. Though our writing implements have improved remarkably since the heyday of the goose quill pen, the physical writing skills of many of us leave much to be desired. This is merely a casual commentary upon one of the numerous shortcomings of our time, and this chapter will not constitute a treatise upon handwriting, abominable or otherwise. It will instead concern itself with some of the delightful and interesting collectible objects associated with the gentle art of writing. Ink wells and ink stands have been written about before, and I will not belabor them here except to suggest that you may have been overlooking some of the intriguing novelty ones, such as the twin reversible metal ink wells that were made in combination with a one-day clock and calendar in the 1890's. Although this chapter will not explore verbally the matter of ornate ink wells and stands, you will find a number of them illustrated.

What I would like to discuss at greater length are such writing accessories as blotters, ink bottles, early novelty pencils, writing sets, and even the fabulous typewriter, which has helped revolutionize both business and personal correspondence and is more or less of a godsend for those whose handwriting is as atrocious as my own. I'd also like to comment on such adjuncts as letter openers, letter racks, and pen wipers.

Ink is not so recent an invention as you may suspect; its use dates back more than 3,000 years. Since the earliest ink appeared in dry cake or stick form, however, ink bottles and ink wells do not go back so far, even though they have been in use, in one form or another, for several centuries.

Blotters as we know them today were preceded by sanders, which continued in use for some time after blotting paper was invented,

Early twentieth-century ink stands and combination stands and pen racks. Many of the metal stands could be had in a choice of finishes, including bronze, ebony and gold, maroon, and sienna and red. The wells in the stand in the center of the second row from top revolved as did those shown at bottom left. The combination shown at bottom right consists of an ink well, a barometer and a pen rack. The fine swirled bottle at bottom center, had a sterling silver top.

or until a little after the middle of last century. Sanders were small boxes made in a variety of shapes with perforated tops much like those of pepper shakers. From these the sand was sprinkled across the newly written page, soaking up the surplus ink. Since our an-

Early twentieth-century ink stands, most of them with plain crystal or cut blass bottles. The one at extreme right on the second row has a pen wiper in the bottle top.

cestors were generally thrifty, they poured the sand back into the container after it had performed its chore of blotting. Many a traveling or lap desk of yesterday contained a sander. Many sanders were made of turned wood, but a variety of other materials were also used in their production, including papier-mâché and lacquer, pottery and porcelain, and such metals and metal and mineral derivatives as gold, silver, brass, bronze, copper, tin, Sheffield plate, and iron. There were sanders of glass and others of marble and other substances.

Collecting ink bottles can be fun. These all date about the turn of this century. The one at far right on the top row is a "traveller's" ink case, designed to be taken along on trips.

Sanders from the nineteenth-century and earlier are fun to collect but are becoming scarce, even though some may still be found priced at only a few dollars. In recent months there have been advertised an olivewood sander for $4.50, one of tin for $3.50, and other wooden ones at prices of $3.50 to $10.

Sanders finally gave way to blotters of other types and in the final quarter of last century "rocking" blotters (blotting paper attached to semicircular metal base attached, in turn, to a flat top metal surface with a handle) were in use. These blotters should be of much interest today, because they were manufactured in many novel and ornate forms and are still obtainable in some quantities.

The knobs (or handles) of these rocker-type blotters are of major interest. Late last century one appeared with the cast metal figure of a horse as its handle. The metal surface was plated with silver. Large numbers of these blotters were contrived with silver-plated embossed decorations such as flowers, geometrical designs, and assorted scrolls. Other animals in addition to horses were sometimes used as handles on this type. An illustration in an 1893 magazine depicts one with a metal figure of a dog.

In addition to the semicircular blotter, which was rocked back and forth by hand, there was a somewhat similar type that revolved completely. The blotting paper was wrapped around a core, held in a metal frame attached to a metal handle. The blotter-covered core was rolled up and down the paper to be blotted. Not only were these made in silver plate but also with handles of sterling silver (as were some of the rocker type). A fine group of these is illustrated in the 1902 "Twentieth-Century Jewelry Catalogue" of Oskamp, Nolting & Co., of Cincinnati, priced at 36 cents to $1.75 each. Several of both the rocker-type and the rolling blotters are shown in the illustrations accompanying this chapter. One most interesting type, shown in an early twentieth-century catalogue of M. S. Benedict Manufacturing Company, of East Syracuse, New York, features a combination rocking blotter-stamp box: the knob itself provides the receptacle for stamps.

A rocking blotter made of black enameled iron with a large metal screw for a cap was introduced early in this century but is not of much interest for collectors. There also was a type with a long handle that could be opened or closed with a slight pressure on the clasp to insert a new blotting pad when the old one had worn out. Others were made with wooden knobs as handles and with nickelplated pads to which the blotters were attached.

Produced in greater numbers and in a wide diversity of shapes and designs were letter openers, sometimes called "paper knives" or "paper openers" in dealers' catalogues. These were offered for

Rocking and rolling blotters. Most of these have sterling silver handles and tops except the Sill's flexible blotters shown at left in the center, the rolling blotter at bottom left, and the Moore's New Improved blotter at top right. Dates of the blotters shown include, top row from left: 1893, 1890's, and 1903. Second row: 1892, and 1905. Third row: Sill's flexible, 1908. The remaining blotters were originally advertised between 1902 and 1905.

sale not only by office supply companies but often by jewelry concerns, the latter type of firm selling those with handles of sterling silver.

Many elaborate letter openers were made with decorated sterling silver handles and pearl blades; thousands of others were manufactured with blades of steel. Some handles were made with enameled gold, which imparted an appearance of costly luxuriousness, even though they could be bought early in this century for only a few dollars.

Blades themselves appeared in various shapes with fairly dull or blunt edges so as to minimize the chance of being wounded while opening a letter. Some blades tapered to a sharp point, more or less like a stiletto; but the majority were broad blades with a semi-curve at the cutting extremity. Still others had a long blade, slightly rounded at the tip, thicker in the center than at the edges.

Letter openers of numerous types are illustrated in nearly all late nineteenth- and early twentieth-century wholesale jewelry catalogues, and you will find a number of illustrations in this chapter taken from some of these. Interestingly enough, many such dealers frequently listed manicure implements and letter openers in the same section of their catalogues. One reason was that both types of implements were usually produced in the same factories and their handles and blades were quite often made of the same materials. Also, writing sets (which some firms called "library sets") are pictured and offered in numerous catalogues in the sections showing manicure sets.

A typical writing set would include one or two crystal glass ink bottles with sterling tops, a rolling blotter, a letter opener, a pen, a seal, and a metal erasing implement. These were neatly packaged in plush-lined leatherette cases, which wholesaled early in this century at prices of $5 or $6 up.

There were book marks with flat blades that could be utilized for opening letters, newspaper wrappers, and the like. Some of these had pearl handles, others had handles of celluloid or metal.

Matching letter openers and seals were produced, too, with precisely the same types of sterling handles.

One early twentieth-century letter opener featured a long handle fashioned of embossed sterling grapes and leaves. Embossed floral designs prdominated on handles of large numbers of these implements produced half a century or more ago. Otto Young & Co. in its 1907 catalogue depicts a variety of these paper knives with sterling handles and pearl blades at wholesale prices of from $4.25 to $18 a dozen.

Other designs encountered on paper knives include human heads, four-leaf clovers, crosses, geometrical arrangements, and—

Paper knives with metal and pearl blades of the early 1900's, all with sterling silver handles except the one second from left on the second row, which has a wooden handle. The last five articles on the second row are combination book marks and paper cutters.

occasionally—heads of animals. One unusual type was made in the shape of a crescent, resembling a miniature weed-cutting blade. A combination silver paper cutter and bookmark was made in the shape of a painter's palette and measured only 3 inches in length. In addition to the metal handles, which predominated, there were some paper cutters with handles of ebony, trimmed with silver. The M. S. Benedict Company, which made many plated and silver novelties, turned out some knives with handles in the flowing "Art Nouveau" designs around 1905. It also made some openers with handles of stag horn.

Another combination to watch for is a paper cutter combined with a small magnifying glass. These are handy gadgets when one is trying to decipher torturous handwriting. Decorations featuring full-length figures on the handles of paper cutters are fairly scarce, but you may occasionally find them, this type having been offered in half-dozen assorted lots on counter cards at the turn of the century.

Small metal-bladed erasers in widespread use less than three-quarters of a century ago were made in numerous handle designs matching those of the paper cutters, and there were a great many inexpensive writing sets that offered, on a card, a sterling handled paper cutter, eraser, and seal. Sets such as these sold for a dollar to $2 in 1900. The eraser blades were small, tapering to fine edges from a thicker center. Some were double-edged and others had only a single blade edge designed to erase by abrasive action. Handles also were made of bone, ebony wood, and rubber.

Letter seals, once popular but rarely used these days, had handles similar in design and shape to those on· the letter openers and erasers with a round base for the seals. Although most handles were of sterling silver, some were made of pearl, silver-mounted.

You'll find letter racks of metal in some antiques shops these days. Many were quite lavishly adorned and customarily consisted of a metal front and back attached to opposite sides of a flat base, providing a space between them for holding letters. Some with open work or pierced designs are especially worthy of attention. Of somewhat similar shape and design were post card holders, some of which were made in combination with a stamp box. The letter holders were termed "paper and envelope racks" by manufacturers. The majority were made of plated silver, and a convenient size was about 8 inches long by 5 inches high. They made attractive ornaments on milady's desk and were pressed into service to hold letters that required an answer. I have a desk set made of enameled iron that includes a small letter rack measuring about $4\frac{1}{4}$ by $3\frac{1}{4}$ inches in size. It is edged in gold leaf with enameled flowers at the front

Here are sterling silver letter seals; steel erasers with handles of silver, stag, hard rubber, and bone; an ebony-handled rubber eraser holder (second from right in second row), and a five-piece "library set." All date in the early 1900's.

Early silver and silverplated letter racks are seen on the top row. Three calendar frames are on the second row, and stamp boxes in various shapes and sizes are shown below.

corners. The other pieces in this set are a letter opener with a copperplated blade, a combination ink stand and pen holder, and a handled flat-bottom paperweight. The entire set cost me only $6 a few years ago.

The spiral Universal pen rack (1903).

Numerous types of pen racks were made in addition to the ink standpen rack combinations. A group of these were horseshoe-shaped devices of decorated metal (frequently bronzed). The two horseshoe-shaped end pieces were attached with metal rods. A group of brackets around the two end pieces held the pens. But a great many other shapes also prevailed. One made of brass had the appearance of a series of gnarled tree branches. Others had front ends that sloped backward toward the top with a series of step-like brackets to hold pens. Still others had ends with semi-circular tops around which the pen brackets were attached. Some racks were flat and oblong. The "Star" rack, shown in a 1903 catalogue, consisted of two oval end pieces with metal stars cut out in their centers and to which was attached a flexible spiral wire formed into grooves between which pens could be placed and held securely. Other types of spiral wire racks were produced. There was even a combination spiral wire pen rack and crystal glass paperweight.

Small racks of sterling silver designed for only two or three pens will appeal to many collectors.

If you're going to collect writing accessories, you may wish to be on the lookout for the more unusual pen cleaners or wipers. Most commonplace were those of chamois (sometimes several pieces joined together), many having colored illustrations on their top surfaces. These were made in the shapes of rugs, envelopes, palettes, and so on. They are scarce, because they were usually discarded after rather constant use. Of more interest are the pen cleaners of glass, metal, and decorated porcelain with wiping surfaces in their tops. Adelphi Silver Plate Company offered an extremely attractive combination ink well of glass and pen wiper top. The pen wiper was held in the ink well's silverplated top or cap.

In a somewhat similar category are sponge cups and envelope

Elaborate letter clips are shown on the top row and at left on the second row. Also on the second row at extreme right on the bottom are harp letter files. Straight letter hooks or files are shown at bottom.

moisteners. Richissin's envelope sealer, patented November 5, 1907, is probably a rarity today. It had a rubber reservoir handle to hold water, a felt moistener attached to a nickelplated feeder, and a small rubber roller on the back of the moistener. The reservoir was sealed with a screw cap. The whole affair, looking almost like a modern-day safety razor in shape, measured 6½ inches in length.

Sponge cups were produced of glass (including cut glass) in numerous designs. One came equipped with a fountain-type reservoir for holding an extra supply of water. There were other mois-

At top from left are a glass block paperweight, a combination glass paperweight and clamp, and two cast figure paperweights. Second row: A glass cube paperweight, a decorated metal weight, and a chamois pen wiper. Third row: two elaborate pen wipers with sponge tops and another chamois wiper. Fourth row: three glass sponge cups, the one at left being of cut glass. Bottom left is a Richissin letter sealer and at right is another sponge cup.

teners consisting of oblong glass trays in which either glass or felt-covered rollers were set. Novelty types of small moisteners were turned out, also.

Novelty paperweights, which are discussed in my book *The Coming Collecting Boom,* merit serious attention in my estimation. Since I first wrote about them in the earlier book, a number of additional types have come to my attention. M. S. Benedict Manufacturing Co. made animal weights, one featuring an elephant and another a rampaging steer on oval plated bases. These weights were available in French grey, Venetian bronze, or ormulu gold finishes at wholesale prices ranging from $15 to $21 a dozen. Benedict made a metal dog weight without a separate base (the bottom of the stretched-out dog providing its own base). This same company produced metal statuettes of feminine figures on round bases that could be used as paperweights.

Paperweights of oblong, cubed or oval glass and metal are certainly worth the search it may require to find them today. A glass clamp-paperweight, combining an oblong paperweight of crystal with a metal decorated paper clamp or clip attached to the top, was patented on December 5, 1893. Advertising paperweights are discussed in the earlier chapter of this book entitled "Free Enterprise: A World of Collectibles."

You'll also find decorated paper clips and paper files discussed in *The Coming Collecting Boom,* but we're illustrating some of these in this chapter. Stamp boxes were and are an important adjunct of writing. A number were fabricated in the shape of miniature porch mail boxes and were made in nickelplated iron. This and other collectible types are illustrated in this chapter.

Hundreds of thousands of novelty-type goldplated and sterling silver pencils have been manufactured over the years, and it is surprising that they seem to be scarce today. But perhaps the reason that they are so seldom encountered is that their present owners have stashed them away somewhere for safekeeping, and, in the meantime, may have forgotten them.

Actually, these little pencils are of small monetary value, but a collection of numerous different types can be of interest. Their decorated barrels of silver or rolled gold plate or pearl can make a striking display when they are arranged alongside one another in an exhibition case. A great many of them were intended to be worn as charm pieces, and they were made with attached metal rings.

Top-quality silver pencils of this type were not particularly inexpensive originally, retailing early in this century for as much as $5 and $6 each. In shape and appearance they were very much like the sterling and the goldplated toothpicks, once in high style.

Sadly neglected thus far are the forerunners of today's fabulous

A diversified group of fine rolled-goldplated and sterling silver pencils dating about 1900 is pictured on the first six rows from top. On the seventh row left is the "Tom Tit" fountain pen and to its right is the "Red Dwarf" Stylographic ink pencil. A Stylographic pen is seen at the left on the eighth row with a Russet Stylographic ink pencil at the right. Two goldplated ladies' pencils of 1891 are seen on the ninth row and at right on the tenth row. At bottom left are two 1905 pocket pencils with silver cases; in the center are two Johnson's solid gold charm pencils, and at right, two novelty erasers of 1903.

typewriters, but these are the machines that helped revolutionize American business and that have enabled many a man (and more than a few women, too) to conceal the deficiencies of their handwriting.

Although we look upon the typewriter as a fairly modern invention, its basic idea was known more than two and a half centuries

Nineteenth-century typewriters. Top row from left: the Densmore; the National (National Typewriter Co.); the Crandall (Crandall Machine Co.); and the Hall (National Typewriter Co.). Second row: the Chicago; Caligraph; and the $6 American (American Typewriter Co.). Third row: Remington; Munson; and Columbia Typewriter Mfg. Co's. Bar-Lock No. 4. Fourth row: Victor (The Tilton Mfg. Co.); Smith Premier (the Smith Premier Typewriter Co.); and the Oliver. Fifth row: the Sun (Sun Type Writer Co.); Hammond (The Hammond Typewriter Co.); the World; and the American Toy Typewriter (bottom left), and the Fox (Fox Typewriter Co.) at bottom right.

ago. Such an idea was incorporated in Royal Letters Patent granted an English engineer named Henry Mill in January, 1714, although whether Mr. Mill ever actually made a typewriter fitting the description in his patent papers remains open to question. No one seems to know just who did build the very first writing machine of this kind, but the first American typewriter was devised by a resident of Michigan named William Austin Burt in 1828.

We will not delve here into the progress of the typewriter; but it does constitute a remarkable story and those who would like to read it will find it nicely detailed in a well-illustrated book written by Bruce Bliven, Jr., and published under the title *The Wonderful Writing Machine* by Random House in 1954. A good many copies of this book were distributed with the compliments of the Royal Typewriter Company, Inc., of New York City.

Numerous kinds of typewriters were invented not long after Burt had patented his machine. Models of the earliest ones are extremely scarce, including models of what is said to have been the first practical commercial typewriter invented by Christopher Latham Sholes a little over a century ago and named, appropriately enough, a Type-Writer. Nevertheless, there are still available for collectors interested in numerous late nineteenth- and early twentieth-century typewriters marketed under various names and produced by various firms, some of which subsequently became giants in the typewriter manufacturing field, including Remington, Underwood, L. C. Smith, and Royal.

You'll encounter many names, some of them no longer known, on early typewriters. There was "The Chicago," made by Chicago Writing Machine Company in its namesake city, which sold for $35 in 1901. "The Densmore" was being made by The Densmore Typewriter Company, of New York City, in the 1890's. The "Caligraph" was a product of The American Writing Machine Company, of Hartford, Connecticut, in the early 1890's with models selling in 1891 at prices of $70 to $100. Several typewriters of the 1890's were little more than toys, and typewriters designed specifically as toys had been made even earlier. One of these was the "American Toy Typewriter," offered as a premium by *The Youth's Companion* in 1889. It could be purchased outright for 85 cents, plus an additional 15 cents for packing and postage. Another well-known early commercial typewriter name was the "Blickensderfer." Still another was the "Oliver." My parents presented me with an Oliver as a birthday gift when I was a high school student somewhere back in the dark ages, and I treasured and used it for years.

For some reason that I cannot recall at the moment, I began collecting early models of typewriters myself about 1949 and had acquired a dozen or more fascinating machines when a fire originated in the building in which I had them housed and burned them to a crisp. Even now, however, I am fascinated by advertisements for used typewriters and always have at least three of the machines on hand, though I doubt that I shall ever again get back up to a dozen.

I do remember such typewriter names, in addition to those mentioned above, as the "Pearl," originally manufactured by Pearl Typewriter Company and retailing for only $5 in 1893; the Hall, made by National Typewriter Co., of Boston; the "American," a $6 seller in the late nineteenth century; the "National," produced by National Typewriter Co., Philadelphia; the "Fox," a product of Fox Typewriter Co., Grand Rapids; the "Hammond," from The Hammond Typewriter Company, New York City; and the "Sun," made by Sun Type Writer Co., New York City.

In your foraging you may also encounter machines with such names as Merritt, Odell, Columbia, Pullman, Franklin, Travis, and Edison "Mimeograph."

I have recently noted advertisements of early typewriters for sale at what seem to me to be quite low prices. These have included a Hall (1887) at $15; an early Remington model with original tin cover at $20; and a Blickensderfer (patented in 1892) at $30. Confidentially, I paid an average of about $7.50 each for those I bought between 1949 and 1954.

Other early writing accessories and adjuncts you may want to investigate include fountain pens and desk calendar frames of decorated metal. You may not think that a desk calendar is an adjunct of writing, but you'd be surprised by the number of persons who apparently cannot write a letter without first ascertaining the date on a handy desk calendar.

[16]

Collectors' Medley

☞ *The time has come, the Walrus said, to speak of many things . . .*

Were Lewis Carroll's Walrus speaking today, he would talk not only *of shoes and ships and sealing wax and cabbages and kings,* but perhaps also of music rolls and hearing aids and luggage tags and rings. Of these and also of fluting irons and spectacles and nickels made of wood, of fire extinguishers of glass and bookends with a hood.

What else is new that's old? What kinds of oddments are people collecting today to add excitement and verve to the pursuit of the newly old? I thought you might enjoy taking a look at some of what may seem to you a strange assortment of articles that are just beginning to entrap the offbeat collectors. You may even want to join the chase while it's still young.

Eyeglasses, or spectacles, are by no means new; the estimable Roger Bacon, thirteenth-century English philosopher and scientist, is credited by some with having invented them or at least with having delineated the principles of their use. Because of his excursions into optics, alchemy, and chemistry and their impact upon the mores of his times, Dr. Bacon was accused of being a practitioner of witchcraft. But thanks to his discoveries and those of other pioneers, there are hundreds of thousands of us today with vision who might otherwise waste a couple of hours daily trying to fit a key into a keyhole that seems to be moving about incognito.

Who *really* did invent eyeglasses? Perhaps no one knows for sure, but there is a long and scholarly article relating to their discovery in the *Journal of History of Medicine,* Volume 11, 1956. It was written by Edward Rosen and appeared in two parts under the title *The Invention of Eyeglasses.* If you're research-minded, you may want to look it up.

These early spectacles and frames are now in the Museum of Optometry, which was created not long ago as a section of the Library of the American Optometric Association, headquartered in St. Louis, Missouri. These early types of spectacles and frames have moved into the category of collectible objects.

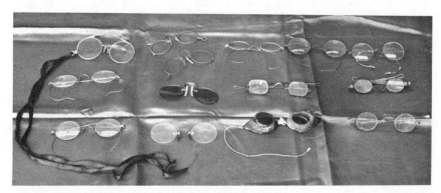

Assortment of early spectacles and frames, some of which date back to the nineteenth century. Assembled from private collections of optometry, these are a part now of the Museum of Optometry, a section of the Library of the American Optometric Association, St. Louis, Missouri, by whose courtesy they are reproduced.

Today, some persons and at least one professional organization are collecting or beginning to collect early examples of spectacles, which truly have proved one of mankind's boons. One can, in fact, get together, with some effort, a remarkable collection of early eyeglasses with iron and steel rims or frames. Nineteenth-century spectacles with tempered steel frames, often nickelplated, are still around in abundance. So, too, are those with frames of gold alloy and what now seem to us quaint wire temple pieces. A striking and highly educational collection of antique spectacles and allied materials has been assembled by the American Optometric Association, of St. Louis, Missouri, for a national museum of optometry.

Spectacle frames also were made of rubber and of coin silver in the nineteenth century, and frameless eyeglasses date back many years. In the 1890's one could purchase a nice pair of eyeglasses for only a few dollars, and some types sold at wholesale for only $2 a dozen pairs! These prices, naturally, did not include the eye examination we now know to be necessary for properly prescribed glasses. Even so, "refracting" and "dispensing" opticians were practicing fairly early last century, and the profession of optometry was licensed early in this century.

Goggles also date back to last century and were available in various colors, including green and blue. Driving goggles had their heyday with the mass advent of the horseless carriage.

You will find pictured in this chapter several types of nineteenth-century spectacles and goggles that may be collected with a very small outlay of cash. Worth seeking also are early spectacle cases of morocco and other leathers, papier-mâché, embossed aluminum, or steel.

Eyeglasses kept in place by a spring which pinches against the nose are generally referred to now as "pince-nez" (from the French meaning "pinch nose"), but early in this century they were listed as "grab fronts."

Protective goggles, in addition to having been made for motorists and cyclists, also were produced for those working at occupations providing eye hazards, including millers and others. Some were made of glass, others of mica, or isinglass. Eye shields were manufactured to be worn over eyeglasses; some of these came with smoke and blue or green lenses. The largest users of goggles early in this century were automobile drivers (and passengers), cyclists, engineers, farmers (while threshing), miners, mill workers, and stone workers.

Another of mankind's beneficial crutches has been the hearing aid—an instrument that has helped thousands (including me) to hear the birds sing again after a period of silence. Today's compact, efficient hearing aids are a far cry indeed from the cumbersome, bulky devices used less than three-quarters of a century ago. The

Goggles, spectacles and cases of 1905. From left at top: Lamb's Patent mica eye shields; eye shield fitting in a cup over the eyes; and the Eureka green eye shade that went well with a handlebar mustache. Second row: eye shield adapted for wearing over glasses; aluminum black japanned and funnel-shaped eye protectors; and collapsible goggles, shown closed. Third row: glazed spectacles for shooting or for use on the seashore and in the mountains; and a pair of Hold-rite Shur-on eyeglasses. Fourth row: a pair of Spectaclettes, and a pair of "grab fronts." Fifth row: eye protectors; a leatherette eyeglass case, and a leather open-end case. At bottom is a straight temple chatelaine eyeglass case.

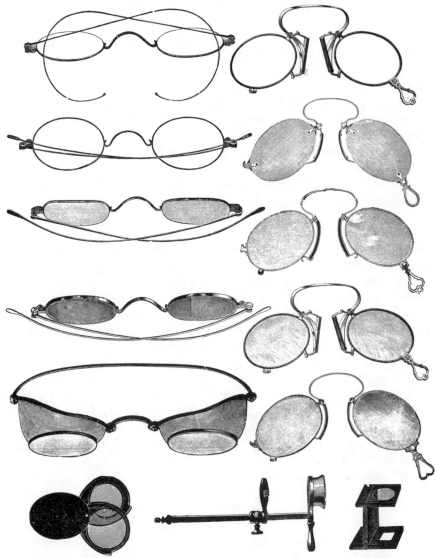

Spectacles of the early 1890's. Top left, a pair with tempered steel riding bow frames, and, right, a pair of "New Style," with adjustable cork guard. Second row: pair with tempered steel frames and "Skeleton" eye glasses with nickel trimmings. Third row: "Pantascope" spectacles with the lenses slanted, and a pair of eye glasses with round wire frames and cork guard. Fourth row: "Cataract" spectacles with straight temples, and a pair of "New Style." Fifth row: miller's spectacles, and "Royal Alloy" eye glasses. Bottom: a double lens pocket magnifier, a nickelplated optimeter or eye tester, and linen tester.

early "conversation tubes" and "hearing horns" are truly relics of the past, outmoded by the scientific explosion of the mid-twentieth century; but they are a part of the American past, and some of them are still around, awaiting collectors intrigued by offbeat "antiques."

What was once known as the "ear trumpet" was a widely used device during the Victorian era. In appearance, it resembled a miniature saxaphone, having a small end that was held against the ear and a horn-like end at the other extremity into which one spoke—or rather usually shouted. At the turn of this century, this type of device was called an "adjustable conversation tube," with silk, mohair, or hard rubber covering the flexible tube that separated the two ends.

Then there was the "London hearing horn," constructed of light metal and somewhat resembling an even smaller saxophone. This could be carried in the hand when in use and placed in one's pocket or purse when not needed. They were made in several sizes and in 1905 were wholesaled at only $2 each! Perhaps the price bespoke their effectiveness.

So-called "bone conduction" hearing aids, however, are not new. They were used during the late eighteenth century, according to *Hearing Progress,* published by Maico Hearing Instruments, a major manufacturer of hearing aids, of Minneapolis. The publication described one of these early devices as follows:

"Typical of these was a device that looked like a fan. The hard of hearing person held the narrow end in his teeth. Sound vibrations were picked up by the fan and transmitted to the teeth, through the jawbone to the skull, and finally to the auditory nerves of the inner ear. This device was of course cumbersome, and its effectiveness as a hearing aid minimal, although, for some, it was better than not hearing at all."

In addition to their inefficiency, early hearing aids had the added drawback of being, in many instances, large and awkward to handle. The size of the horn, for example, had a direct effect upon the device's efficiency. Its shape affected its sound-transmitting qualities.

With the dawn of the twentieth century came the electrical hearing aid, which converted sound energy into electrical energy, transmitting it along wires or through space and finally converting it back into sound energy. In a way, the electrical hearing aid was similar to the telephone, although there were some substantial differences, too. But even these early carbon-type aids were bulky, utilizing large earphones held by a headband and large microphones strapped to the chest. *Hearing Progress* points out that the receiver and microphone of these aids was connected by heavy cords to two quite sizeable batteries, normally attached to one's legs, and that "In those days, wearing a hearing aid was not the sort of thing you took lightly."

Hearing instruments of an earlier day are pictured here, along with a modern instrument of far greater efficiency and much smaller proportions. Note the variety of hearing horns and tubes. (Photo courtesy of Maico Hearing Instruments.)

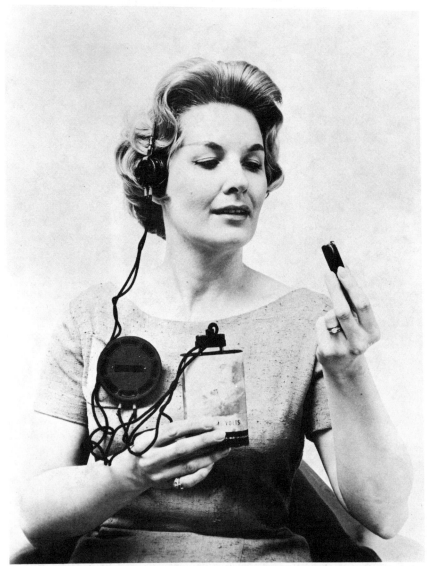

This bulky early hearing aid is a far cry from today's small and efficient instruments and is among the many miscellaneous objects for which collectors are on the lookout. (Photo courtesy of Maico Hearing Instruments.)

The awkward carbon-type aid was used for about four decades, but began to be supplanted around 1938 by one utilizing a glass vacuum tube, similar to those used in radios. Wearing a hearing aid became at least practicable. Today, vacuum tubes have been replaced by transistors as the amplifying elements and sizes of the devices have literally been shrunk to the point that they are almost unnoticeable. Meanwhile, their efficiency has been vastly improved, and hundreds of thousands of users have been enabled to return to a normal life.

This is not intended to be a treatise upon hearing aids but merely to suggest that early ones will never be made again and are collectible.

Silver deposit glasswares have been produced for about a century. This type of glass was decorated by an electro-deposit method, an electrolytic process long used to coat articles with metals. Relatively, this process was inexpensive, and it was simplified after its discovery. Large quantities of this type of decorated glass were produced early in this century (although it also had been made prior to that time). Quantity production continued until about the 1920's.

Two early twentieth-century adjustable conversation tubes and a London hearing horn once used by the hard of hearing. The hearing horn was made of a lightweight metal.

In his excellent book *Nineteenth Century Glass: Its Genesis and Development,* a new edition of which was published by Thomas Nelson & Sons in 1967, Albert Christian Revi, an outstanding authority on glass, points out that several methods for depositing silver (as well as other metals) on glass were patented in the latter half of last century. Those who would like to know more about the technicalities of the processes will find some of them described in his book. Even some of Frederick Carder's Steuben Aurene glass was made with decorative silver trim, electrolytically applied.

Silver deposit glass usually had raised designs or ornamentation

Silver deposit glasswares made at the turn of this century. From left, top: oil or vinegar bottle, water set, another oil bottle, and a candlestick. Second row: sugar and cream set on each end and puff box. Third row: sherbet glass with plate, sandwich plate, and compote. Bottom: cologne bottle, salt or pepper shaker, two vases, jelly dish, and pitcher.

on the outside of the article. Many pieces are quite attractive; in other cases constant handling has worn much of the silver off. Many of the earlier pieces will be found tarnished, although a process to retard or prevent tarnishing was perfected earlier in this century. Among types of glass decorated with silver deposit was some Mother-of-Pearl Satin glass.

Numerous articles of silver deposit glass are shown in early trade catalogues. Among the items produced were cologne bottles, water sets, miscellaneous pitchers, vinegar bottles, sugar and cream sets, puff boxes, sherbet glasses, plates, compotes of various kinds, vases, jelly dishes, condiment sets, sandwich trays, and nut and candy dishes and jars.

In 1914, silver deposit glass candlesticks were being advertised at wholesale prices of $2.30 a pair, compotes at $1.75, pint-capacity pitchers at $2, sugar and cream sets at $1.50, and cologne bottles at 68 cents. In 1919, Marshall Field & Company had silver deposit sandwich trays at prices of $4 to $7.30, candy jars at $5.50, oil or vinegar bottles at $5, and small handled baskets at $1.40.

Even now, excellent articles of silver deposit glass may be found at quite low prices, and they are beginning to be collected. Don't let the pieces whose silver has tarnished somewhat disappoint you: you'll be surprised at how much a good silver polish and a bit of elbow grease can accomplish with these.

Although silver deposit is not, generally speaking, a "highbrow" type of glass, it is interesting, and many pieces of it can be put into service. You may be interested in the following prices recently asked for certain pieces of it:

Pair of candlesticks, 5½ inches high, $8.50; cruet, $12; set consisting of creamer, sugar bowl, syrup pitcher, and plate, $18; 9-inch-tall decanter with stopper, $20; cologne bottle with original stopper, $8.50; large relish dish, $22.50; 5-inch-tall vase, amethyst, $9; and sugar and cream set, $15.

Novelty hand mirrors of the nineteenth and early twentieth centuries were produced in dozens of shapes and designs and will still be found in numerous older homes. Thousands of these, particularly the silverplated ones, featured the florid embossed decorations that apparently had a strong appeal to our late Victorian ancestors. Their designers probably wouldn't take any prizes in design competitions today, but these old mirrors should have an interest for us in reflecting the tastes of their times. Those with backs of sterling silver will have some monetary value as well.

The mirrors were frequently a part of matching toilet sets that included also an ornate brush and comb, and, sometimes, such articles as manicure brushes, cloth brushes, puff boxes, and cuticle knives as well. As was the case with so many other decorated articles

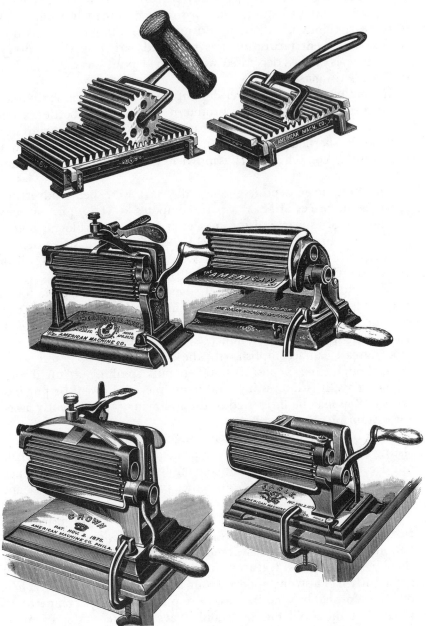

Hand fluters (top) and fluting machines of the 1880's.

of the latter part of last century, scrolls and flowers were prominent in the designs on the backs. Some catalogues described the decorated mirror borders as "rococo." Most were in that rather dull finish called "French gray."

Arrange a group of these elaborately decorated old mirrors along a wall, with the glass toward the wall, and you can have yourself a rather striking display. But don't turn the reflecting glass surfaces outward, or you may have your feminine visitors staring at the display for hours.

Youngsters of earlier generations who took music lessons outside their homes (and frequently at the insistence of their parents) often carried their sheet music in leather carrying cases. The oval and oblong carriers, called simply "music rolls," were made of various materials, but generally some type of leather with a hand or shoulder strap attached, and, in some instances, adorned also with a sterling silver name plate.

I don't know what's happened to the many thousands of these old music rolls, but one rarely sees them these days, either inside or outside of antique shops. Nevertheless, they are interesting to encounter; and the adventurous collector can have a lot of fun seeking them.

The carriers (or rolls, if you prefer) measured about 14 to 16 inches in length, and the sheet music or scores could be wrapped neatly inside without folding or the danger of tearing. As a matter of fact, the rolls also were known early in this century as "music wrappers." Their prices depended upon their quality, which, in turn, depended to a large extent on the material of which they were made. This included "leatherette," seal leather, sheepskin, walrus hide, keratol, doe skin, alligator hide, cow hide, Turkish morocco, and other leathers, as well as various types of cloth. In 1906, the firm of Lyon & Healy, of Chicago, offered for $45 a dozen rolls of "delicate genuine Offenback cloth and a rare leather never before used in the manufacture of Music Wrappers and well known for its beautiful and delicate finish." Some of the finer carriers wholesaled for as much as $100 a dozen.

In addition to the oval and oblong rolls, carriers, or wrappers, there also were music bags made in shapes similar to small valises. These were manufactured of the same materials as the rolls and had attached carrying handles at the top. They were fastened, as were most of the rolls, by a leather strap and buckle. Some bags had open ends, others closed ends.

Looking even more like miniature suitcases were combination music bags and satchels, including an oversized band music satchel.

All of these types of carriers are worth seeking, and chances are you can buy them for almost a pittance. Besides, you'll be looking for something apparently no one else is yet collecting.

Ornately-decorated hand mirrors of the late nineteenth and early twentieth centuries. The two on the left on the top and second rows and the top one at right are of sterling silver; the others are silverplated.

I have no idea, earthly or unearthly, why; but there is some interest being whipped up right now in early fluting irons. These were used before the days of woman's emancipation from the kitchen and the laundry to press ruffles on dresses.

The fluting iron was a cumbersome contrivance, heavy and difficult to handle—but then, the ruffles had to be pressed. I am not sure to what modern day use you can convert fluting irons, but I am certain the ladies will think of something, if indeed they have not already done so. I guess one could convert them into lamps, though I shudder at the prospect of encountering one so used.

The more elaborate fluting machines were operated by the use of a crank handle, but there were smaller much less expensive hand fluters with wooden or iron handles attached, and some of the latter types wholesaled in 1884 for as little as $10.50 per dozen. The American Machine Company made many of the fluting machines and the smaller hand fluters. The machines were designed so they could be attached by a clamp to a table top. They consisted of two mangles, or grooved rollers, of metal, which engaged one another when in operation. The hand fluters were operated by pushing a grooved roller across a flat grooved surface. You'll find both types illustrated in the accompanying illustrations, and you may be surprised to note that the machines look rather like the old-fashioned clothes wringers except for the type of mangles.

Luggage identification tags of paper, cardboard, or leather have now largely replaced the metal tags with leather straps once used by travelers to identify their suitcases, trunks, satchels and allied paraphernalia on their journeys. But some years ago no traveler who valued his property would ship luggage without a metal-and-leather identification tag attached. The finest of these consisted of sterling silver plates in various shapes to which leather straps for fastening to luggage were attached. Even though those accessories of travel were virtual necessities, they usually were classified in trade catalogues as "sterling silver novelties." Perhaps this characterization derived in part from the novel shapes in which so many of them were turned out.

Less expensive tags were made of nickelplated German silver. You should be able to find a good many of the early metal tags still attached to old pieces of luggage that have been in storage for some years. Most of those you find are likely to have the original owner's name and address engraved on the plate.

Because of the variety of their shapes and decorations, a large collection of these tags may be assembled without duplication. They were produced in round, oblong, oval, square and heart shapes with rococo-type ornamentation or beaded borders. They can be displayed under glass, mounted on boards, or simply hung along a part

Group of early twentieth-century bag tags with sterling silver identi-fication plates.

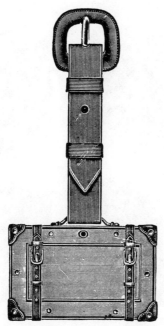

A pre-World War I satchel tag in the shape of a satchel.

of a wall. Those of sterling silver may cost you a few dollars now but those in nickel plate are likely to come cheaper. The all-leather tags may be collected but are not of as much interest as those of leather and metal.

The fern is not much favored in home decoration now, but these cool and languid green plants had a special appeal to our ancestors of last century, who may have found their gentle appearance a compensating factor for the garish appeal of so much of their home decor. The fern graced the table of many of our grandparents' and great-grandparents' homes with the result that there was a great demand for fern dishes of various kinds.

One favorite type in the late nineteenth century was the silver-plated fern dish, the decoration of which sometimes offset the pleasant simplicity of the fern itself. These were customarily footed and often had handles attached to their outer casings. Most fern dishes were round but oblong shapes also are encountered. Although they are generally referred to as fern dishes, these receptacles were frequently used for other flowers as well. Some truly gorgeous arrangements of ferns with various flowers were devised by our feminine forebears, who looked upon this chore as an art, which it often was. Linings of metal, pottery, and poreclain were used in various of these silverplated containers.

These interesting silverplated fern dishes were offered by the Adelphi Silver Plate Company late last century. The dish at bottom right is a silverplated flower pot, taller than a fern dish but otherwise similar.

Among the outstanding producers of silverplated fern dishes that had a wide appeal in their day was the Adelphi Silver Plate Company, of New York City. Other silverplating companies also made them.

Those you find today may need replating, but they can serve as exceedingly attractive containers for flower arrangements of various types as may be evident in illustrations accompanying this chapter from an early catalogue.

Who collects nineteenth-century silk-fringed gift books? They probably have been largely overlooked by both dealers and book collectors who specialize in such categories as Americana, first editions, and even limited editions and special press books; but there was a fairly brisk trade in them years ago when they were utilized as gifts of the inspirational type. Many such books ("booklets" might be a more apt word) featured well-known hymns of the day as the following sampling of titles will indicate: *Abide with Me, The Glorious Song of Old, My Faith Looks up to Thee, Rock of Ages,* and *From Greenland's Icy Mountains.*

These gift books were beautifully printed with sentimental lithographed illustrations in color on their front covers, which were fringed with silk on three sides. In a way they resembled elaborate sentimental or inspirational greeting cards. Naturally they were often sent as gifts to friends who were troubled or had suffered some grievous loss.

Other books of this type were referred to as Gift Annuals, and the publication of them dates back to as early as the first part of the nineteenth century. Their covers were elaborately decorated with gilt. Some, even though designed primarily for consumption in the United States, were printed in England, and their contents were devoted to foreign countries. One of this type, dealing largely with India and produced in England, was entitled *The Parlour Scrap Book,* edited by Willis Gaylord Clark. It was decorated with steel-engraved plates. One edition of this was published in 1836 and another the following year.

Many somewhat similar Gift Annuals containing a miscellany of reading material were published by houses in New York and Boston around the middle of last century. Titles included *Rural Wreath, Ladies' Wreath, Golden Gift, The Choice Gift, Young Lady's Cabinet of Gems, The Oasis, The Token, The Pearl Offering,* and *The Moss Rose.*

Although most of them are of little artistic merit and not much monetary value, metal mantel ornaments made in the late nineteenth century and during the early years of this one are beginning to be collected. These were cast figures—some made of bronze and others of so-called "white metal"—that were quite similar to mantel

Music rolls or wrappers, music bags, and combination music bags and satchels. The combinations are shown down the page at right, and the music bags with closed ends are on the bottom two rows (left and center). These all date 1906, and were offered by the distinguished firm of Lyon & Healy, which still operates in Chicago.

clock ornaments of the same period. In fact, many were advertised as "artistic clock and mantel ornaments."

The cast figures ranged from just a few inches to more than 20 inches in height and included a great variety of subjects. There were numerous cast animals—dogs, deer, horses, lions, and other creatures —ferocious and domesticated. There were representations of brigands and warriors on horseback, mythological characters, trumpeters, Arabs, Indian scouts, and females clad in flimsey garments.

Some of their names will give an indication of the character of these ornaments that "graced" many a Victorian mantel: "Diana," "Arminius," "Olympia and Chloris," "Musician," "Cossack," "Hannibal," "Hunter," "Indian Warrior," and "Horse Tamer."

Similar ornaments also were made in plaster of paris, or chalk, painted to resemble bronze. These can fool you at a distance, as one of them once fooled me when I failed to heed my own advice. The advice I'm talking about is never to bid at auction on anything you haven't personally examined. On one occasion a clock which I had not examined beforehand came up for bids at an auction I was attending. It was really a fantastic contrivance with a large figure of a girl feeding numerous birds and with other bird effigies atop the clock and on its sides. I was certain the clock housing was bronze and I was rather astonished when it was knocked down to me for only $15. But when I picked it up at the close of the auction, I discovered that far from being bronze, the entire housing was made of plaster of paris. I have been careful to heed my own advice about bidding ever since.

The metal ornaments were originally inexpensive, wholesaling at prices of a dollar to about $10 with the exception of some elaborate ones that stood nearly two feet tall and were wholesaled in pairs at a bit more than $40 for the two. Some of the latter were listed in a 1905 catalogue as being made of "Syrian bronze."

Even though you may not find these ornaments of much value from either an artistic or a monetary standpoint, you can assemble a striking collection of them and derive much enjoyment from your search. A number of them are shown in the illustrations. You may find some of these ornaments with holes drilled in them, indicating that earlier owners had converted them to lamps. You can use them as lamps now if you wish. In spirit, at least, the metal mantel ornaments were akin to the Staffordshire figures made of pottery at a slightly earlier date.

The perils of fire have been with us since time immemorial, and through the years a great variety of fire extinguishers for use in the home have been produced. These extinguishers usually contain a mixture of chemicals charged with water. Some of the earlier fire extinguishers were made of glass in the shape of a bottle or cylinder.

Bronze mantel ornaments were produced in a wide range of figures and presentations as indicated in this illustration.

Metal mantel ornaments of the early twentieth century. Those at bottom were cast in "Syrian bronze."

Among the agents used in creating fire extinguishers are sulphuric acid and bicarbonate of soda.

Many of the early hand extinguishers in the shape of bottles are still around, awaiting collectors. One that should be of interest is the Hayward Hand Grenade, made in the last quarter of the nineteenth century by the Hayward Hand Grenade Fire Extinguisher Company, whose headquarters in 1885 were located at 407 Broadway, New York City. These "grenades" were glass bottles containing chemicals. They were thrown into a fire to generate a gas which extinguished the flames within a reasonable distance. In 1885, they sold for $10 a dozen. Some early types of hand fire extinguishers have been offered for sale of late at prices of $12 to $15 each.

A fairly large number of different types of these bottle fire extinguishers were made through the years. They were produced in shades of green, blue, purple, amber, and clear glass. In addition to the Hayward mentioned earlier, there was the Harden Hand Grenade Extinguisher, and the General Fire Extinguisher Company, of New York City, also produced them in grenade types. Many were marked with labels originally, and some bore patent dates.

Some of the grenade bottles were ribbed; others had sunbursts on their bottoms; and still others had diamond patterns in the glass. Bottle collectors will naturally be interested in them, but they can make a fine collection by themselves.

You may think that the washing machine is a modern invention, but automatic dish washers were being offered for sale in the 1890's. One producer was the Stevens Dish Washing Machine Company, of Cleveland, Ohio. One of its advertisements illustrated a dish washing machine that resembled a console television set on legs, without the viewing screen. The top could be raised so that the dirty dishes could be placed inside the cabinet.

What could a housewife do with such a machine? Here is what the manufacturers said about that question:

"She can wash, rinse and dry 10 or 100 dishes at one time, with a machine, without chipping or breaking a dish, and without using a dish mop or towel; she can save from two to three hours per day of disagreeable work, and prevent the destruction of her hands, by simply purchasing the lightrunning and noiseless Stevens Dish Washing Machine."

These dish washing machine cabinets, if you can find them, can be converted to housing for hi-fi sets or home bars.

The collector of glass and of other small objects should be interested in nineteenth-century glass curtain pins. These were screws in a small shaft to whose front glass knobs, usually oval in shape, were attached. Scores of these glass curtain pins are exceptionally attractive, particularly those whose flat top surfaces were made of silvered or white enameled glass with colored flowers.

The glass surfaces were made in diameters of 2½ to 4½ inches. In the 1880's those made of plain silvered glass wholesaled for only $1.15 a dozen. Those of silvered or enameled glass with flowers ranged in wholesale price from about $2.05 to $3.20 a dozen, depending on size. Some were fashioned in the shape of rosettes, and some bore engraved designs. Also collectible are curtain pins with decorated porcelain centers or surfaces.

In the category of small boxes, you may not have considered the plush photograph boxes used last century to hold collections of photographs. Most of these were wooden boxes covered and lined with silk and, often, with nickel trimmings on the cover. Many such boxes had two partitions inside, each measuring about 5 inches in length by about 3½ inches deep. They held pictures of one's family and friends and were frequently brought out at home gatherings so the photographs could be displayed. Metal trinket boxes also were sometimes used for the storage of photos.

You know, of course, that match book covers are being collected, but did you know that small individual sugar sack covers also are being sought? One ardent collector of these colorful little sacks is Miss Betty Gau, of 11209 South Sawyer Avenue, Chicago, who calls her preoccupation with them "the sweetest hobby in the world." She says there are 100 or more collectors of these sacks (or envelopes or wrappers if you prefer) in a club of which she is a member, and that the hobby is known as "sucre sacology," or the science of collecting sugar sacks.

Miss Gau has assembled considerably more than 3,500 such sacks, used largely by cafes and food-serving institutions for sugar servings. The sacks customarily are issued in two sizes—one-fourth of an ounce and one-sixth of an ounce. Some companies print their own sacks with their own advertising messages on them; other sacks are made by printing firms for specific customers and contain advertising printed to order on either one or both sides.

Collecting wrappers has been a hobby in Europe for some years. but the collecting of sugar sacks is relatively recent in the United States. The club of which Miss Gau is a member is known as "Sucre-Sac-Ologists Society, International, with members in this country and abroad.

Some collectors mount the sacks in loose-leaf books for display. Some sacks are issued in sets, and the full sets are earnestly sought. There are often seven or eight different sacks (each with a different illustration) in the sets. Sacks often contain company or institution advertising on one side and colored illustrations—birds, flowers, foods, etc.—on the other. Collectors often swap duplicate envelopes for envelopes of a type they do not already have, and

Small portion of the collection of antique automobile sugar sacks of Miss Betty Gau, 11209 South Sawyer Avenue, Chicago.

Offbeat collectibles: Left to right, *top row: a Hayward Hand Grenade fire extinguisher (1886); a pistol flashlight (1914); an 1892 dish washing machine, and the "Penniston" food warmer. Second row: The "Dandy" wall shoe shiner (1902), and illustrations of the "Champion" egg opener in use as contrasted with the opening of an egg by the use of a knife. Third row: a curtain pin with a glass center and one with a porcelain center (both 1884), and a silk plush photograph box (1889). Bottom: two silk-friged gift books of the late nineteenth century, an early luggage tag (just below), and a pictorial advertisement for the Hayward Hand Grenade fire extinguisher.*

that is particularly true in the case of the sacks called "national," imprinted with the advertising of hotels, restaurant chains, and so on that operate largely in limited states or regions.

A precursor of the thermos bottle as we know it today was the nineteenth-century traveling food warmer. This was intended primarily to keep certain foods and liquids warm (or cool) for infants or invalids. One type was essentially a hot water bag with pockets in an outside cover. One filled the bag with hot water, then put sterilized milk, other liquids or foods in bottles in the outer pockets, and they would be kept warm for some time.

An advertisement of 1894 for the "Penniston" food warmer, described it as "a hot water bag with pockets on the side for holding the ordinary nursing or sterilizing bottles." To keep foods cool instead of hot, one filled the bag with ice water instead of hot water. The "Penniston" was manufactured by the Davol Rubber Company, of Providence, Rhode Island, and was characterized as "invaluable to travelers or invalids."

There are literally dozens of other "oddball" collectibles that may appeal to many. Have you ever thought of such articles as early novelty flashlights, mechanical egg openers, wall-attached shoe shiners, or advertising cloth bags? There's a collector in Glencoe, Illinois, seeking early wooden peck and half-peck measures. Down in Texas, another collector wants glass lightning rod balls. A lady in Connecticut advertised for brass monkeys "any size over 12 inches."

Other types of items for which collectors have been advertising include manuscripts about whaling, articles related to early dentistry, old automobile sales brochures, ship logs, photographs of midgets, prehistoric teeth, cowboy chaps, mule shoes, ornamental embellishments from old homes, peanut roasters, and home movies.

So you see there's really no need to follow the well-worn paths of collecting unless you want to: you can beat a path of your own. And in so doing, you may be able to become an expert in a field about which others know little. That's much more satisfactory than knowing little about a field that abounds in experts!

[17]

Selected Bibliography

(These suggestions for further reading include both books and magazine articles. Back issues of magazines will often be found in the larger public libraries and may sometimes be purchased from the original publishers, or dealers handling magazine back issues. The arrangements below are by chapter and, where feasible, by subjects within each chapter.)

FREE ENTERPRISE: A WORLD OF COLLECTIBLES

Advertising Novelties, Gifts, Etc.

ANONYMOUS. *Early Gift Advertising.* Article in August, 1952, *Hobbies.*

FELGER, DONNA. *Advertising Spoons.* Article in September, 1966, *Western Collector.*

GARRETT, FRANKLIN M. *Coca-Cola Collectibles.* Article in July, 1968, *The Antiques Journal.*

MUNSEY, CECIL. *Coca-Cola.* Two-part series in August and September, 1967, *Western Collector.*

PALMER, BROOKS. *The Sidney Advertising Clock.* Article in September, 1952, *The Antiques Journal.*

Inventions and Patent Models

ANONYMOUS. *Dreams of the Past . . . Realities of the Present.* Article in June, 1952, *Hobbies.*

LARSEN, CEDRIC. *The Patent Office Models, 1836–1890.* Article in March, 1950, *The Antiques Journal.*

Lithographs

BARTLETT, F. J. *Commercial Americana!* Article in September, 1952, *Hobbies.*

Mirrors

ANONYMOUS. *Early Business Advertising.* Article in September, 1952, *Hobbies.*

Packages

McCLINTON, KATHARINE MORRISON. *The Complete Book of Country Antiques.* New York: Coward-McCann, Inc.

Shelf Jars

COLE, ANN KILBORN. *How to Collect the "New Antiques."* New York: David McKay Company, Inc.

Signs and Signboards

ENDELL, FRITZ. *Old Tavern Signs. An Excursion in the Story of Hospitality.* Boston: Houghton Mifflin Company.

Thermometers and Barometers

ANONYMOUS. *Early Business Advertising.* Article in September, 1952, *Hobbies.*

Trade Cards

(LAUNDAUER, DELLA C.) *Early American Trade Cards from the Collection of Della C. Laundauer.* Notes by Adele Jenny. New York: William E. Rudge.

MACCOUN, BILL. *Collecting 19th Century Trade Cards.* Article in July, 1966, *Western Collector.*

MAUST, DON. *The American Trade Card.* Article in June, 1967, *The Antiques Journal.*

MEBANE, JOHN. *New Horizons in Collecting: Cinderella Antiques.* Cranbury, New Jersey: A. S. Barnes and Company, Inc.

EVERYTHING SHORT OF LIFE EVERLASTING

Bottles

KENDRICK, GRACE. *Antique Bottles.* Article in December, 1963, *The Antiques Journal.*

PUTNAM, H. *Bottle Identification.* Duarte, California: The Author.

REVI, ALBERT CHRISTIAN. *American Pressed Glass and Figure Bottles.* Camden, New Jersey: Thomas Nelson & Sons.

SILVA, BEVERLY J. *Take One Wineglassful Every Forty Five Minutes.* Article in March, 1967, *Western Collector.*

TIBBITTS, JOHN C. *John Doe, Bottle Collector.* Sacramento, California: The Little Glass Shack.

WATSON, RICHARD. *Bitters Bottles.* Camden, New Jersey: Thomas Nelson & Sons.

General

CARSON, GERALD. *One for a Man, Two for a Horse.* Garden City, New York: Doubleday & Company, Inc.

COOK, JAMES. *Remedies and Rackets.* New York: W. W. Norton & Company, Inc.

DARLING, ADA. *Gems and Drugs.* Article in July, 1947, *The American Antiques Journal.*

FISHBEIN, MORRIS. *Fads and Quackery in Healing*. New York: Covici, Friede.

HOLBROOK, STEWART HALL. *Golden Age of Quackery*. New York: The Macmillan Company.

JAMESON, ERIC. *Natural History of Quackery*. Springfield, Illinois: Charles C. Thomas, Publisher.

SMITH, RALPH LEE. *Health Hucksters*. New York: Thomas Y. Crowell Company.

OUR GRANDPARENTS' TOYS

DAIKEN, LESLIE. *Children's Toys through the Ages*. London: Spring Books.

FISHER, ELIZABETH ANDREWS. *Miniature Stuff*. Middletown, Connecticut: The Author.

FOLEY, DANIEL J. *Toys through the Ages*. Philadelphia: Chilton Company.

FREEMAN, RUTH and LARRY. *Yesterday's Toys*. Watkins Glen, New York: Century House.

FRITZSCH, KARL EWALD, and MANFRED BACHMANN. *An Illustrated History of Toys*. London: Abbey Library.

HERTZ, LOUIS H. *The Handbook of Old American Toys*. Wethersfield, Connecticut: Mark Haber.

HILLIER, MARY. *Pageant of Toys*. New York: Taplinger Publishing Company, Inc.

JONES, VERE. *Victorian Toys*. Article in July, 1967, *The Antiques Journal*.

MAUST, DON. *Before We Put the Toys Away*. Article in February, 1967, *The Antiques Journal*.

MEBANE, JOHN. *Treasure at Home*. Cranbury, New Jersey: A. S. Barnes and Company, Inc.

WHOOPEE, BOYS! ELON'S GOT THE BALL!

General

DEMING, CLARENCE. *Athletics in College Life*. Article in July 1, 1905, *Outlook*.

DURAND, JOHN, and OTTO BETTMANN. *Pictorial History of American Sports*. (Revised edition.) Cranbury, New Jersey: A. S. Barnes and Company, Inc.

GEIST, ROLAND C. *Old Vehicles: 60 Items for the Cyclana Collector*. Article in October, 1955, *Hobbies*.

KROUT, JOHN A. *Annals of American Sport*. New York: United States Publishers Association, Inc.

MARR, HARRIET WEBSTER. *Amusements and Athletics in the Old New England Academies*. Article in Winter, 1954, *Old-Time New England*, The Bulletin of the Society for the Preservation of New England Antiquities.

MENKE, FRANK G. *Encyclopedia of Sports.* (Revised edition.) Cranbury, New Jersey: A. S. Barnes and Company, Inc.

MOSS, PETER. *Sports and Pastimes through the Ages.* London: George G. Harrap & Company, Ltd.

PRATT, JOHN L., and J. BENAGH (Eds.). *Official Encyclopedia of Sports.* New York: Franklin Watts, Inc.

SULLIVAN, JOHN. *Football Program Mania.* Article in September, 1960, *Hobbies.*

WARE, W. PORTER. *Antique Sports.* Series of articles in *Hobbies,* February-April, 1963.

Decoys

BARBER, JOEL. *Wild Fowl Decoys.* New York: Peter Smith. Also, reprint edition by Dover Publications, Inc., New York.

EARNEST, ADELE. *Art of the Decoy: American Bird Carvings.* New York: Clarkson N. Potter.

MACKEY, W. *American Bird Decoys.* New York: E. P. Dutton Company.

STARR, GEORGE ROSS, JR., M.D. *Old New England Decoys.* Article in Fall, 1952, *Old-Time New England,* The Bulletin of the Society for the Preservation of New England Antiquities.

FOR THE LADIES: A CHOICE MISCELLANY

Fans

ANONYMOUS. *Fans in San Juan.* Article in August, 1967, *Hobbies.*

OLDHAM, ESTHER. *Fans East and West.* Article in February, 1948, *Antiques.*

———. *Fans of Freedom.* Article in March, 1964, *The Antiques Journal.*

PRINCEHORN, HARRIET H. *The Romance of Old Fans.* Article in July, 1949, *The American Antiques Journal.*

SHULL, THELMA. *Victorian Antiques.* Rutland, Vermont: Charles E. Tuttle Company, Inc.

STICKELL, DOROTHY ALBAUGH. *Little Engines of Love or How to Flirt a Fan.* Article in July, 1949, *The American Antiques Journal.*

Hat Trimmings

HUBBARD, CLARENCE T. *About Hats.* Article in October, 1963, *The Antiques Journal.*

Paper Dolls

ANONYMOUS. *Paper Dolls.* Article in September, 1962, *The Spinning Wheel.*

FAWCETT, CLARA HALLARD. *An American Publisher of Paper Dolls.* Article in August, 1953, *Hobbies.*

———. *About Paper Dolls.* Article in March, 1952, *Hobbies.*

———. *On Dressing "Lady" Dolls of the Late Nineteenth Century.* Article in October, 1966, *Hobbies.*

HOWARD, MARION B. *Advertising Paper Dolls.* Two-part article in March and April, 1955, *The Toy Trader.*

Parasols and Umbrellas

ANONYMOUS. *Umbrellas for Sale.* Article in September, 1967, *The Spinning Wheel.*

MURRAY, ANNE WOOD. *Sunshades, Parasols, and Umbrellas.* Article in April, 1967, *Antiques.*

SHULL, THELMA. *Victorian Antiques.* Rutland, Vermont: Charles E. Tuttle Company, Inc.

FOR THE GENTLEMEN: A CHOICE MISCELLANY

Cribbage

JARVIS, ALLEN J. *Cribbage as I Think it Should Be Played.* Boston: Bruce Humphries, Inc.

Dice

GARCIA, FRANK. *Marked Cards and Loaded Dice.* Hackensack, New Jersey. Wehman Bros.

SCARNE, JOHN, and CLAYTON RAWSON. *Scarne on Dice.* (Revised edition.) Harrisonburg, Pennsylvania: Stackpole Books.

Knives

PETERSON, HAROLD L. *History of Knives.* New York: Charles Scribner's Sons.

Shaving Mugs

KIM, GEORGE. *Shaving Mugs.* Article in January, 1967, *The Antiques Journal.*

TO THE BOILING POT THE FLIES COME NOT

General

ADAMS, LOUISE G. *Quilt Making in the United States.* Article in March, 1947, *The American Antiques Journal.*

BAKER, MURIEL L. *A Handbook of American Crewel Embroidery.* Rutland, Vermont: Charles E. Tuttle Company, Inc.

FINLEY, RUTH E. *Old Patchwork Quilts and the Women Who Made Them.* Philadelphia: J. B. Lippincott Company.

ICKIS, MARGUERITE. *The Standard Book of Quilt Making and Collecting.* New York: Dover Publications, Inc.

LITZ, JOYCE. *Quilting Is an Art.* Article in August, 1937, *The Antiques Journal.*

LOWES, EMILY LEIGH. *Chats on Old Lace and Needlework.* London: T. Fisher Unwin, Ltd.

SALYER, PAULINE A. *Great Artists of China Decoration.* Oklahoma City, Oklahoma: Salyer Publishing Company.

UNDERHILL, VERA BISBEE, and ARTHUR J. BURKE. *Creating Hooked Rugs.* New York: Coward-McCann.

Jewelry Making

FRANKE, LOIS E. and W. L. *Handwrought Jewelry.* New York: Taplinger Publishing Company.

ROSE, AUGUSTUS F., and ANTONIO CIRINO. *Jewelry Making and Design.* New York: Dover Publications, Inc.

ZECHLIN, KATHERINA. *Creative Enameling and Jewelry-Making.* New
York: Sterling Publishing Company.

THE SOUNDS OF MUSIC

BAINES, ANTHONY. *European and American Musical Instruments.*
New York: (Studio Books) The Viking Press, Inc.

———. (Ed.). *Musical Instruments.* Baltimore: Penguin Books, Inc.

———. (Ed.). *Musical Instruments through the Ages.* Gloucester,
Massachusetts: Peter Smith.

BUCHNER, ALEXANDER. *Musical Instruments through the Ages.* New
York: Tudor Publishing Company.

EDGERLY, BEATRICE. *From the Hunter's Bow.* (New edition edited by
Boris Erich Nelson.) New York: G. P. Putnam's Sons.

GEIRINGER, KARL. *Musical Instruments: Their History in Western
Culture from the Stone Age to the Present.* New York: Oxford
University Press.

HUBBARD, CLARENCE T. *Clavichords, Virginals, Spinets and Grand
Pianos.* Article in April, 1967, *The Antiques Journal.*

LANG, PAUL H., and OTTO BETTMANN. *Pictorial History of Music.*
New York: W. W. Norton & Company, Inc.

MICHAELS, MARILYN. *Antique Musical Instruments.* Article in January, 1964, *The Antiques Journal.*

SACHS, CURT. *History of Musical Instruments.* New York: W. W.
Norton & Company, Inc.

SCHWARTZ, H. WAYNE. *Story of Musical Instruments from Shepherd's
Pipe to Symphony.* Garden City, New York: Doubleday & Company, Inc.

SCOTT, JANE. *Old Musical Instruments Play Again at the Sanders Old
Music Store.* Article in October, 1952, *The Spinning Wheel.*

WELSH, ROGER L. *American Antique Folk Stringed Instruments.* Two-
part article in December, 1966, and January-February, 1967, *The
Spinning Wheel.*

HIS MASTER'S VOICE—AND OTHERS

FRENCH, BILL. *Talking Machine Doctor.* Article in November, 1961,
The Spinning Wheel.

FAVIA-ARTSAY, AIDA. *Historical Records.* A regular monthly column in
Hobbies.

GELATT, ROLAND. *Fabulous Phonograph: From Tin Foil to High
Fidelity.* Philadelphia: J. B. Lippincott Company.

MAUST, DON. *Victrolas, Violins, and an Ancient Viola.* Article in
January, 1965, *The Antiques Journal.*

MILLER, W. H. *Antique Mechanical Musical Phonographs Offered for Sale.* Troy, Ohio: The Author.

WALSH, JIM. *Favorite Pioneer Recording Artists.* A regular monthly column in *Hobbies.*

THOSE FASCINATING MATCH SAFES

ANONYMOUS. *Match Safes as a Collector's Item.* Article in October, 1952, *The Spinning Wheel.*

MCCLINTON, KATHARINE MORRISON. *Late Victorian Match Safes.* Article in the January-February, 1967, *The Spinning Wheel.*

WENTWORTH, RAY E. *The Match Box Story.* Article in October, 1965, *Western Collector.*

WATCH THE BIRDIE

ANDREWS, RALPH W. Picture Gallery Pioneers. Seattle, Washington: Superior Publishing Company.

BLIVEN, FLOYD. *The Daguerreotype Story.* New York: Vantage Press.

GERNSHEIM, HELMUT and ADDISON. *History of Photography.* New York: Oxford University Press.

——— and ———. *L. J. M. Daguerre.* Cleveland: World Publishing Company.

GROSS, HARRY I. *Antique and Classic Cameras.* Philadelphia: Chilton.

HORAN, JAMES D. *Mathew Brady, Historian with a Camera.* New York: Crown Publishers.

MEREDITH, ROY. *Mr. Lincoln's Camera Man.* New York: Charles Scribner's Sons.

NEWHALL, BEAUMONT. *The Daguerreotype in America.* New York: Duell, Sloan and Pearce, Inc.

———. *The History of Photography from 1839 to the Present Day.* (Revised edition.) New York: The Museum of Modern Art and the George Eastman House.

———and NANCY. *T. H. O'Sullivan: Photographer.* Rochester, New York: The George Eastman House and the Amon Carter Museum of Western Art.

POLLACK, PETER. *History of Photography.* New York: Harry N. Abrams.

RINHART, FLOYD and MARION. *American Daguerrian Art.* New York: Clarkson N. Potter, Inc., Publisher.

SIPLEY, LOUIS W. *Collector's Guide to American Photography.* Philadelphia: American Museum of Photography.

———. *Photography's Great Inventors.* Philadelphia: American Museum of Photography.

THE CLUTTERED TABLE

BOULTINGHOUSE, MARK. *Art and Colored Glass Toothpick Holders.* Reynolds, Illinois: The Author.

KOVEL, RALPH M. and TERRY H. *Directory of American Silver, Pewter and Silver Plate.* (Revised edition.) New York: Crown Publishers.

LONG, WILLIAM HERBERT. *Bonanza King's Treasure Trove.* Article in May, 1966, *Western Collector.*

MCCLINTON, KATHARINE MORRISON. *Collecting American 19th Century Silver.* New York: Charles Scribner's Sons.

RAINWATER, DOROTHY T. *American Art Nouveau Silver.* Article in July-August, 1967, *The Spinning Wheel.*

WARDLE, PATRICIA. *Victorian Silver and Silverplate.* Camden, New Jersey: Thomas Nelson & Sons.

FROM METALLIC STYLUS TO BALL POINT PEN

BLIVEN, BRUCE, JR. *The Wonderful Writing Machine.* New York: Random House.

DEAN, H. I. *Writing Materials through the Ages.* American Classical League.

EDITORIAL STAFF. *Sanders, the Blotters of Yesterday as Items for Collectors Today.* Article in September, 1952, *The Spinning Wheel.*

GARD, CARROLL. *Writing Past and Present: The Story of Writing and Writing Tools.* Chicago: A. N. Palmer.

IRWIN, KEITH GORDON. *Romance of Writing: From Egyptian Hieroglyphics to Modern Letters, Numbers and Signs.* New York: The Viking Press, Inc.

WHITED, GENE. *Inks that Left Their Mark.* Article in October, 1967, *Western Collector.*

COLLECTOR'S MEDLEY

HUBBARD, CLARENCE T. *Nursing Bottles.* Article in January, 1967, *Western Collector.*

TIBBITTS, JOHN C. *John Doe, Bottle Collector.* Sacramento, California: The Little Glass Shack.

Index